Praise for *West of the West*

"By turns lucid, harrowing, and comical, this collection of dispatches paints a darkly impressionistic portrait of modern California. A journalist and native son, Arax puts paid to vestigial West Coast clichés and replaces them with ominous realities and discontents encountered during four years of intrastate travel. Migrants, exiles, dreamers, schemers, murderers, hippies, fundamentalists, conspiracists, environmentalists—all share space in these pages and in that vast Golden State. The possibility of crazy-quilt discursion looms high, but Arax calmly sews the diverse stories and dramatic studies into coherence and poignancy. The effortless mix here—memoir and reportage, psychography and geography—coolly achieves the author's aim: 'to find the truth and the lie of the California myth.'"
—*The Atlantic*

"These swift, penetrating essays from former *Los Angeles Times* writer Arax (*In My Father's Name*) take the measure of contemporary California with a sure and supple hand, consciously but deservedly taking their place alongside Didion's and Saroyan's great social portraits. Expect the unexpected from Arax's reports up and down the state: on the last of the Okies, the latest migrants from Mexico, the treesitters of Berkeley, Bay Area conspiracy theorists, an Armenian chicken giant's infamous fall or the mammoth marijuana economy of Humboldt County, among much else. For Arax, a third-generation Californian of Armenian heritage who spent years covering the Central Valley as an investigative reporter, the state's outré reputation and self-representation are a complex dance of myth and memory that includes his own family lore and personal history. It's partly this personal connection, running subtly but consistently throughout, that pushes the collection past mere reportage to a high literary enterprise that beautifully integrates the private and idiosyncratic with the sweep of great historical forces."
—*Publishers Weekly*, starred review

"Arax is the perfect cicerone through the heavenly and hellish landscapes and historical evolutions he has chosen to chronicle. . . . He knows how to write colorfully. . . . The tales are never hurried but unfolded in a measured, controlled manner for maximum context and texture. And he has come up with some doozies! Haunting."
—*San Francisco Chronicle*

"I intended to spend half an hour and spent half a day. This is that kind of book. You think you know California? Think again, and settle in."
—Jack Miles, author of *God: A Biography*

"Arax dug deep into the dirt of California, and he didn't come away with his hands clean."
—*San Diego Union Tribune*

"The many strengths of *West of the West* include solid reporting, taut writing, and an author who has a firm grasp on his subject. Arax's California isn't about beaches or Hollywood or Disneyland. It's about a mix of real people who live there, mostly not in the limelight. You can trust that when Arax writes about this subject, he knows what he's talking about."
—*Las Vegas Review Journal*

"Pick up a copy of *West of the West* and absorb it. It's a delight to read."
—*Huntington News*

"In *West of the West*, Arax demonstrates the same uncanny ability to get closer to his subjects than you would ever think possible. These are compelling, sometimes heart-rending, eminently readable stories."
—*Contra Costa Times*

"Native son Mark Arax travels the state side-to-side, end-to-end to gather its stories, writing about the 'real' California lost in the gloss of tourism teasers."

—*Sacramento Bee*

"Arax is drawn to stories of mysterious loss, and he tells them so beautifully that his writing rises above the often tragic subject matter, lending mythic value to little-known lives."

—*OCMetro*

"*West of the West* is immediate in the best ways, sometimes intemperate, but always interesting."

—*Minneapolis StarTribune*

"Wherever he goes, Arax takes a remarkably crafted personal prose vision. His essays are gorgeously written, poignant and funny."

—Bookotron.com

WEST OF THE WEST

ALSO BY MARK ARAX

The King of California:
J. G. Boswell and the Making of a Secret American Empire

In My Father's Name: A Family, a Town, a Murder

WEST OF THE WEST

DREAMERS, BELIEVERS, BUILDERS, AND KILLERS IN THE GOLDEN STATE

MARK ARAX

PublicAffairs
New York

Book Design by Jeff Williams

The Library of Congress has catalogued the hardcover as follows:
Arax, Mark, 1956–
  West of the west : dreamers, believers, builders, and killers in the Golden State / Mark Arax.
    p. cm.
  ISBN: 978-1-58648-390-6
  1. Arax, Mark, 1965–. 2. Travel—California. 3. California—Description and travel. 4. California—History.
  F866.2.A73 2009
  917 9404—dc22

Paperback ISBN: 978-1-58648-983-0

To my three children, Ash, Joe, and Jake.

My heart, always.

"When I am in California,
I am not in the West. I am west of the West."

—THEODORE ROOSEVELT

Contents

A Prologue

The first letter postmarked "Fresno, California" arrived at the doorstep of my grandfather's flat in Istanbul, Turkey, in the late winter of 1920. "Watermelons the size of small boats. Grapes that hang like jade eggs." The words were written by an uncle who had started a new life in America after his wife and children had been massacred five years earlier in a village in Turkey. This uncle had gotten his revenge by killing one or more Turks—the number was the storyteller's whim—and now he was farming raisins seven thousand miles away in the San Joaquin Valley. My grandfather, an Armenian who had survived the genocide by hiding in an attic, had no intention of following the same path. He had hatched a plan to leave Istanbul and move to Paris, where he would study literature and become a great proletarian poet. But the letters kept coming from the uncle in Fresno who had no one else, each letter more dramatic than the one before it. "Here find an

Eden of pomegranate and peach." My grandfather was nineteen when he took the bait.

The roads that lead to California are long roads. They are
journeys, migrations, exiles. My grandfather's road in the
spring of 1920 took him past the Statue of Liberty, the nation's
capital, the new factories of Detroit, but it wasn't until the
tracks crossed the San Joaquin River and reached the irrigated
desert of California's middle that he could see what his uncle
had seen. Outside his window, beneath the snowy caps of the
Sierra, vineyards and orchards and vegetable fields, row after
perfect row, shimmered in the late afternoon sun. As the train
chugged into Fresno, he kept muttering in Armenian, "Just
like the old land."

So who could say that the myth of California isn't true? He
had crossed two seas and an ocean and found the same place he
had left. California had taken him back home, or so he thought.
In time, he would see that the myth was merely a distillation, a
cleaned-up version of a messy struggle that was fought on the
ground and constituted the real California. He would come to
understand that this new land, even as it allowed him to resur-
rect a piece of the old land, is not kind to memory. Its power
would erase the old land in the hearts of his children and
grandchildren so that years later, as he confronted death, he
would call this effacement the "white genocide."

I was the first of his grandchildren to be born here, and for
more than half my life, in one story or another, I have worked
to find the truth and the lie of the California myth. What is
not mythical about its desert, its Sierra, its farms, its redwood
forest, its Hollywood, its Silicon Valley, its Golden Gate, its
prisons, its ghettos of Little Tokyo, Seoul, Managua, Michoacán, San Salvador, Yerevan, Saigon, Beijing, Addis Ababa,

Tehran, and Tel Aviv? Then to dig down in any one of these places and discover a mirage, a chimera, a poverty, a greed, a hubris, a crime—the lie that was the antithesis of the original myth, which by its very dimension had become a new myth. Simply put, this is where it was done like nowhere else—for the best of it, for the worst of it.

Our vastness is a vastness of heft, yes, but also a vastness of idea and projection and execution. And our myth, at least the best part of it, continues to act as a powerful lure to a new generation of seekers who come, as my grandfather had come, to change the future. So how to capture such a place? I had been covering California long enough to know that each region, by virtue of its geography and psychology and history, gives rise to its own drama. I began where I always begin, with the great Central Valley, my home turf, and then worked outward to the extremes. This book is not a memoir, though the *I* does pop up here and there and sometimes everywhere. Neither is it told in the voice of an essayist, though I admit to occasional lapses of jaundiced eye. And while it may be considered a collection of individual stories, I have intended them as a kind of integrated journey. If the stories run a certain ominous course, I happened to be following a road trenched by 9/11 and the War on Terror and the anomie of the digital age and the greatest financial collapse since the Great Depression.

In his lifetime, my grandfather became a migrant fruit picker, a farmer, a grocer, a communist, a capitalist, an atheist, a believer—in other words, a consummate Californian. He became everything but a writer. This was no small defeat considering he had come to this country not with his real surname, Hovsepian, but with the pen name of Arax, the mother river of the murdered nation of Armenia. The uncle who had lured him to America waited a few days and then put my grandfather on another road—down the long, hot valley to the town of Weedpatch. There, long before the Okies and Steinbeck arrived, he dropped to his hands and knees and started picking. There, eighty-five years later, in the powdery loam, I found a young Mixteca who had arrived the week before from deep in Mexico, her land turning to dust. She had been smuggled in the back of a Suburban and was using her wages from the bell pepper fields to pay off a $1,900 debt to the coyote, a trafficker of humanity. I asked her why she had come, and she began to tear up. She had left two young children in their village with her mother. "For their future," she told me.

chapter one | The Last Valley

On the eve of the 2008 presidential election, I found myself standing in line at the U-Haul on Blackstone Avenue in Fresno, waiting to rent a truck. I had been living in a condo for the past year and a half, ever since my wife and I parted. Now, thanks to the fire sale prices of the nation's foreclosure mess, I was moving into a new house not far from my old house.

The line at the U-Haul was long, but the two clerks manning the four-clerk counter worked quickly. Before I knew it, my turn had come.

"Now that's what I call customer service," I said, without a hint of smart ass.

The young female clerk was not amused. "It don't take long when you run their card through the machine and find out they ain't got no credit left," she said.

As I waited for my truck to be brought out, I watched those who had come in behind me. Cash or not, they needed to produce a working credit card to rent a moving van. Nearly half of them could not. Still, they had reached into their wallets and purses and did the ritual swipe. Maybe the bank had changed its mind.

"I got more money than God," one man turned down at the counter mumbled.

Behind the wheel of my truck, adjusting the giant side view mirror, I counted myself among the lucky. No region of the country had seen the value of its houses shoot up farther and faster during the boom years than the San Joaquin Valley. And now no region in America had fallen deeper and darker into the hell of the bust than us. In and out, the dispossessed scurried without even the services of U-Haul to ease them from house to apartment. And here I was making the trip in reverse with a $29.95-a-day truck and a hired hand named Juan.

I had once read that Alexis de Tocqueville, in his journey across a callow America, had puzzled over a nation whose inhabitants were such a restless lot that "they started to build a house and left before the roof was finished." What would he make now, I thought, of a country where the roofs had left the people?

I had been happily paying $1,400 a month in rent, but my thinking began to change when I realized that $800,000 houses in old Fig Garden were now selling for $400,000. With a solid 20 percent down, I calculated, my monthly mortgage payment would be the same as my rent. So that summer I started studying the local real estate offerings and chasing down foreclosures in pursuit of a house that had the same open feel as my old house, with enough backyard dirt to grow a few fruits and vegetables.

The list of foreclosures, as you might imagine, had no end. Up and down California, $100 billion worth of houses had been repossessed by the banks over the previous two years. Each business day, 1,300 more houses joined the ranks of the emptied. For all that volume, I kept running into the same two houses: the house that was too good to be true, in which case my offer to buy always seemed to arrive a few minutes late. Or the house that looked promising on the outside only to reveal on the inside the anger of the family that had been pried from it. Plumbing lines filled with cement, microwaves torn from cabinets, holes kicked into walls, and even a "Fuck You" scrawled in purple lipstick on a vanity mirror. For two months, I hunted without luck, and then I adopted a vulture's strategy: Pick out a desired neighborhood and look for the lawn that was starting to turn brown. Then, before a For Sale sign can be put up, find the real estate agent representing the bank and make an offer for full price.

In two weeks time, I had landed a classic 1958 ranch house—3,100 square feet, side garden, and Olympic-size pool—for $99.69 a square foot.

That night, after Juan and I had finished moving the last load, I sat in my new garage and picked through the boxes of old notebooks from a quarter century of reporting on California. Why I had lugged them from L.A. to Pasadena to Fresno, from apartment to house to condo to house again, I wasn't sure. The stories had been written. The stories had been read. People and places I had captured in scrawls so intimate at the time. It was as if they had been thrown into boxes and sealed up too. This is what a journalist does, I reasoned. You can't afford to look back. There is the next one, and then the next one. I kept on doing the next one until the newspaper of record in California—a state that is eight hundred miles long and two hundred miles wide, boasting a population nearing 40 million and an economy greater than all but nine nations, that built the greatest agricultural machine and prison industrial complex the world had ever known—no longer needed a journalist roaming the middle to find its untold stories.

It struck me that night that I had an opportunity a social scientist might kill for. The story I had been covering for half my life—the migrations at the core of California, the grafting of old onto new, the capacity of the newly arrived to reinvent themselves—had not ended with the -30- I typed under the last line. Here was a chance to freshen up those notebooks and find old friends, to hit the open road and see how the story of California had evolved over a distance of twenty-five years, an eternity, after all. Was the dreamer still dreaming? The seeker still seeking? The builder still building? What had become of the places where I had done time?

My phone was ringing, a caller from the 702 area code, Las Vegas or its sprawl. The stranger on the other end started fishing; he sounded like maybe a cop or a hit man.

"I'm calling regarding Tai Lam. Do you know where he is?"

"First of all, who in the heck are you?"

"I'm an investigator. Background checks. Tai Lam listed you as a reference on his application. Says he worked for you as a translator at the *Los Angeles Times*."

"Is this about a job he's applied for? Because I can confirm that he worked for me."

"Not exactly. I need to find him. Do you have his number or know where he might be living?"

"Look, I don't know you from Adam. You sound like you might want to do him some harm."

"I'm trying to help him, sir. If you find him, please tell him to contact me." He repeated his name and number.

"I'll see what I can do."

"Tell him our patience isn't infinite."

Tai Lam. Where to begin? Let me begin on Valley Boulevard in the year 1986:

I was a strange animal, something called a "suburban reporter" for the *L.A. Times*, a newspaper whose commitment to covering the "Southland," as the Chandler family had dubbed it, extended to five suburban sections planted across the basin with reporters who had been stars at the *Baltimore Sun*, the *Philadelphia Inquirer*, the *San Francisco Examiner*. The Moscow bureau chief of the United Press International had left his job to cover the growing Jewish community on the Westside. Each staff produced its own weekly full of local news and features inserted into the fat pages of the main paper. The Sunday paper, if it landed wrong, could kill your toy poodle. "Own the suburbs" was our battle cry. I was assigned to the San Gabriel Valley section, our office a cinderblock building that sat on a dead end street in the town of Temple City. We shared a parking lot with a metal plating sweatshop where the workers, men and women from Mexico, came and went at all hours of the night. I knew this because I didn't work a normal shift like my colleagues. Much to the dismay of our editor, Don Hunt, I checked in at noon and headed out to prowl the streets. My favorite was Valley Boulevard, an epic that shoots through the towns of Monterey Park, San Gabriel, Alhambra, and Rosemead—all the way out to Walnut. Here, the newest supermarkets were now Pagoda-roofed and the storefront signs of dentist, launderer, and baker written in Chinese. For lunch, I would stop at my favorite Pho house and let my face feel the steam of the piquant broth of Hu tiu tom cua, a complete soup meal of shrimp, crab, greens, and thin noodles. And then I'd make my way to the Turning Point Bar and spend the evening watching the dancing bear girls play $200-a-drink footsie with the highflying businessmen from Taiwan.

Over the next year, I documented one of the most sweeping demographic and social transitions ever experienced by a suburban region—the rise of America's first suburban Chinatowns along the corridors of Valley and Atlantic boulevards. The arrival of hundreds of thousands of ethnic Chinese from Taiwan, Vietnam, Hong Kong, and China had altered every institution of civic life. Teachers talked of being missionaries in their own country. Old-timers spoke of feeling alienated from the only home they'd ever known. For every Asian migrating there, another white or Latino resident was leaving.

The voices of flight captured in my notebooks sounded like this:

"I know I cringe when I hear my friends make racial remarks. But when they tell me that the sheer numbers of Chinese are overwhelming, I can't tell them otherwise. When they tell me that they go shopping and are pushed over by Chinese women behind carts, I can't disagree because the same thing's happened to me."

"I feel like an outsider. I have withdrawn, and in my withdrawal, I feel a great loss. I'm a citizen of a town that has gone beyond me. The only thing the same is that I live on the same piece of dirt."

"I remember the Garvey Hardware Store. We'd go there every Saturday to chew the fat. In one afternoon, you'd be able to catch up on all the city news and politics and also get the widget you needed to get. When I go there now, I'm watched very carefully by the new owners. And when it's time to pay and I pull out my credit card, they ask for my driver's license and phone number. Am I entitled to feel a little resentful after shopping at a store for thirty-two years and living in a community for thirty-two years and suddenly having to feel like a stranger?"

"We barely find out that the old neighbors have left when, puff, the new neighbors bulldoze the house and yard and begin building not one house but a two-story monster. It's a dozen condos with walls that extend from lot line to lot line. Open space is a foreign concept to them."

The voices of the newcomers weren't so easy to capture. One Saturday evening in the winter of 1986, I stumbled upon a little wood frame house on Muscatel Drive in Rosemead. From inside the living room came a shout, "Dap no! Dap no, Howk Hogan!" Through the front window, I could see a shirtless man with pants rolled up to his knees, standing in front of the TV, his arms flailing crazily. In Vietnamese and pidgin English, he gave out another belly roar. "Go get 'em, Howk Hogan. Beat 'em. Dap no!"

One of his sons, a teenager named Tai, appeared from the back and assured me that all was well inside his home. Hulk Hogan, the professional wrestler and his father's favorite American, had just dispensed with another opponent.

"He goes crazy. We tell him that it's fake, but he doesn't believe us. When they bleed, he turns to us and says, 'Is that fake? Is that fake?' We've stopped trying to convince him."

Tai opened the door and I walked into the lives of the Lams: Xuong Lam and his sweet wife, Ngoc Lam, and his eighty-year-old mother, Vien Tran, a devout Buddhist, and his thirteen children ranging in age from thirty-one to thirteen, six girls and seven boys, all under one roof. "We're used to being crowded," Tai explained. "We Chinese can make bedrooms out of anything."

He and his brother Bao were twins who looked nothing alike. Bao lived in fear of his grandmother, who called him a "four-legged Vietnamese animal" whenever he didn't speak Chinese. She told him to bring home nothing less than a Chinese spouse, and she'd better be able to speak her particular Chinese dialect, Chiuchou. "We like American women," Bao said, "but my grandmother told us if we ever dated an American girl, she will sweep her out of the house with a broom."

Over the next several weeks, I returned to the house on Muscatel again and again. The Lams stood out as a remarkable example of getting ahead by pooling resources, delaying gratification, and assigning each family member a role based on his or her potential in America. I was never quite sure who made this call—the father or the children—but it was a decision based on purely objective measures. Thus the oldest children with the poorest English skills put aside dreams of college and went to work for the U.S. Post Office. They didn't spend their paychecks on themselves but turned over their earnings to their father, a brilliant and fair-minded man who had been a paper mill tycoon in Vietnam before the Communists took everything. With that money (and a little welfare dough kicked in from Uncle Sam) Xuong Lam was buying and rehabbing rundown houses and renting them out to refugees like himself. Five years in L.A., and already he was a paper millionaire. His middle children, perfect fifty-fifty grafts of old and new, were winning straight As and making plans for professional careers. Then there were the youngest ones, the brothers Tai, Bao, and Qui, who recalled little of the Thai refugee camps and even less of Vietnam. America for them was an exaggeration, a place to surrender their souls to the pursuit of easy money. They woke up and went to bed with games of high-stakes poker in their head.

Tai was the tallest, the most handsome, and every bit as bright as his father. When he wasn't beside me, I was greeted by the newcomers as the "white ghost" or the "FBI man." With Tai as my translator, I gained the trust of scores of families. He called me "Markie Boy" and taught me the right way to hold chopsticks and not to cringe when the whole table of Chinese Vietnamese boat people gobbled furiously from the same plate of noodles. I took him home to meet my wife, Coby, and our little baby, Ash, and before long he became part of the family. He loved the way Coby dressed her salads—olive oil, wine vinegar, fresh garlic, and lemon juice—and the lamb chops we barbecued on Sundays. He'd spend hours teaching Ash puzzles and reading her books, and then he'd fall asleep on our couch. Every so often, in the middle of the night, we'd hear him scream. One night, he told us about the church man in Pittsburgh whose good Christian family had sponsored their resettlement to the United States—and then molested Tai.

"Sometimes I wonder if there is anybody in the world that I love," he said. "My father, mother, brothers, and sisters. I never told someone I loved them. The Chinese way is not to say, 'I love you.' Americans say it all the time, even when they don't mean it. I'm not sure which is worse.

"If I told my father I loved him, he'd probably laugh at me. Sometimes I get the urge to say 'I love you' to someone. I almost told a girl that once. I guess deep down inside, I'm still very Chinese. Sometimes I stay up late at night and wonder who I am. I keep thinking and thinking . . . I guess I think too much."

He was making plans for college when he got a part-time job at a casino dealing Pai Gow. The Asian winners tipped him big, but as soon as his shift ended, he turned into a player and gave it all back. His gambling losses piled up to the tens of thousands of dollars, and he borrowed from friends who were always willing to bail him out because he had bailed them out a few months earlier. If their generosity wasn't enough, he'd visit the Chinese loan sharks and, if he really got desperate, his father. There was no greater loss of face than watching his father dig into his pockets to cover a debt that they both knew wouldn't be his last. "He doesn't have to say a word, Markie Boy. I just see the look in his eyes and it says everything."

After a friend of his who owed a hundred grand was murdered, I persuaded Tai to break clean of the casino life and join us in Fresno. I got him a job busing tables at a local Vietnamese restaurant, but he lasted only a few weeks. At the Indian casino in the hills above town, he had met Crystal, a rich Chinese girl from Singapore who was attending Fresno State. For the next five years, Tai lived in Fresno on Crystal's dole. His father and mother would drive up to visit, always bringing us a fifth of cognac and two jars of Hawaiian macadamia nuts. "Mr. Mark," his father would say, bowing his head as he shook my hand. "Thank you for helping Tai."

Then one day, Crystal left for graduate school in Ohio, and Tai returned to Los Angeles. He'd check in with us every few months, the news never good. He was dealing at Larry Flynt's Hustler Casino in Gardena and trying to raise a baby son from a short-lived relationship with a Cambodian prostitute. Finally he decided that the boy would be better off living with one of his younger sisters and her husband; his son called them Mom and Dad, and he was "Daddy Tai." Twice he called from the Los Angeles County jail, where he was locked up for drunk driving. He drank to forget the long nights of losing big.

"I'm in deep, deep, deep, Markie Boy, and I need a fast way out. I owe about thirty grand. I borrowed from the juice man."

"You need to swallow your pride and go back home, Tai. One last loan from your father, and then make it right."

"I'd rather die than do that. The plan is already in motion. I can't do anything to stop it."

"Plan? What plan?"

He said he was going to rig his Pai Gow table to make sure the house lost. The winners would then split the proceeds with him. He wanted me to say it was all right.

"I'll be out of this mess in three months. I'll be standing at your door."

"You're not a thief, Tai."

"Don't do that to me, Markie Boy. You know I'm not what you think I am. I don't believe in anything. Not Buddha. Not God."

"That's bullshit, Tai."

"I wish I could have a wife like you. Kids like you. But I've never had anybody or anything I've cared about enough."

This was why I would never tell anyone, much less a stranger calling from Las Vegas, where Tai Lam could be found. This is how I found myself one winter evening in 2008 driving east again on Valley Boulevard, straining my eyes to locate the street sign that said the 3000 block of Muscatel Drive. The Turning Point Bar was still standing, the same awning out front. There were hotel high-rises fronting the boulevard, built by investors from the Far East, just as the Taiwanese boomers had predicted two decades before. The all-night jostle that had once been confined to Monterey Park had busted out to the city of San Gabriel and beyond. A profusion of new restaurants—Vietnamese French bakeries, Texas Gulf–style shrimp houses—told me that the established community of ethnic Chinese had been joined by a newer community of ethnic Vietnamese, some of whom had migrated from America's Southwest. I could see that a small war had broken out between the Asian foot massage houses. Prices had been slashed to $9.99 for a half-hour of reflexology.

I might not have recognized the house, but there was the father, in a suit and tie, walking down the driveway.

"Mr. Lam," I shouted. "Mr. Lam."

Before he could answer, I saw a head pop up in the garage that served as a back living area, where the grandmother, long since dead, used to burn her holy paper and change the fresh fruit she offered at the base of her ancestor shrine.

"Markie Boy. Is that you?"

He shuffled outside in his slippers and we hugged. He must have weighed a hundred pounds, and one of his front teeth was missing. "I got into a fight with that crazy Cambodian, and she knocked it out," he said sheepishly. We both knew that his affair with crack years ago had rotted every tooth in his mouth. Soon they would all be missing.

"I wasn't sure if I'd find you dead or alive, my man."

"Barely, Markie boy."

His mother, gray and shrunken, kept bowing and grasping my hand. Ngoc Lam still spoke little English. I bowed back and embraced her, and then she hurried off to the kitchen.

"Tai, what's happened?"

"I lost my job. I lost my car. Another DUI, Markie Boy. This time a year in jail. I just got out."

I could see a laptop sitting on the bed, the screen frozen to an online football betting pool.

"I'm stuck here, right where you found me. What was that? Twenty or twenty-five years ago? I'm a forty-year-old man now. But look, no gray. You, no gray either."

"How's Brandon?"

He pulled out a photo, a beautiful boy. "He's five years old. I don't see him much. It's better that way. Why confuse him."

His mother handed me a cup of hot tea, opened the dresser drawer, and began pulling out family albums. She pointed to a faded Polaroid of the church people in Pittsburgh who had sponsored them. "Very nice," she said. And then one by one, with snapshots filling in for words, she took me through the arc of her children's lives. There was Nga, the middle daughter, the one with a sassy mouth. She had grown up to be a lawyer and married a Jewish man, a lawyer too, and they had one girl. There was Le, the serious one who had attended Cal Poly Pomona with a double major in math and computer science. She was now an optometrist living outside Cleveland with a Chinese husband and two children. There was Dung, the tiniest one, always smiling with a mystery book under her arm. She had become a high school teacher and married another teacher, a Mexican man, and they were raising one son and Brandon. The oldest Lam children had all married Chinese spouses and still worked at the U.S. Post Office and lived nearby.

Mrs. Lam stuck a half dozen photos in an envelope and asked me to take them home to show my wife. Tai was watching with a funny smile, face puckered, as if to say he understood his mother's pride and understood her disappointments too. Twin son Bao and youngest son, Qui, had found decent jobs, but trouble was never far away. The mother knew this even if she didn't know the details of how Bao and Qui were both moonlighting as bookmakers for the Asian mafia. She was happy that Tai was back at home, living in the converted garage where she lived too. But it wouldn't be for long, she knew. He would soon find his way back to the casino life.

She held a studio portrait of little Brandon, a miniature businessman in suit and tie with a cell phone stuck to his ear. "Very hand . . . some," she said. "Very smart."

It was getting late and neither Tai nor I had eaten. "There's this Vietnamese restaurant down Valley," he said. "Spicy catfish soup."

He went to grab his shoes. His mother reached out and held my hand. "Tai, Tai. You help. You talk."

We ate and drank a few beers, and he reminisced about Jenny, his high school sweetheart who had lived down the block and kept her bedroom window open for him at night. He talked at length about the wagers he placed on pro football, games in which the point spread always fell the bookie's way because of some last-second fluke on the field. I listened and nodded and tried not to say all the things I had said in the past: "You're too smart for this life, Tai." "You've got plenty of time to turn it around." "Get that real estate license and help your dad buy and rent houses." His father was finished buying and renting. He was getting ready to pass on his fortune to his married children and their children.

I took him home, and we walked into the backyard where I had seen so much of their lives play out. The garden where the hens used to peck amid the vegetables they had brought over from Vietnam, and China before that, was gone. With his grandmother dead and his mother turned old, there was no one to tend to them now. He lit a cigarette and took a puff.

"I hate that you came here tonight, Markie Boy. I hate that Ash is in college and Joe is a senior in high school and Jakey is ten. I hate that you and Coby aren't together anymore. It reminds me of everything I've missed."

"A lot of life went by fast, Tai."

All the cages where his brother Ta used to keep his exotic birds were empty. Only one songbird remained.

"I've lived in this country for almost thirty years, and you guys are the only white people I ever really knew, the only white people I ever cared about. I love you guys."

I wanted him to know how much we loved him too. I told the story of how Joe, before he ever uttered the word "Daddy," had learned to say "Tai."

"The little shit. I kept repeating 'Daddy, Daddy' and he kept saying, 'Tai-Tai, Tai-Tai.'"

"It bugged you to no end, didn't it Markie Boy," he said, cackling.

He followed me back down the driveway, and we pledged to see each other soon. "Sometimes I wonder what my life would have been like had we never met," he said. "You know our paths crossed that day by luck. That's why I can't believe in fate or destiny. The game is chance, chance encounters. Luck . . . That's what makes sense to me."

From Valley Boulevard, it was a short drive to downtown Los Angeles. I circled past the skyscrapers and looked for the big beam of light that used to shine down on the *Times Mirror* building. Another seventy-five of my old colleagues, prize winners who had made the paper one of the world's best, had been told that their services were no longer needed. In a matter of three years, a newsroom of 1,300 had been slashed in half by a succession of publishers who were convinced that readers wanted their morning paper to mimic the quick and dirty of the Internet. What counted in the Digital Age wasn't news written in a compelling style or hard-hitting investigative reports or absorbing narratives. What counted were the hits that landed on a newspaper's website. It hardly mattered that the thousands of hits prompted by a small feature story on "shaved" ice, for instance, had nothing to do with snow cones and everything to do with the "shaved" pubis of Britney Spears. The carpetbaggers from Chicago who now owned the paper, and the underwhelming editor they had chosen to run it, were determined to usher in nothing short of a remaking. If it meant giving up the qualities that made us unique, the very service we did best that hundreds of thousands of readers relied on us to do, it was a necessary shedding to attract a new generation of information consumers. A few among us argued that it was a theory of desperation, a violation of the principle that you waltz with the one who brought you to the dance. The fact that it was being imposed by the Tribune Company, a second-rate media chain that wanted nothing more than to see the haughty *L.A. Times* knocked down a few pegs, made it all the more difficult to swallow. Of course, if we were looking for someone easy to blame, they were right here in the San Marino suburbs of Los Angeles. All those blue-blooded Chandler cousins who ached for John Birch to return had finally gotten even with Otis for turning their rag into a newspaper. In the months following his 2006 death, their years of scheming to see that none of Otis's sons would ever become his successor had come to this: The paper was now owned by a midget on a Harley who had made his fortune raising rents on the poor.

Maybe no one family could have held on forever. Bloodlines thin, dynasties are genetically geared to implode. The city, as cities are wont to do, had unfolded along an arc of power that had moved inexorably outward. There was that early epoch of boomers, speculators and wheat farmers, growers of citrus and herders of goats. They gave way to a long run of clubby white capitalists who, one generation removed from the goat glands their fathers harvested to bring back their virility, liked to think of themselves as "old money." They were the latter-day corporate elites whose moment was crowned with the 1984 Olympics they sponsored. Finally the power splintered off into many pieces, with no single node of control but rather a diffusion of union Latinos, Hollywood Jews, Armenian entrepreneurs, and Asians who were building satellites of Tokyo, Seoul, and Hong Kong. Otis Chandler had foreseen the challenges to a newspaper whose model of growth was predicated on the continuing expansion of white suburbia. What would happen when hundreds of thousands of Third World Latinos and Asians began migrating to those suburbs, driving whites to Orange County and San Diego and Phoenix and Las Vegas—places beyond the pale of the *L.A. Times*? Should he open new bureaus to serve them and become the paper of record for the entire West? Or should he redouble his efforts to reach the children of the immigrants and make them his new readers? The paper had attempted to do both with varying degrees of commitment, and mostly failed. I didn't know of a single Chinese patriarch in the San Gabriel Valley who subscribed to the *Times*.

A handful of billionaire industrialists and philanthropists did their best to influence civic affairs in the fashion of the Chandlers. But L.A. had become too flattened out, too inclined to

dispute, for any beneficent rule. Of the twenty-four billion-
aires who called the city home, I found myself most fascinated
by Stewart Resnick who, like Harry Chandler a century before, had leveraged his wealth to buy vast stretches of California farmland and stockpile hundreds of millions of dollars
worth of river water. In less than two decades, Resnick had
purchased 120,000 acres and planted the largest groves of almonds, pistachios, pomegranates, and citrus under the control
of any one man in the world. Only the footprint of J. G.
Boswell, whose family came west from Georgia in the 1920s
and dried up Tulare Lake to carve out the world's richest cotton fields, was bigger. Boswell boasted 140,000 acres and controlled a full 15 percent of the Kings River, which irrigated
more farmland (one million-plus acres) than any other river
except the Nile and Indus. But when it came to the sheer dollars that one man's crops brought in—and the marketing of
those products to the world—Resnick was clearly the new king
of California.

Both men were the sons of terrible drunks. Both ran their
empires from headquarters in Los Angeles and hired the best
college-trained agriculturalists to watch over their distant
fields. Boswell was hardly a dirt-under-the-nails farmer, but
cotton at least ran deep in his plantation past. Resnick, by contrast, was the son of Jewish bar owner in Highland Park, New
Jersey, who headed west in 1956 after his dad gambled away
everything. He made his first million while still in law school
at UCLA, waxing floors and cleaning carpets under the business name of Clean Time Building Maintenance. ("When it's
time to clean, it's Clean Time.") Then he took those same
commercial buildings and began watching over them with security guards and alarm systems. By the 1970s, Resnick con-

trolled half the commercial alarm accounts in Los Angeles, a $100 million business.

This became a springboard to Teleflora, the giant flower-delivery service that his second wife, Lynda, revolutionized with the concept of a "flower in a gift." Roses were short-lived, she reasoned, but the teapot or watering can that the flowers arrived in was a keepsake. Experts in knickknacks, the Resnicks then bought the ultimate house of knickknacks—the Franklin Mint—for the sum of $167.5 million. Lynda shoved aside the commemorative coins and medallions that were the mint's stock-in-trade and introduced a Scarlett O'Hara doll that, all by itself, generated $35 million in sales. From there, it was the John Wayne collector plate and the precise replica, scaled down, of the beaded gown and matching bolero jacket—à la Elvis—worn by Princess Di. By the year 2000, annual sales at the Franklin Mint approached $1 billion.

Looking for a hedge against inflation, Resnick got the idea of dabbling in real dirt. In the late 1970s, he traveled to Delano, the farm town where Cesar Chavez and his union had made so much history, and purchased his first grove—2,500 acres of citrus with a packing plant. Soon after, the Kern County oil companies, looking to unload their farms, approached him with chunks of twenty and forty thousand acres. They were practically giving the land away. That his nearest field in Lost Hills sat more than a hundred miles from his gilded palace in Beverly Hills made for some easy incongruity. But Resnick was only following in the tradition of the late-nineteenth-century industrial tycoons who had developed from afar the first farms in California's interior. What made him different from them and all their progeny was his belief that the city and the farm are part of the same possibility. He had taken the Big Middle culture of co-ops and farmers and wedded it to the L.A. culture of marketing and celebrity, turning his crops into heart-friendly snacks and antioxidant elixirs and chi-chi potions.

I had been trying to get Resnick to tell me his story since the early 2000s, but I could never maneuver past his farm managers or succession of personal secretaries (during one six-month period, three different women held the title). He and Lynda had plucked the nearly forgotten pomegranate and squeezed its ancient, bittersweet fruit into POMWonderful, the ruby-colored juice in the figure-eight bottle (two pomegranates making love) that fought heart disease and prostate troubles. If these claims seemed familiar, the Resnicks had hired some of the world's best medical scientists—to the tune of $25 million in research—to bear them out. Single-handedly they turned the fruit into a rage. On Oscar night, the gift bags handed to the stars carried POMWonderful. Bartenders were mixing Pom martinis, and cosmetologists were giving Pom facials.

On every floor of their high-rise that overlooked West Olympic Boulevard, employees were engaged in the far-flung operations of Roll International—from Paramount Farms to Fiji Water to Teleflora. Yet there was no one in the building that a reporter with a simple question could turn to. Resnick had no office of media relations for the simple reason that he had no media relations. The first time I called looking for a comment, I was working on a story about how Resnick had wrested control of a Kern County water bank built with $74 million in public funds. I explained to the secretary that this private grab didn't put her boss in the best light, and I needed his version of events. "We don't talk to the press," she said. "Good-bye." Click.

My persistence had won over Boswell, and he was a man who abided by the family motto that "As long as the whale never surfaces, it is never harpooned." So I kept trying with Resnick. Then one day in 2008, after reading the Boswell book, he returned my phone call. "I've never given an interview before," he explained. *"Forbes, Business Week, Fortune,* the *New York Times,* I've told them all no. When you're making the kind of money we're making, what's the upside? I'd rather be unknown than known.

"On the other hand, I'm not going to live forever, even with the massive amounts of pomegranate juice I'm drinking. It might be nice if my kids and grandkids could turn to a book someday and read about what we've built."

With that, he invited me to his 25,000-square-foot mansion on Sunset Boulevard, described by a harpist who had performed there as "something akin to Versailles, only grander." That first Saturday, the massive gates opened and I was greeted on the front steps by the Chinese housekeeper and two identical, blow-dried dogs of some high breed. They led me to the rear parlor where Resnick, fresh from a ride on his stationary bike, was expected any moment. I tried to eye the eighteenth-century paintings of Jean-Honoré Fragonard and the marble statues of Napoleon, but there was too much show in the way. Either that or I was on the wrong floor.

He was a short man, right around five foot five, with thin gray hair and a fit build. He wore a Paramount Farms shirt tucked neatly into blue jeans and the most stunning pair of pink, purple, and turquoise socks. "I tell my children no birthday gifts. Just give me real wild socks." A piece of red string was tied around his wrist, part of his flirtation, I had been told, with kabbalah, the occult rituals of the old-world rabbis.

"My life is about California," he said. "I didn't grow up here, but if it wasn't for California, its openness and opportunities, I wouldn't be sitting where I'm sitting. When I arrived in the mid 1950s, it was real simple. You work hard, you get ahead. It was a great time. Everything was like 'wow.' We'll never see those times again."

He recalled his first entrepreneurial inspiration as a thirteen-year-old in Highland Park: selling Christmas to the Christian families of east Jersey. "People didn't have cameras in those days so after a snow, I'd take a picture of their house with the Christmas displays all lit up and sell it to them. I had good technique, but not much artistry."

His pals were all Jewish kids from middle- and upper-class families. It wasn't easy being the poorest one, he said, knowing his father was capable at any moment of losing the few comforts they had. "I remember one time in high school, the car was gone. He lost it in a bet. He was very tough, bull-like, and didn't take crap off anyone. But inside he had these weaknesses. Compulsive gambler and alcoholic."

I wondered, as I wondered with all wealthy men, what accounted for his ambition. Was it the financial insecurity he knew as a child? The insecurity of the small ethnic outsider? Or was money just a grand game?

"Not a game. My father was a great negative role model. The lessons I got from him were all what not to do. About the only positive he taught me was never let anyone push me around. So, yes, I had this drive that came from the financial insecurity I saw as a child. My idea was never to go backward. Always live below my means, so it would give me the flexibility to take risks."

"Living below your means?" I said, smiling.

"Well, none of this is my idea. If I had my way, I'd probably still be living in Culver City in a little ranch house. This is my wife. This is Lynda."

She had recently posed for a photograph in the *New Yorker* to accompany a profile entitled the "Pomegranate Princess." It was a classic shot, a background of heavy-legged gold furniture and paintings in thick gold frames and gold-leafed carpet and gold-fringed drapes. There she stood in the foreground in a black pants suit with open-toed silver pumps and a single piece of jewelry around her neck. In case you mistook her for a woman of understatement, her short auburn hair was teased big and her thin eyebrows arched high. In the distant background, under the gaze of a ten-foot-tall marble goddess, sat husband Stewart in a gold-skirted chair. He was head down in an orbit of paperwork.

"She wanted to tell the story of the pomegranate," he said. "For a long time, she got no credit. Now she's getting lots of credit."

"You kind of got left out of the piece."

"I'm sort of back there signing checks," he said, chuckling. "She's the face. Fine. I'm good with it. But when I decided to plant that first 640 acres of pomegranates, about half the pomegranates in the country at the time, there was absolutely zero market. My farm manager thought I was nuts. 'At worst,' I told him, 'we can make some juice out of it.'"

He said he was looking for a modest return, maybe $500 an acre. But like every other crop he bet on—almonds, pistachios, Clementine "Cutie" tangerines—pomegranates hit big. "I've never had a bum investment in my life. While I'd like to take all the credit, I'd have to say that fully half of my success has been luck. Now in farming we're in a unique position. The crops we grow can only be grown in a few places in the world. But none of it would have happened without luck."

He had caught each crop at the front end of a boom that still showed no signs of abating. Almond sales were rising 10 percent a year in the United States and 25 percent overseas. From one year to the next, the number of almond-bearing trees in California had jumped by 50,000 acres. This wasn't competition because Resnick, in addition to being a grower, sat as a full processor and pusher of nuts. No other farmer, not even Gallo, had cornered a market the way Resnick had, controlling the growing, buying, and selling of pistachios. Of the 400 million pounds produced each year in the United States, 120 million pounds came off Resnick's perfectly groomed fields. Another 140 million pounds were grown by farmers who took their pistachios to Paramount to process and market. Thus Resnick had his hands on 65 percent of the nation's harvest.

"If you want to buy a half million pounds of pistachios anywhere in the world, you have to come to us," he said.

All by himself (with a little help from his lawyers) he had killed the venerable California Pistachio Commission. Here he was, funding the lion's share of the commission's marketing, and not a single Paramount employee was on its board. Worse yet, he claimed, the programs were all geared to helping the small guy. "We were underwriting the costs of programs that were actually doing harm to Paramount. That's not a situation we could tolerate for very long."

To his critics, Resnick represented one of the more evil forces in California agriculture, a behemoth willing to employ teams of lawyers and tens of millions of dollars to shove his agenda down the throats of growers who dared to be independent. A member of the pistachio commission, on the eve of its demise, had told me, "Stewart wants to be a benevolent dictator. But if he thinks you're defying him, he'll start with 'Nobody respects me. Nobody realizes the good I've done for agriculture.' Then he'll move on to, 'Do you know who I am? Do you know what I am? I'm a billionaire.' He's got an awful temper that he's trying to control through kabbalah. That little red string is supposed to remind him to count to ten. But his ego, there's no controlling that. And Lynda, well, she's just over the top. A TV reality show waiting to be discovered."

Resnick had heard it all before. He was the bad guy in agriculture for no bigger offense than he was big. "Look, these farmers go back two, three, and sometimes four generations. Me, I'm the carpetbagger from Beverly Hills. I've never driven a tractor. I've never turned on an irrigation pump. But you ask the growers we process and they'll tell you that year in and year out, no one offers a better price. No one pushes their product harder."

I had one last question I wanted to ask. I told Resnick I had never stopped admiring writer Carey McWilliams for his undying commitment to the agrarian ideal. But more than seventy years after his "Factories in the Fields," we had to be honest about the economics of small farming. Old farmers attached to the soil try to hang on, but their children—professionals and tradesmen—are softened by no such nostalgia. Not when they're getting the same price for a box of plums that their fathers got in 1981. So who could blame the small guy for selling out to a developer for one hundred grand an acre?

I wondered if this meant that our best hope for keeping the valley's farmland from becoming a new century's Los Angeles rested with the Resnicks of agriculture, their economies of scale and marketing genius.

"Are you truly a farmer?" I asked. "Or just another developer in waiting?"

"The valley is the most fertile area for farming that I know of in the world," he said, dodging. "And there's an awful lot of acres."

"The reason I ask is because you've already begun selling farm water, at least on paper, to other big agricultural concerns—Newhall Ranch, Castle & Cook—so they can turn their fields into suburbs."

"We're not talking about taking water and committing it forever to these projects. We're just saying we believe we have enough water to occasionally pump some for them. Our first loyalty is to our trees."

"For how long?" I asked.

His answer was the answer of a billionaire. "If there's some big opportunity for us to take a couple thousand acres and build a nice industrial park out there, we're going to do it. I don't see it as 'Oh my God, we're paving over farmland.' That's just life. But on balance, unless there's a really big opportunity, there's a continuity to farming that I like."

Every time I barrel down the steep descent of the Tehachapi and cross the Mason-Dixon line that divides the sprawl of Southern California from the farm fields of the Central Valley, the same question occurs to me: Am I a fool for believing that this valley's birthright is agriculture, that if God intended a place to be something, He intended this place to be farmland? Nowhere else in the world brings together land, sun, soil, and water in such harmony. Then I think of the fools like me in Pasadena and Valencia and Van Nuys who believed those orange groves would always be orange groves.

It was Saroyan and later Stegner and Didion who taught me that every writer who comes from the land must eventually confront a deep ambivalence about the place that nurtured him. The writer does this one of two ways. He leaves and writes about his place from afar, hoping the distance gives him not only perspective but a rein on his anger and a check on his heart. Or he stays and tries to work it out from within, the past and present knocking heads and confusing his feelings. If he stays, his writing sometimes misses the mark. This is because the immediacy he has gained by being so close to his subject can bring too much heat, too much passion. At the halfway point in my newspaper career, after stints in New York, Baltimore, and Los Angeles, I chose the latter, returning home to the valley, digging my heels into native ground. It has been a messy affair, but I am still here, trying to put my finger on this place.

If I brought a different passion to the stories I did on the valley, most of my editors didn't seem to mind. Whether the issue was growing new towns in the middle of the vineyards or the tens of millions of dollars in crop subsidies that went to the richest families in Fresno, the stakes always seemed higher here than when I was writing about L.A. The reasons were obvious in one respect—it was my home—and yet I sensed a deeper explanation that had to do with how we as a society related to place. I began to consider the different ways—three by my count—that Americans connect to place, each one a way of living.

The first evolves out of the idea that place is moveable, that you can take home with you or create home wherever you are. This becomes an easier proposition because so much of what makes a place unique has been lost in America, swallowed up by the tide of homogenization. If one place looks identical to the other place, then place is no big deal. And losing place is no big tragedy. Place is not only moveable, it is disposable. The second notion of place is the way a historian or social scientist sees it. Place becomes your subject and as a subject it must be kept separate from your soul. You can live in such a place, become a student of such a place, and even find a measure of accord with that place, because it is your home and your laboratory. But the place is never you and the changes that come to it are never taken personally. You live above the fray. This was the sense of place that informed my writing about Los Angeles. The third notion of place is one of deep roots and intimacy, a direct connection between a person and place, right down to its earth. I am bound to this place. You cannot separate me from it. As the land is being remade, where is my place? I am tied to this place, and yet as it abandons itself, does it also abandon me? In this way, place is not simply geography but a spiritual relationship to the geography, and it is this relationship that gets lost as the land becomes transformed. This was the sense of place that I brought to bear in my writing about the valley from the day I touched down in the foggy winter of 1990.

I had arrived at the cusp of an era of stunning growth. A half million acres of the state's best farmland was being converted to new Targets and Home Depots and terra cotta subdivisions with Orwellian names such as The Orchards. Up and down Highway 99, city council agendas were filled with pages and pages of applications for rezoning. As far as I could tell, not a single one was ever denied. In the County of Kern, supervisors decided that the planning commission, the last bridle to boom, needed to be eliminated. Developers were building residential tracts without even the sewer lines to service them. In Bakersfield, the most sprawled city in the West, a whole new side of town was taking shape with nothing more than septic tanks. In Fresno, the Planning Department had been renamed the Development Department. The salaries of the development director and all his staff were now funded by the builders themselves; the faster they pushed each project through the pipeline (the fewer questions they asked) the faster the fees from the developers poured in.

The local newspapers, their Saturday and Sunday editions fat with builder ads, weren't in a mood to ask questions either. One question seemed obvious: At a time of boom, why were cities scrambling to balance their budgets? Why had the unemployment rate of 14 percent not budged? Why were drivers getting killed on one-lane country roads that served as the only route in and out of Apricot Estates? Why was the main lobbyist for the building industry driving around town in a fancy car with the license plate REZONE?

I spent months digging through planning documents, sitting through public meetings, and comparing decades of local budgets. What I found did not please the building industry associations or the chambers of commerce or the publishers of the Bees. From Bakersfield in the south to Stockton in the north, the boom was scarcely reaping economic prosperity. In a paradoxical twist, growth was actually draining the coffers of every city and town in a 250-mile stretch of middle California. For every dollar that the boom was generating, cities were spending roughly two dollars to provide streets and sewers and cops to serve the new suburbs. To cover the loss, one city after another had taken on record bond debt. The builders had city hall in a classic bind. Cities needed the

front-end revenue from property and sales taxes to cover the
hefty back-end costs of sprawl. This meant that each new losing subdivision was being approved to pay for the losing subdivision before it. It was a giant Ponzi scheme.

The immediate source of the problem was in plain view.
Valley towns, in a lavish gift to a handful of local builders, were
failing to charge the development fees that cities to the north
and south were charging. In San Jose or Glendale, for instance, a three-bedroom, two-bath house was generating
$45,000 in fees—everything from a fee for roads, sewers, and
police stations to a fee to beautify downtowns and build parks.
Modesto, Visalia, Stockton, Bakersfield, and Fresno, on the
other hand, were charging less than four grand for the same
house. It didn't take a lot of math to figure out that during a
sustained boom—tens of thousands of new houses rising up on
farmland—valley cities were forgoing hundreds of millions of
dollars to build a better place.

This is why Bakersfield smelled the way it did and looked
the way it did. Why the roads were full of peril and a fifteen-
minute drive across town—red light to red light—took thirty
minutes. (Synchronization is a fee too.) This is why Fresno
had one of the lowest parks-to-people ratio in the nation and
why downtown had become a roost for pigeons. Why a dozen
valley men with names such as Spanos, Bonadelle, McCaffrey,
Wathen, and Assemi were multimillionaires making a 40 to 50
percent profit on each house they built, an unheard return in
the nation's building industry.

With its patchwork services, Fresno had consigned itself to
the status of a third-rate city. "It's pretty basic," Walt Kieser,
an expert on municipal financing, told me. "Good infrastruc-
ture is what the best industries and retailers are looking for

when they locate to a city. In Fresno, they've done such a miserable job with the roads, parks, libraries, and schools that they haven't created a nice place to live. Instead, they've allowed developers to just maximize their profits."

In Bakersfield, at least one politician was sorry. "I knew residential development wasn't paying its way," Pauline Larwood, a Kern County supervisor, said. "Yes, I voted for my share of developer projects in other supervisors' districts. I did so because if I wanted something in my district, I was going to need their vote."

In Fresno, there were no such apologies. "Slowing growth is elitist and anti-market and anti–free enterprise," Ken Steitz, a real estate lender who moonlighted as a Fresno city councilman, told me. "If a builder comes before the council and meets all the requirements, I don't believe we have a right to tell that developer no. And let's call developer fees what they are: hidden taxes. We don't need any more taxes."

Had Steitz, a born-again Christian, been more honest, he would have added that he was a drunk and a philanderer in the clutches of a half dozen developers. He and his fellow council members were pushing the view that California environmental laws did not apply to Fresno. Developers needn't fuss with the environmental impact reports that were basic in every other major city. The San Joaquin Valley had overtaken L.A. as the nation's smog capital, but the council refused to consider how the new subdivisions on the far fringe of town were polluting the air. When the city's own economic impact studies began showing that each housing tract was putting Fresno deeper in the red, Mayor Jim Patterson stepped in. The city, he said, could no longer afford to do economic analysis. The studies were shit canned.

I talked to one longtime builder from Southern California who couldn't believe his good fortune upon landing in Fresno. "The first time I stood at the Development Department's front counter and realized what they were requiring me to do— which was nothing—I thought I had died and gone to heaven," he told me.

To further my indoctrination, I paid a visit to the father of American sprawl himself, Eli Broad. He had built more houses across suburbia than any other man in history, changing the face of cities from New Jersey to California. Now, in a second act that could not have been further removed from those days at Kaufman & Broad, he seemed to be doing penance. He was trying to revive downtown Los Angeles, a core that had been gutted by the subdivisions he had planted across the basin. As we sat in his Sun America building thirty-eight stories above Century City, his office at the very top, he traced his rise from the shy, big-eared son of Jewish socialists to a billionaire philanthropist trying to change the culture of the city he had come to love. To better illustrate his vision of downtown, we got into the backseat of his limo and took a drive.

"You're a very dangerous man," he said.

"Why do you say that?"

"Because you make me feel comfortable."

Then, with a missionary's glare, he made a remarkable confession. The way he and every other home builder paved over the landscape was wrong. The growth they were bringing— cookie cutter houses with strip malls on fertile farmland—was no longer tenable. "The costs of urban sprawl are very expensive," he said. "We've got to build closer in, higher densities and do whatever's necessary to save the farmland." Maybe he really believed it. Or maybe the old developer in him merely understood that the future of growth, or at least the hippest growth, was moving away from the exurbs and back to the neglected city centers.

A few days after my first story appeared in the *Times* exposing the low fees and high costs of growth, I awoke to the heat of a community-wide blowback. The head of the building industry association used his weekly column in the *Bee* to call me a liar. On the news pages, a *Bee* reporter dug up a whole new set of figures that contradicted the numbers I had come up with. The conclusion was clear: I had cooked my analysis to make Fresno and its developers look bad. The popular host of a local radio talk show ranted on the air: "This is the same Mark Arax whose father was murdered in this town in 1972, a crime that was never solved. He's a bitter kid who has let his anger get in the way of objective reporting." A few days later, the *Bee* discovered that its story had been wrong. A city bureaucrat had given the paper false information to discredit my story and make it appear as if developers were paying their fair share. None of it mattered now. In the minds of the powerful, I was the prodigal son who, chip on his shoulder, had come home to dump on the home team.

True, I knew things about the valley, secrets that were whispered but never chronicled in any official way. I knew that Ed Kashian, one of the wealthiest developers in Fresno, had learned how to influence politicians from an old technician, his father. Big Mike Kashian, straight from Detroit, became card-playing friends with my grandparents and was never very careful when he boasted that his buildings downtown, fronts for prostitution, were protected by the mayor, police chief, and district attorney. I knew that Harold Zinkin, Kashian's partner, was having an affair with a councilman's wife, paying her a salary while the councilman was voting to approve his rezones. •

And I knew that John Bonadelle, the most formidable builder in Fresno, had been a cattle rustler who was caught three times hauling off steers from neighbor ranches during the worst deprivations of World War II. After a stint at San Quentin, he changed his name from Bontadelli to Bonadelle and went into the construction trade. He was a short, thick man in his mid-seventies who was rumored to have stared down the Mafia in a land deal gone bad. I saw for myself how intimidating he could be during a city council meeting to consider one of his applications for rezoning. He wanted to build hundreds of houses in a part of town that had been deemed off-limits to growth because it lacked water, sewer, and roads. He took a seat front and center where no council member could possibly miss him and waited with a smile that wasn't a smile. The wording of the motion was confusing, and councilwoman Esther Padilla, a Bonadelle lapdog, looked flustered as she cast her vote. She ended up voting, much to her surprise, against the rezone. By a 4 to 3 margin, John Bonadelle had suffered a rare defeat. His face turned red with rage, and he summoned Padilla to the outer hall. I followed right behind and watched as he backed her into a corner. I couldn't hear their words, but Padilla appeared to be begging for forgiveness. After the break, the council reconvened, and Padilla raised her hand to speak.

"Would it be possible," she pleaded, "to return to the last item so I could change my vote?" The council voted again, and Bonadelle got his rezone.

His office sat on old fig ground in the northwest part of town not far from where I lived. When I called to set up an appointment, he did not remember that I was the kid who grew up on Lafayette Avenue just behind his mansion. It took up nearly a full block of Van Ness Extension, the lawn so wide that the USC marching band (his children were Trojans) came there every summer to play at a fund-raiser. In the far backyard, Bonadelle kept a pen of squawking peacocks that occasionally broke out and showed up, in full plumage, on our front lawn. The old cattle rustler had no trouble herding them back home.

I knocked on his office door, but there was no answer. I walked in and stood in front of the secretary's desk, but there was no secretary. From the other room came the sound of snoring, and I followed it to the doorway. There was Bonadelle, cowboy boots on his desk, taking an afternoon nap. I tiptoed back into the lobby and studied the mounted photos of the rare African long-horned cattle he kept at a small spread west of the highway. At some point he awakened and invited me into the conference room, where I proceeded to ask him about every rumor I ever heard about his payoffs to politicians—cash, booze, and whores. He stopped me only one time to lodge a protest, and that was when I told him I was planning to write a profile about him that would include his time in San Quentin.

"Would you mind turning off that tape recorder?" he asked in a gruff voice.

"Sure."

"Now, I've got a wife and three kids who know nothing about my prison time. And I'm an old man with grandchildren who think I'm pretty special. You wouldn't want to destroy all that, would you?"

He started to horse trade. "I'll give you what you want if you leave that out."

I promised to leave his prison time out of the story, but he gave me nothing that was worth a damn. As it turned out, I didn't need his assistance. With a little more digging, I found out that Bonadelle, in an effort to get his housing tracts green-lighted in the little boomtown of Clovis, had bribed several local politicians. At least one of them, a councilwoman named Pat Wynne, had turned him down flat. At first, Wynne didn't want to tell the story, fearing what Bonadelle might do to her. But the FBI already was in town, snooping around. So she decided to go on the record:

"John Bonadelle invited me to coffee one day and said he thought every pretty girl ought to be driving a Mercedes or Cadillac. I told him I liked my Toyota. Then he said I could be making $250,000 a year selling real estate, and all I needed was for him to open the door. He said, 'Tonight, when you lay your pretty head on your pillow and think about your future, I want you to think of John Bonadelle.' I kept thinking, 'My God, how blatant. This only happens in cheap paperback novels.'"

The FBI and assistant U.S. attorney in Sacramento couldn't believe how blatant it was: cash handed over in paper bags at the country club; politicians selling votes for a new set of car brakes, an oil job, a contract to build a fence. Before it was over, sixteen politicians and developers pleaded guilty or were found guilty. Farid Assemi, the builder who liked to finger a string of worry beads and play bridge on the international circuit, came to a teary-eyed deal with the feds. His main lobbyist, Jeff Roberts, the man with the REZONE license plates, took the fall and was hauled off to prison. Right behind him was old man Bonadelle.

I went to federal court to hear the guilty plea of Big Bob Lung, the blustery city councilman who had whined that my reporting was nothing more than the get-even of a murdered man's son. The evidence showed that Lung had sold his votes to Bonadelle for, among other things, a new blue suit. As he stood up to come clean, I couldn't believe my eyes. He was pleading guilty wearing the same blue suit.

As the mortgage industry imploded and the foreclosure notices stacked high, reporters for the national dailies kept heading to the north valley, to the delta towns of Manteca and Stockton and Lathrop, where the housing crisis had hit harder than in any other region of the country. I kept waiting for one of them to find Norman Jarrett, the South African developer who in the 1990s had gone from city to city in Northern California peddling a creation he called Gold Rush City. Not until he came upon Lathrop, a town of 8,859, untouched by cynicism and surrounded by cheap open land, three freeways and the outspread tail of the San Joaquin River, did he find a taker. The town had been incorporated only two years before and was looking to land something big. If Gold Rush City seemed long on swagger and short on capital, Jarrett had already found a local partner, a sugar beet farmer with 4,500 acres in the floodplain.

That the actual Gold Rush never made it anywhere close to those sugar beet fields seemed forgivable once you stepped inside Jarrett's office. Prospector's picks and pans and gold-plated spittoons lined the perimeter and Tiffany lamps were swagged overhead. The phone number ended in 1-8-4-9 and the fax number in 1-8-4-8, the year the first nugget was found at Sutter's sawmill along the American River, touching off the madness of the El Dorado ("the Gilded"). Jarrett's car, a Cadillac El Dorado, had been fitted with the license plate "Gldrsh2," presumably because someone else had already taken "Gldrsh" and "Gldrsh1."

As he turned off the lights and fired up the projector, he wanted to make one thing clear. No slide show on earth could possibly do justice to his $4 billion project—its four theme parks, its Barbary Coast, its 1849 mining town, its Boot Hill, Fisherman's Wharf, Safari Zoo, Hungarian horse show, Chinese circus, 120,000-seat auto speedway, sports arena, performing arts center, three golf courses, four world-class hotels, and 8,500 houses done in Italian, German, English, and Chinese motifs on a single boggy island called the Stewart Tract.

"Other than Disney World," he said, "this is probably the biggest project of its kind in the United States."

On the far white wall of his office, the dream assumed vivid color. "Water is the reason we came here. You'll be able to get to the site from Old Sacramento and Pier 39 in San Francisco by smaller craft. We're going to have a marina, a water bus. There'll be high noon gun battles in the streets. We would like to recreate the mountains, the rivers, the lakes and pan for gold. Whatever gold you find, you get to keep. You might hit it big, as they say."

He would hear no talk that Lathrop, saddled with some of the worst tule fog in winter and satanic heat in summer, would be anything less than a destination spot for vacationing families. "We'll have lions, leopards, and tigers. A giant grizzly bear statue will announce the site. We don't think it would be as large as the Statue of Liberty or the Statue of Christ in Rio but certainly big enough to see from all points."

As I left Jarrett that day, he was wearing a suit and tie and standing in the muck of a January flood that had left the entire island under water for three months. He was vowing to build a levee that no man on earth had ever attempted, a bulwark that would hold back everything but the thousand-year flood. Now, eighteen years later, the local newspaper headlines told of another deluge: FORECLOSURES HIT RECORD HEIGHTS; 170% INCREASE IN SAN JOAQUIN COUNTY.

"Norman isn't here any longer. And Gold Rush City is now River Islands at Lathrop," Susan Dell'Osso, who ran the new office, informed me. "I used to work with Norman. He was a pure visionary, that's for sure. I'm now the project manager."

An Englishman whose family fortune came from the shipping business had already dumped $150 million into erecting a levee and bringing in gas and electrical lines. Not one of River Islands' 11,000 houses had been built yet. As for the theme park, and all those commercial and industrial businesses that would rise in its wake, well, they had to be jettisoned.

"We've gone through a few changes. After all, it's been eighteen years," Dell'Osso said. "But our enthusiasm for this project hasn't diminished. You're welcome to visit and look for yourself. I promise no slide shows."

I headed north up 99 past the town of Madera, where a Kaufman & Broad tract called Orchard Pointe had been halted after a third of the 340 houses were built. The mobile trailer where the KB sales staff had worked in a fever alongside the lenders from Countrywide Financial was shuttered. The lots were laid out and streets all paved, but not a single house stood on Apple Drive or Pomegranate Lane. Along Mandarin and Blueberry Way, tumbleweeds had popped up through the hardpan. The whole north valley had become a land of yard sales. The sign twirler on the street corner pointed the way to a Mervyn's closeout with 50 percent discounts.

As I followed the river's bend and veered toward the Lathrop city hall, I found myself in the middle of the Mossdale master planned community. It was 1,500 new houses and 1,500 empty lots. No one could tell when phase 2 might come. Every third house had been foreclosed upon, the official notices tacked onto the front door telling a grim tale. From the bank: You didn't make your meeting to discuss your interest rate hike. From the utility: You're three months behind in your electricity payment. From the code enforcement arm of Lathrop: You've violated sections 8.24.030—the removal of furniture, garbage, junk and/or debris.

On Mossdale's commercial drag, the community's one restaurant and home design store were plastered with giant "Now Open" signs; they were now closed. The new city hall was still sparkling, but it had been financed with the revenue stream from the developer. And that revenue was drying up as Mossdale fell on hard times. To meet the building's debt, Lathrop was dipping into its reserve funds. "We're good for a few more years," the grim-faced assistant city manager said. "But if this lasts for four or five years, we're going to have some issues."

River Islands sat on the other side of the bank, its owners now grateful for every environmental roadblock that had kept them from building a single house and following Mossdale into foreclosure's descent. "Thank goodness it collapsed when it collapsed," Dell'Osso said. "Can you imagine us trying to sell million dollar houses in this market?" The levee that now rose to protect River Islands was nothing like the twenty-five-foot-wide levee that guarded Mossdale and was breached in the 1997 flood. This levee was a "super levee" in the words of Dell'Osso's husband, Ron, a third-generation farmer who grew pumpkins next door. "Hop in my truck, and I'll show it to you," he said. I had seen the granddaddy of California dikes on the lake bottom land that J. G. Boswell farmed, but this was some other phenomenon. It measured three hundred feet at the crown, and there was no edge to it. So much earth had been moved that its sides now blended into the field that once sat below. "It's going to take a storm of biblical proportions for the water to top this levee," the farmer said. "We haven't trumped nature. There is no such thing. But the whole state of California would have to be under water for this levee to give way."

I turned around and headed south, all the way past Tulare and Pixley, until I reached a place that had no name in the middle of a vineyard along the Southern Pacific railroad tracks. It was here, almost a decade earlier, that I knocked on the door of a tarpaper shack that seemed lifted right out of the Mississippi Delta, circa 1930. Out came a black man bent and holding a cane, his drawl a stutter. He said his name was James Dixon, and he took out his driver's license to prove it. I assured him that I was no official from the housing authority, no officer of the law. Just a writer wondering how he landed here, from where and how long ago.

He was part of a lost tribe of black Okies who had been living in the alkali dust of Tulare County for more than a half century. They were the great exception to America's great migration. Unlike millions of other blacks who had fled the rural South for the promise of the northern city, they had come west looking to keep alive their rural souls, all the way down to the cotton picking. He was ninety-five years old and slept on a fifty-year-old bed of iron with a barley sack for a pillow. The bed wasn't quite long enough for his five-foot-five frame, so he rested his pillow on a beekeeper's wooden box. He was throwing the last limbs of a pecan tree his uncle had planted years ago into a potbellied stove to keep warm. Weather and rats had chewed a gaping hole in his ceiling. To keep it from falling, he wedged empty Vienna sausage cans into the crevices. Chickens in the San Joaquin Valley lived in a better roost.

"Soon as I get into bed at night, I go to praying and singing," he said. "Church songs. I keep in good spirits."

Now Barack Obama was president and James Dixon was dead, as were so many of the other black Okies whose lives I had captured with photographer Matt Black. I drove farther out until I reached the spot in the road where Highway 43 meets the town of Allensworth. Here, exactly a century ago, a black colonel from the U.S. Army, Allen Allensworth, came to plant his hope on the salt desert of California. He would build the first black settlement, by and for black people, west of the West.

"If we expect to be given due credit for our efforts and achievements, they must be made where they will stand out distinctively and alone," the colonel said during the town's formal opening in the summer of 1908. "To do this, people of our race must live in a community where the responsibilities of its municipal government are upon them and them alone. This cannot be the case in a city controlled by Caucasians. We would not expect them . . . to turn their cities over to others. They build for themselves and their children; we must do as they did—settle upon the bare desert and cause it to blossom as a rose."

The rose would bloom—church, schoolhouse, store—and then wither when the wells with good water turned up poisoned and dry. I drove into what is now Allensworth State Park and found the faded turquoise house on a patch of prairie so thick with salt that it appeared in the distance as fallen snow. Hallie Jones and her husband, Ed, and their three children used to live here. They moved away not long after their son Eric was found in the cotton field across the tracks with nine bullet holes in his back, burns from electrical wires, and a wooden handle protruding from his rectum. "There's no word to describe his end," she told me. "'Torture' doesn't do it. Neither does 'desecration.' What they did to my son is unlisted."

On the far end of the old settlement, I met Reverend Dennis Hutson, a retired Air Force chaplain who had bought fifty-eight acres at the end of the road where his mother lived. "There's Allensworth of the past," he said, pointing back toward the town site. "And up this road right here is Allensworth of the future."

He had never farmed in his life, but he had spent more than eighty-five grand digging a well 720 feet deep and prepping the land to plant a crop of wheat. Next he would bring in tens of thousands of New Zealand white rabbits to raise for their meat, using their pellets to grow onions, peppers, and garlic.

Why, I asked, would he plant so much time and money in a place that has brought so much heartache to black people?

He looked across the flat horizon to the cemetery on the other side of the field where the original settlers had been buried. "This is one of the poorest places in all of California," he said. "And the basis of any surviving economy must first of all be agriculture. People have to eat. And once you can do that, you can expand and create a revenue base, a tax base, that will be able to afford other amenities into the future."

"Okay, but why here? There is better land all across this valley?"

"I am a minister," he said. "Colonel Allensworth was a minister. He was a military chaplain. I was a military chaplain. This is where the dream for black folks in California began. It's just been laying in the soil. It's been laying dormant for someone to catch the vision, to see the value in the vision and to put in the time and resources to make it grow again. The dream never died."

chapter two

The Agent

Before the wins and losses get tallied up and the war on terror finally goes down in the books as either wisdom or folly, it may be useful to recall what took place on a spring day in 2006 on the thirteenth floor of the federal courthouse in Sacramento. There, in a perfectly dignified room, in front of prosecutors, defense attorneys, and a judge, a tall gaunt man named James Wedick Jr. was fighting for a chance to testify, to tell jurors about the thirty-five years he had spent in the FBI and how it came to be that he was standing before them not on the side of the U.S. government but next to two Pakistani Muslims, son and father, whose scrapbooks and prayers and immigrant dreams were now being picked over in the first terrorism trial in California.

From his seat at the defense table, Wedick stared straight ahead as the prosecutor from Washington, a stocky guy with a little too much bounce in his step, called him a hired gun for the terrorists, arguing that any criticisms the former FBI agent had about the investigation would only confuse the jury and waste the court's time. Wedick might have stood up and shouted that he was the most decorated FBI agent ever to work out of the state capital, that for years prosecutors, judges, and juries had nothing but time to consider the way he busted dirty state senators and cracked open the biggest health care scam in California history. But now he could only sit and listen as the judge ruled that the highlights in his career—Abscam, Operation Fountain Pen, Shrimpscam, Bonanno—were no reason to believe he had anything of value to offer about the FBI's conduct in the age of terror or, more to the point, about the government's case against Hamid Hayat, the cherry packer, and his father Umer, the neighborhood ice cream man. By order of the court, Wedick was muzzled.

In eight weeks of trial, fifteen witnesses for the prosecution and seven witnesses for the defense took the stand, yet the one witness whose testimony might have struck a devastating blow to the claims of the U.S. government never got to tell his story. He never got to trace his metamorphosis from agent's agent to turncoat to a Sunday morning in June 2005, when he woke up thinking he had seen all the absurdities that a life of crime fighting had to offer only to find the FBI videotape—the confession that would lie at the heart of the case—on his doorstep.

It had arrived with no small hype. Down the road on Highway 99, the feds had busted up an Al Qaeda sleeper cell in the farming burg of Lodi, population 60,000, the apparent inspiration for Credence Clearwater's "Stuck in Lodi Again." The town sits at the far northern edge of the San Joaquin Valley and has gone from the "watermelon capital of the world" in the 1880s to the "Tokay grape capital of the world" in the

1920s to the "Zinfandel capital of the world" today. The community boasts sixty wineries, thirty-six tasting rooms, a Zinfest in May, and its own appellation: Lodi-Woodbridge. Somehow burrowed into the 90,000 acres of grape fields that pleat the rich flat loam of the Mokelumne River basin was a radical young Muslim carrying a prayer of jihad in his wallet.

Hamid Hayat had just returned home to Lodi from a terrorist camp in the hills of his ancestral Pakistan. He had been trained there with Kalishnikov rifles and curved swords and target dummies wearing the faces of Bush and Rumsfeld. He was awaiting instructions, via a letter in his mailbox, to bomb hospitals and supermarkets in California's heartland. In the meantime, he was processing Bing cherries on the outskirts of town. The two imams at the small marigold mosque across the street from the Lodi Boys and Girls Club directed the cell at the behest of Osama bin Laden. They were building a multimillion-dollar school to spread the seeds of Islamic holy war to Pakistani immigrant children up and down the farm belt. If the story sounded too bizarre to be true, the twenty-two-year-old cherry packer and his forty-seven-year-old father, Umer Hayat, the ice cream man known to the kids of Lodi as "Mike," had confessed to everything on camera.

At home in the Gold River suburbs of Sacramento, Jim Wedick agreed to study the FBI video as a favor to one of the defense attorneys. He fully expected that he would be calling the attorney back and advising him that son and father, guilty as charged, needed to strike a quick plea deal. After all, it is hard to trump a confession, and in this instance the feds were holding not one confession but two. As Wedick stuck the video in his player and sat back on the couch to watch the grainy images, he recognized the setting right off. It was the old polygraph room at the FBI's regional headquarters on the north side of the capital. Despite the blanked-out faces, he recognized several of the agents too. They had come a long way, he thought, from the days when he ran the white-collar crime squad and they handled $1,000 thefts by bank tellers. In the year since his retirement, after the office had been completely reorganized in the wake of 9/11, these same agents had become experts on counterterrorism. Now, two at a time, they began the five-hour interrogation that would crack a Muslim suicide bomber in the making.

Wedick could see that Hamid Hayat was cold and scared. To keep from fidgeting, he locked his hands between his legs like a kid trying not to pee. He was rail thin with sunken eyes and eyebrows so wonderfully arched that he had the gaze of perpetual befuddlement. Even with his long black beard, he looked more teenager than man.

The agents gave him a blanket and pulled their chairs closer. We're here to listen, not judge. Whatever you tell us about the training camp won't come as a surprise. We have spy satellites over Pakistan, so if you're thinking about lying, you may want to think again. Wedick knew all too well the game they were playing, the back-and-forth between trust and fear. It might take hours, but if trust and fear were maneuvered the right way, the whole room suddenly would turn. One moment the suspect was way up here—seeing the world his way. And the next moment he was way down here—seeing it your way. The free fall, Wedick called it, the release that came from finally shedding the weight of lies. It happened with even the most cunning of crooks.

Hayat shifted in his chair, and his voice grew submissive. One hour, two hours, yawns, cigarette break, yawns, candy break, exhaustion. The free fall never came. Instead, each revelation, each new dramatic turn in his story, was coming from the mouths of the agents first. Rather than ask Hayat to describe what happened, they were describing what happened for him and then taking his "uh-uhs" and "uh-hmms" as solemn declarations. The kid was so open to suggestion that the camp itself went from being a village of mud huts to a building the size of the ARCO basketball arena. His fellow trainees numbered thirty-five, forty, fifty, how about two hundred? The camp was run by a political group, a religious school, maybe his uncle, maybe his grandfather, yes, it was Al Qaeda. The camp's location was all over the map too, from Afghanistan to Kashmir to a village in Pakistan called Balakot. As for weapons training, the camp owned one pistol, two rifles, and a knife to cut vegetables.

Deep into the confession, as the agents kept trying to pin down the contours of one believable story, they succeeded only in betraying their own ignorance. They didn't seem to know the terrain of Pakistan or the month of Ramadan. They didn't seem to fully appreciate that they were dealing with an immigrant kid from a lowly Pashtun tribe whose sixth grade education and poor command of the English language ("Martyred? What does that mean, sir?") demanded a more skeptical approach. And then there was the matter of the father's confession, which veered wildly from his son's account. Umer Hayat described visiting the camp and finding a thousand men wearing black Ninja Turtle masks and performing "pole vaulting" exercises in huge basement rooms. The camp wasn't located in Balakot but one hundred miles in the other direction. Even so, the agents going back and forth between the two interrogations never attempted to reconcile the stark differences in the confessions.

Maybe it couldn't be helped, Wedick thought. Maybe the Hayats' ties to terrorism had popped up out of nowhere and the agents were scrambling to catch up. Yet Wedick would soon find out that this wasn't the first night the agents had encountered the Hayats. They had been tracking them, recording them for three years in an operation launched just weeks after 9/11. It began when a Pakistani undercover informant, fresh from working at McDonald's and Taco Bell, passed on an incredible tip: Dr. Ayman Zawahiri, one of the world's most wanted terrorists, Osama bin Laden's number two man, had been living and praying in Lodi.

The video ended and Wedick picked up the phone and called defense attorney Johnny Griffin. Whatever hesitation he had about taking on the FBI office that he, more than anyone, had put on the map—the office where his wife still worked as an agent—was now gone.

"Johnny, it's the sorriest interrogation, the sorriest confession, I've ever seen."

They speculated that the government had its best evidence still tucked away. "There's got to be a silver bullet, Johnny. Because without it, I just can't see the bureau or the U.S. attorney going forward with this case."

It would take Wedick another year to fully appreciate that this was a different Justice Department, charged with a more righteous task, than the one he had sworn his allegiance to.

Whether the terrorist in our midst is Timothy McVeigh or Mohammed Atta, we, the citizens of the United States, expect the FBI to catch him and his cohorts before they strike. The national conversation about vigilance rarely concedes that no amount of vigilance can ever be enough. No politician dares say that we are too vast a land, too diverse a people blessed with too many freedoms to ferret out every madman. So whenever a madman does strike, we go into overdrive to turn the FBI into something it isn't. From the start, it was more accountant than cop, a bureaucracy (the Bureau) whose turf wars and play-it-safe culture made it tough on any risk taker. For every Melvin Purvis, the G-man who ran down John Dillinger and Baby Face Nelson and earned the jealous wrath of J. Edgar Hoover, there were a dozen agents who sat in the corner and worked nine to five, answering phones and pushing paper.

Jim Wedick had no intention of being one of those faceless agents. Even as a kid growing up in the Bronx in the 1950s, he could tell you the stories that make up FBI lore. Out there was a new Public Enemy No. 1, and he wrote the bureau saying he'd like to join. A month later, an agent from New York was on the phone, wondering if he would come in for an interview. Wedick paused and stammered. He must have forgotten to mention in his letter that he was barely fourteen years old. Nine years later, an accounting degree from Fordham University in his back pocket, he was standing inside the FBI Academy when he received his first posting: Indiana. "How in the hell did that happen?" his fellow graduates wanted to know. All through training, as the other rookies set their sights on San Diego or Miami Beach, Wedick kept telling them about his dream job in Gary, Indiana. That's where Purvis worked. That's where Dillinger carved the gun out of soap to escape from prison. That's where the Lady in Red who fingered Dillinger ran her brothels.

Within a week of landing in Gary, Wedick was trailing a ring of thieves who were hijacking big rigs loaded with steel.

He leaned so hard on one crook that the local mob assumed the guy was blabbing to the new agent with the blue eyes. As a favor to the guy, Wedick faked a late-night confrontation in an underworld bar to show that the crook hadn't sold out to the feds. The crook was so pleased to have his loyalty to the mob restored that he agreed to turn informant. The next day, he led Wedick to a sprawling industrial yard outside of town where a chop shop was hidden inside a giant silo. The hijacked trucks and all their cargo were being cut up like cattle for market.

Wedick's hustle had caught the eye of Jack Brennan, the star of the office who had grown up in Alabama as the son and grandson of FBI agents. Brennan asked Wedick to join him in an undercover operation known as Fountain Pen that was exploring the growing ties between white-collar executives and the Mafia. The investigation had begun to focus on a brilliant Minnesota swindler named Phil Kitzer who was using paper banks to sell phony lines of credit to businessmen, looking to bilk real banks out of millions of dollars in loans. Posing as a pair of young cons, Wedick and Brennan slowly worked themselves into the role of Kitzer's protégés, meeting clients in Germany, Pakistan, Japan, and the Bahamas before flying back to New York City where the flamboyant swindler wined and dined them at the fanciest restaurants, ordering without the benefit of menus. "Give us one of every item you serve," Kitzer would tell the waiters.

Operation Fountain Pen ended with the conviction of dozens of con men and Mafioso across the country. Kitzer himself did six years in a federal penitentiary, but his loyalty to Wedick never wavered. "Jimmy, you and I can talk forever," he'd say. Freed from prison, Kitzer would go on to become one of the FBI's best cooperating witnesses, mailing Christmas cards to Wedick from wherever the bureau had posted him. The Mafia boys, though, never got over their grudge. Fearing reprisal, the FBI decided to ship Wedick all the way out west— to the safety (slumber) of Sacramento.

He arrived in the summer of 1978. The regional headquarters and its satellite offices covered the largest federal beat in the country—from Bakersfield to the Oregon border—with fewer than one hundred agents. It had a reputation, as far back as Prohibition, as a graveyard for federal agents who wanted no part of the front lines. Soon after settling in, Wedick created a splash by snaring Joseph Bonanno Jr. for wire fraud and the chairman of the state teachers retirement system for stealing $1.5 million from the pension fund. As he made his way around town, he kept hearing the same rumor from Sacramento insiders: the state legislature was rife with corruption; $30,000 passed to the right politicians could buy you any law.

Even the most committed undercover agents, working a new angle, took off now and then to relax with their families. Wedick was so obsessed with finding a way to infiltrate the statehouse that he began skipping meals and sleep. During one long stretch, he came home only long enough to watch his first wife leave him. "I was so lost in work I didn't even see it happening. She was packing her bags right in front of me, and it didn't sink in. She ran off with somebody else, and it nearly destroyed me. I kept the house exactly the way she left it for almost two years. Same pictures, same calendars, same notes affixed to the refrigerator."

One day, driving by a Sacramento fish market, the perfect setup struck him. Why not create a dummy business that would import gourmet shrimp from the Gulf of Mexico to Northern California? The company—phony papers, phony home office in Alabama, phony president Jack E. Gordon (a.k.a. FBI agent Jack Brennan)—would require the passage of special legislation to qualify for state loans. If lawmakers and their staff were corrupt and payoffs were needed, the FBI would write the checks. And so it began, Wedick's most brazen sting. From start to finish, Shrimpscam took a decade and became the most ambitious political corruption investigation in California history, netting seventeen convictions and ending the political careers of four state senators and an Assembly leader. When it was over in 1994, Wedick was flown out to Washington, D.C., to receive the Director's Award as the criminal investigator of the year. He shook hands with FBI chief Louis Freeh and then rushed back to Sacramento, where a grand jury was about to hear his next case.

All through the 1990s, as he headed the public corruption squad, Wedick and his team continued to break big cases and make national headlines. They caught developers in Fresno and Clovis buying zoning votes from city councilmen for a set of tires and a brake job. They caught hundreds of medical care providers defrauding the state out of $228 million in health care payments. Prosecutors in the local U.S. attorney's office lined up for a chance to take one of Wedick's cases to court. "Jim brought a New York City pugnacity and abrasiveness to Sacramento and changed the culture of the office," recalled Matt Jacobs, a prosecutor in Shrimpscam. "That detective on TV always in trouble with his supervisors—that was Jim. He didn't go to the shooting range like he was supposed to. He didn't get his physical when he was supposed to. All he did was make big cases."

Wedick's run, like so much else, came to an abrupt end on September 11, 2001. He was in Europe with his wife, Nancy, riding bicycles through the Scottish highlands, when the hijacked planes struck the World Trade Center. His first thought was his deceased father, James, who had been a New York City firefighter for thirty-five years, retiring as battalion chief. He recalled the long campaign his father had waged to keep the Twin Towers from being built. Hours and hours he spent on the phone warning city leaders that the skyscrapers, if hit by a plane, would be a deathtrap for firefighters. "What would Dad think now?" he kept mumbling.

He came home to a different imperative. The war on white-collar crime, his bread and butter, was suddenly an indulgence. In FBI offices across the country, the shift to counterterrorism was swift and unmistakable. In Sacramento alone, dozens of agents from public corruption and other squads were now working foreign intelligence, domestic terrorism, and international terrorism. Federal prosecutions of white-collar crimes would drop by one-third over the next five years. "With everyone looking for bin Laden," Wedick told friends outside the Bureau, "there's no better time for the good old-fashioned American crooks to steal from the people."

Twice he had voted for George W. Bush, but he couldn't help but wonder if the entire war on terror was overblown, based on the false premise of a threat that never went away. He was struck by how willingly people surrendered their civil liberties in a vain experiment to calm themselves, and how they naturally assumed that the federal government must be right when it targeted Muslim communities with moles and wiretaps. Hauling off Arab and Pakistani immigrants to prisons here and abroad without a charge or even a public show of the slightest evidence reminded him of our treatment of Japanese Americans a half century before. What was happening to the

Muslims, of course, was less sweeping than the way fear had been used to wrench Japanese families from their farms and ship them off to internment camps in the desert. Even so, Wedick wondered how a country still haunted by the memory of that injustice could allow these new injustices to take root so casually.

As the Bureau's charge shifted, he felt himself becoming more and more an outcast, until one spring day in 2004 when federal agents, prosecutors, and judges gathered at a restaurant on the grounds of McClellan Air Force Base to pay him tribute. They read a letter from Attorney General John Ashcroft praising his outstanding career and calling his cases "models for other agents to emulate." Then they shook his hand and wished him luck in his new life as a private eye. Whether they realized it or not, they were saying good-bye to the old FBI, as well.

In a cramped little room off the tenth floor of the federal courthouse in downtown Sacramento, a trio of federal officials gathered on the morning of June 8, 2005, to tell the public about the terrorist nest found across the river and down the field in Lodi. The day before, the government officials had leaked word of the arrests to a few trusted reporters at the *Los Angeles Times* and *Sacramento Bee*, who then broke the news in front-page stories that, while careful with the right qualifiers, had the huff and puff of hyperventilation. Now McGregor W. Scott, the tall, handsome son of a Eureka lawyer who had risen from Shasta County district attorney to the top prosecutor in the Eastern District of California, was standing front and center before a bank of TV news cameras. "I wish to emphasize that this investigation is evolving literally by the moment. Every step we have taken—and will take—is examined, reexamined, and vetted by the highest levels of the Justice Department."

The joint terrorism task force, more than a dozen federal, state, and local agencies, was working around the clock with the Department of Homeland Security to pursue all aspects of a Lodi sleeper cell intended to "kill Americans." Agents had searched the residences of the Hayats and two local Muslim clerics, Muhammed Adil Khan and Shabbir Ahmed, who were suspected of leading the plot. The imams were safely tucked away in the arms of U.S. Immigration and Customs. "I would also like to make a statement to the Muslim community in Lodi and elsewhere," Scott said in closing. "We have the greatest respect for the Muslim faith and Muslim members of our community. These are criminal charges and immigration charges against certain individuals, not a religion or people in a community."

By the second day, the feds already were backing away from some of the more damning details they had leaked to the press. In a revised affidavit, the U.S. attorney's office had removed any mention of hospitals and supermarkets as potential targets. Also deleted was the assertion that Hayat's grandfather in Pakistan, a prominent Muslim cleric, was friendly with a man who ran a terrorist camp in Afghanistan. As it turned out, his friend was actually a different man who shared the same last name— Rehman—with the terrorist. It was the Pakistani equivalent of Jones or Johnson.

"Bureaucratic errors," the Justice Department called them, though it hardly mattered to the cable news crews stampeding into Lodi and chasing down everything Muslim: S. Khan's auto repair shop, the Pak India market, the Jehovah's Witnesses kingdom hall turned mosque, and, finally, the terrorist's lair on the side of a wood shed where Hamid Hayat had fed his growing hatred of America.

"Hi everybody. This is *The Big Story*. I'm John Gibson. Fox News has live team coverage and expert analysis of these terror arrests. We begin with Claudia Cowan in Lodi, California."

"Hi John. Well, news crews and a number of curious neighbors have descended on the home of Umer Hayat here in Lodi. He and his twenty-four-year-old son have been arrested on charges of lying to the FBI. But federal agents really believe that this father-son team has been secretly helping America's biggest enemy, Al Qaeda."

Gibson: "The Patriot Act was created to help keep America safe following the terror attacks of 9/11. Does this particular bust prove that the Patriot Act is working or was this a case of being lucky? Joining us now, the former undersecretary of the Department of Homeland Security, Asa Hutchinson."

Hutchinson: "Well, I don't think they just got lucky . . . It is of great concern that a camp in '03, '04 would exist in Pakistan."

Gibson: "Asa Hutchinson, sorry to interrupt. This is a Fox News alert. We have news coming from Santa Maria, California. Trace Gallagher is out there. Trace, we all assume it's a verdict. Yes or no?"

And thus with a seamless tilt of the satellite dish, the "big story" shifted from a suicide bomber in the California vineyards to singer Michael Jackson in a California court on charges of molesting a little boy. The curious among Fox's audience would have to wait another day to learn why the FBI had chosen to target Lodi or how it came to be that a few thousand Pakistani immigrants found themselves living amid "the Grape American Dream," a town built by German Russian wheat farmers from the Dakotas whose descendants still lived in neat brick and stucco houses lined with oak trees and azaleas and every Tuesday still grabbed a bowl of creamy borscht soup for $2.89 at Richmaid's.

It was a familiar story, really. Like the Chinese and Japanese and Mexicans before them, the peasant farmers of the great Indus valley—Hindu, Muslim, and Sikh—had migrated to California in the early 1900s to work the land. They had grown cotton, wheat, sugar cane, and row crops back home and though the soil was fertile and the water plentiful, they were caught at the bottom of a strict caste system. They had traveled thousands of miles only to land smack dab on the same old line of latitude. The Punjab sun was the valley sun. And they had come to a new land only to find the old land's caste, a system where each immigrant group was pitted against the other to keep wages in the fields low. By the 1960s, a few dozen Pakistanis had congregated on Lodi's east side, living and working in the corrugated shadows of the packinghouses and canneries. As long as they were productive and didn't carouse at night, townsfolk looked past the pajama-like pants and long shirts they wore and the goats they brought home to slaughter. They had kept their end of the bargain, until now.

Umer Hayat was eighteen years old, a village boy with few prospects, when he left Pakistan in 1976. He had nothing to show a future wife. No family farm. No schooling beyond the eighth grade. He might have been expected to marry a girl from the village like his father and grandfather, but he had a different idea. He would migrate to Lodi, become a natural-ized U.S. citizen, and use his paper status to attract a city girl back in Pakistan. His scheme worked in a way he could have never imagined. The young woman was the daughter of Qari

Saeed-ur-Rehman, the revered Muslim scholar who operated a religious school or madrassa in Rawalpindi. The marriage was arranged, and to the surprise of Hayat's entire village, her father had said yes. The citizenship paper clutched by the young suitor—the chance for future generations of Hayats and Rehmans to prosper in the United States—was all the assurance the old cleric needed.

That Umer Hayat ended up squandering this opportunity may have been his one true crime. The problem wasn't so much what he had chosen to do with his own life. After all, he had found a job outside the fields and the canneries, driving a beige ice cream van with Homer Simpson painted on the back, learning Spanish to better serve the neighborhood kids. And it wasn't so much the strong ties he kept to Pakistan. He was like so many other immigrants who made their way to America as adults, never quite accepting the country as their own, still looking backward and intending one day to return home. Rather, the problem was his insistence that his four children, each one born in the United States, follow the same path.

Keeping America outside the door of the little yellow frame house proved a monumental task. Because the public schools didn't segregate boys from girls and there were no classrooms at the mosque for his daughters, he insisted that they drop out at thirteen and marry young. He fretted most about his oldest boy, Hamid, and wanted badly for him to become a Muslim scholar like his father-in-law. Toward that goal, he yanked him out of school in the sixth grade and sent him back to Pakistan to live with his grandparents. The boy was there for more than a decade and memorized the entire Koran. Once he returned home, though, he was too lazy to even take the $800 a month job as a cleric in training at the Lodi mosque. So he lived with his father and sick mother and eleven other relatives, sleeping all day and waking up to eat six McDonald's fish sandwiches and watch big-time wrestling and the Pakistani national cricket team on satellite TV. Late at night, all by himself, he'd head down Highway 99 to nowhere. "I'm a speeder," he boasted. "Seventy miles per hour, man."

Caught between two lands, the kid kept a scrapbook in his room with articles he clipped from a Pakistani newspaper that harangued against the United States and "Bush the Worm." He had no friends to speak of, and he whined that no Pakistani girls in the United States would give him a second look. His nose would bleed at the most inopportune times, and he was convinced that a black magic curse by an enemy had jinxed his love life. Maybe things would change, he told himself, if he could ever quit smoking and drink less tea and save more money from his job packing cherries.

Then in the summer of 2002, a real friend walked into his world, a man ten years his senior, a clean-cut guy with neatly pressed pants and shirt always tucked in and wavy black hair brushed back. He had a fancy job at a computer company and drove a shiny SUV and spoke perfect English and fluent Pashto and Urdu, two of the main languages of Pakistan. His name was Naseem Khan, and he had come to the United States with his mother in the late 1980s, living for a time in Lodi.

Umer Hayat wasn't sure about his son's new friend that first day he found him eating beef curry in the living room. Hamid assured him there was no cause for worry. Khan had arrived in town several months earlier and already befriended the two imams, spending the night at their homes and working on the website for the planned Farooqia Islamic Center. This new friend was, above all, a passionate Muslim who believed "we are from God and to God we return."

For Hamid, it quickly became something more than that. Khan was the first friend who actually wanted to see his scrapbook and hear his stories about the mujahideen fighters who attended his grandfather's religious school before heading off to Afghanistan to fight the Soviets. This was jihad in its truest, most righteous sense, Hamid insisted, defending a Muslim country from an invading army.

"Have you watched the news?" Khan asked Hamid, referring to the arrest of one of bin Laden's highest-ranking deputies in March 2003.

"No. About what? The Al Qaeda thing?" Hamid replied. "Al Qaeda is a tough group, man. They're even smarter than the FBI, friend."

"Huh?"

"Smarter than the FBI."

Khan laughed. "Yeah, better than the FBI, huh?"

Whether in Urdu or English, Khan wasn't much of a talker. That he was considerably more comfortable asking questions might have been Hamid's first clue. Yet the kid was so desperate for someone to take him seriously that he didn't seem to notice how every time he talked about the girl who turned down his marriage proposal or his uncle who was the "king of Pakistan," Khan steered their conversation to the same place. Jihad.

"I'm going to fight jihad," Khan declared. "You don't believe, huh?"

"No, man, these days there's no use in doing that," Hamid replied. "Listen, these days we can't go into Afghanistan . . . the American CIA is there."

As for the training camps, Hamid said he had seen one on a video, and it demanded far too much out of its students. Forty days of training. Guard vigil all night. Push-ups in the cold morning. Bazooka practice. "Man, if I had a gun, friend, I wouldn't be able to shoot it," he said.

Over the next six months, Khan would record more than forty hours of conversations with Hamid and his father, mostly in the privacy of their home. As a job, working as a confidential witness for the FBI's war on terror paid considerably better than Taco Bell—more than $225,000 when it was all said and done—and Khan threw himself into the part with such ardor that he looked more FBI than the agents themselves. Still, it wasn't easy doing this to your own people, especially to a kid who had the mental capacity of a nine-year-old and kept referring to him as his "older brother" and to a father who had gotten over his initial distrust and now called Khan his "other son." Khan replied in kind: "If you've accorded me the position of a son, then you're no less than my honored father."

The FBI had come calling on Khan in the weeks after 9/11. He was living in Oregon, working double duty at McDonald's and a convenience store, bringing home $7 an hour to an American girl who was falling in love with him. He did his best to impress the two agents. Yes, he was familiar with the Pakistani community in Lodi. A few years earlier, he had seen Al Qaeda's number two man, Zawahiri, going in and out of the small mosque on Poplar Street. And not only him. Among the men on their hands and knees praying were the main suspects in the 1998 bombings of the U.S. embassies in Kenya and Tanzania and the 1996 bombing of the Khobar Towers military housing complex in Saudi Arabia.

The FBI would later concede that Khan's sightings were almost certainly false. Yet such flights of fancy didn't deter the Bureau from opening the case and giving him the code name Wildcat and sending him back to Lodi in a new Dodge Durango. The two imams would eventually grow uncomfortable with his jihad talk and warn students to steer clear of him. Inside the yellow house, though, he would have no trouble getting Hamid Hayat to pour out his heart.

"I have a friend in Pakistan who starts talking to me over the phone," Hamid confided to Khan. "He cusses America, right? He tells me, 'My friend, don't you get offended? I'm abusing your country.' I said, 'Man, this country is mine in name only, understand? My heart is in Pakistan.'"

Hamid began to cover up his impotence with a tough guy persona that found comfort in Khan's caricature of slickster jihadist. During one visit, Hamid wondered if Khan had read the news about the murder of Daniel Pearl, the *Wall Street Journal* reporter, in Pakistan. "They killed him. So I'm pleased about that. They cut him into pieces and sent him back. That was a good job they did. Now they can't send one Jewish person to Pakistan."

If Hamid felt that strongly, Khan wondered, why was he hesitating to return to Pakistan for more religious training and possibly a camp. "You told me, 'I'm going for jihad,'" Khan said. "What happened?"

"I'm ready, I swear. My father tells me, 'Man, what a better task than this. But when does my mother permit it? Where is a mother's heart? She said, 'I kept you separated for ten years. I won't let you be separated from me again.'"

In the summer of 2003, with his mother's apparent blessing, Hamid did go to Pakistan to meet the girl his parents had arranged for him to marry and bring back an herbal medicine to cure his mother's diseased liver. But the bride-to-be rejected him, and his mother was forced to fly in and go door-to-door in the village until she found another father willing to marry his daughter to Hamid. Two months into his stay in Pakistan, the phone rang and he heard the stern voice of his friend Khan calling from the United States.

"You're just sitting around doing nothing," Khan said.

"I do one thing. I pray. That's it."

"Don't lie to me. Don't talk bullshit."

"Why would I lie to you?" Hamid pleaded. "There's nothing of note regarding our area of interest. Understand?"

"There's nothing at all, eh?" Khan asked.

"Nothing. Absolutely nothing."

"The plan to go. What happened about that?"

"The plan to go where?"

"To the camp."

"That can't be done these days, man. It's too difficult. Strict restrictions have been imposed on the madrassas. There are lots of spies."

"So what kind of Muslims are these, then? Here in the U.S., they're all afraid, too."

"Well, see, my friend, Naseem Khan, what strange times these are!"

To Khan, this sounded like the student lecturing the professor, and he grew angry. "You told me, 'I'm going to a camp. I'll do this. I'll do that.' You're sitting idle. You're wasting time."

"No choice."

"You fucking sleep for half the day. You wake up. You light a fucking cigarette. You eat. You sleep again. That's all you do. You're just walking around like a loafer. A loafer guy."

"What else am I going to do?"

"Yeah. Fuck you in the ass. . . . You sound like a fucking broken bitch. Come on. Be a man. Do something."

"Whatever I can do, I'll do that, man."

"When I come to Pakistan and I see you, I'm going to fucking force you, get you from your throat and fucking throw you in the madrassa."

"I'm not going to go."

"Oh yeah, you will go."

In the months after the arrests and before the trial, even as President Bush congratulated the FBI for a job well done in Lodi and the nation's intelligence czar John Negroponte, in his annual threat assessment, cited a network of "Islamic extremists" in the farm town, it became more and more clear that no case existed beyond the Hayats. The two imams, the so-called big fish who allegedly formed the sleeper cell, were found to have uttered anti-American remarks years earlier during a clamorous time in Pakistan but nothing more. In the end, citing minor immigration violations, the government deported them. "We have gone and will continue to go wherever the evidence takes us," U.S. Attorney Scott pledged a few weeks later. "We have detected, we have disrupted and we have deterred, and whatever was taking shape in Lodi isn't going to happen now."

On an overcast day in mid-February 2006, Jim Wedick strode down the long, polished hall of the thirteenth floor in the U.S. district courthouse and swung open the heavy door to the courtroom of Judge Garland Burrell, the former Marine from south-central Los Angeles who had presided over the Unabomber case. During his FBI years, Wedick had been an overweight agent whose courtroom attire aspired to drab. Now he was bone thin from a thyroid condition and dressed in a blue pinstriped suit and red Windsor-knotted tie, his gray beard and mustache shaved tight. He scooted past defense attorneys Johnny Griffin and Wazhma Mojaddidi and took a seat next to the two defendants. For the last eight months, he had tried to downplay this moment, telling friends that it was all part of the routine of crossing over. He was joining a long line of old FBI agents who retired one day only to hang out their private eye shingle the next. Because of his reputation, he knew that sooner or later he would land a high-stakes case pitting him against his former colleagues, but the Bureau and the U.S. attorney's office would surely understand he was only doing his job. Besides, the only person he owed an explanation to was his wife, Nancy, also an FBI agent. She was the one who had to go to work each day with the same agents who had targeted the Hayats. Yes, she would be in a tough spot, but she told him not to worry about it. As the case headed to trial, Wedick knew where he stood with the government. He wouldn't be sharing old war stories with prosecutors and agents in the halls outside the courtroom, but neither did he expect to encounter outwardly hostile feelings. His former cohorts, he figured, were pros who knew how the system of justice worked.

Anyone watching Wedick find his place that first morning could see that he had underestimated the situation. This wasn't your garden-variety betrayal. If the Hayats greeted his arrival like a good luck charm, the trio of young prosecutors, S. Robert Tice-Raskin, Laura L. Ferris, and David Deitch, went out of their way to ignore his presence. He tried not to make eye contact with the FBI supervisors and agents huddled around the government's table, and they pretended not to see him. In the days to come, his wife would drive home from work in tears, telling Jim that fellow agents were calling him a "traitor." The regional boss would sit her down in his office and remark that Jim would be wise not to attend a retirement luncheon for an old FBI colleague. Some of the more angry agents, the boss suggested, might go after him. Wedick understood that it wasn't simply a matter of bad blood inside the Sacramento office. The entire bureaucracy of the Justice Department, already evangelized by Attorney General John Ashcroft, was being shoved even further to the right by his successor, Alberto Gonzales. Job candidates from Ivy League schools or Stanford—those who spoke Arabic or did volunteer work to clean up the environment or once posted a cartoon on a MySpace page poking fun at President Bush—would be deemed too elitist, too liberal, too soft for the mission at hand. The same sort of quality control was being used to decide which assistant U.S. attorneys would stay or be fired. Even the silliest cases had become worthy of pursuit if they happened to involve a Muslim shooting off his mouth about blowing up a tower in Chicago or, better yet, a Palestinian on American soil sending humanitarian funds to the Holy Land. This was a war of wholesale battlefronts, and Jim Wedick had crossed the line to join sides with the enemy combatant. "I guess I was naive to think that it could be some other way between me and them," he would say later. "But I honestly didn't expect the boss of the FBI office in Sacramento to lean on Nancy the way he did. I didn't expect that they'd actually retrieve my old personnel file to see if they could find some dirt on me. But that's how badly they wanted to keep me off the stand and win this prosecution."

Wedick felt so strongly about the case that he had performed almost all of his duties for free, deconstructing the confessions of father and son and poring over every piece of paper the FBI had handed over. The way he saw it, the trial boiled down to a few basic questions: Why, if this case was so important, did the FBI entrust the investigation to a rookie agent? Why didn't the Bureau use its considerable manpower in Pakistan to follow Hamid and determine if he actually attended a terrorist camp? Hamid had vowed in his last recorded conversation with Khan that he would attend not a camp but a madrassa. "After Ramadan, God willing, I'll study and become a religious scholar," he promised. Khan had booked a flight to Pakistan to see for himself what kind of camp, if any, Hamid had decided to attend. Why, at the last minute, did the FBI scuttle that trip? Why, if Hamid was such a threat to national security, did the FBI take him off a no-fly list and let him reenter the United States? And why, if he was truly confessing, did the agents find it necessary to spend all night spoon-feeding him the answers?

Now Wedick turned a sharp eye on the female prosecutor addressing the jury of six men and six women who had come from one of the most conservative regions in California (it could have been a jury in Texas or Oklahoma, for that matter) to decide Hamid's fate. Ferris, a fit woman with short dark hair and small features, told jurors that Hamid kept a "jihadist" scrapbook and immersed himself in extremist Muslim views before heading off to Pakistan. There he attended an Al Qaeda training camp and returned home to do harm to Americans. "He talked about training camps. He talked about acts of violence," she said. "He talked about jihad, jihad, jihad."

The young man with a fresh haircut and hip goatee and new black sports jacket with matching slacks and tie made no expression as the prosecutor's words came to him, via ear-phones, in Urdu. "Hamid Hayat had three faces. One when he was lying to law enforcement. One when he was confessing to law enforcement. And one when he was talking and didn't know law enforcement was listening."

Hamid's attorney, Mojaddidi, had come to court for her first criminal trial and first federal trial wearing a dark pantsuit with a hot pink blouse and hot pink shoes. Color, she would explain later, was the way a middle child got attention in a large family that escaped war-torn Afghanistan and came to the United States as refugees. Her father, a Kabul banker, had worked at a pizza parlor in Washington to send his children to medical school and law school. She and the Hayats came from the same Pashtun tribe, only they were from the village and her family was from the city. The difference explained everything.

"The government cannot prove that he actually attended a camp," she told jurors in her opening. "It's a crucial missing link." Instead, his time in Pakistan was spent playing cricket and getting married and taking religious classes at a madrassa. As for the confession, Hamid merely uttered "the words the FBI wanted to hear," she said. It was nothing more than garbage in and garbage out.

Then the witnesses began to take the stand.

There was Lawrence Futa, an FBI agent in Japan who testified that on May 30, 2005, a Korean Air Lines flight to San Francisco was diverted to Tokyo because it carried a passenger who appeared on a no-fly list. Futa interviewed Hamid Hayat and found a pleasant young man who denied any links to terrorism. His thin build made it seem unlikely he had recently undergone rigorous training, and Futa permitted him to board a later flight.

There was Pedro Tenoch Aguilar, the rookie agent who headed the government's case and conceded that he could never corroborate whether Hamid had attended a camp or not. "Minus his statement, no," Aguilar said. There was Naseem "Wildcat" Khan, the bureau's mole, who also testified that Hayat expressed a desire to go to camp but never told him that he'd done so.

There was Hassan Abbas, a former high-ranking police official in Pakistan who testified that religious schools in the predominantly Muslim country were centers of terrorist recruitment. When the defense got its chance to cross-examine Abbas, prosecutor Tice-Raskin kept objecting to the questions. After each objection was overruled, Abbas, as if on cue, sidestepped the question with a vague answer. It turned out that he was following a script that the government had laid out for him. In the prosecutor's notes, which were inadvertently turned over to the defense, Abbas was coached to play dumb whenever Tice-Raskin objected to a defense question. It was an eye-opener into the tricks the federal government was willing to pull to win the case, but Judge Burrell let the tactic pass without ever admonishing the government.

There was the professor of Islamic studies who testified that the verse Hamid kept in his wallet—"O Allah, we place you at their throats, and we seek refuge in you from their evil"—may have been the prayer of a traveler seeking divine protection. More likely, though, it was the supplication carried by "fanatics and extremists." Finally, there was the Defense Department analyst who testified that satellite pictures taken in northeastern Pakistan revealed a camp near Balakot that "likely" matched one of the camps described by Hamid.

It was all rather murky, and son and father weren't about to testify to clear things up. The trial, it seemed, would turn on the confession that really didn't become a confession until the early morning hours of June 5, 2005. That's when agent Tim Harrison replaced agent Gary Schaaf as Hamid's main inquisitor.

"The thing I want to talk about, most importantly, is the camp where you went."

"Uh-huh."

"Did they teach you how to read maps?"

"No."

"Did you get to play with GPS . . . global positioning?"

"What's that?"

"Satellite."

"No, no."

"All right. So you came to the United States. They sent you off. 'Allah Ahkbar. You've got to go to jihad.'"

"Uh-huh."

"And you left with marching orders."

"What's that?"

"You know. 'Here's what your mission is. Here's what you do with all this training. You're training to be a good jihadi.'"

"Uh-huh."

"What did they want you to do?"

"They didn't tell me nothing."

"I'm trying to get to the truth here. Because we're going to try to make an argument for you. That you are not one of the big players. So they sent you to the U.S. after you've done your training. You're ready for jihad."

"No. I'm not ready for jihad."

"You're here to take orders."

"No, I didn't take orders from them. They will give me the orders to fight. But they didn't give me no orders right now."

"Who's going to tell you?"

"Maybe, uh, send a letter."

"I don't think they're going to send a letter. I think you're going to have to talk to somebody here in Lodi."

"Yeah, maybe."

"Give me an example of a target. A building?"

"I'll say no buildings. I'll say people."

"Okay, people. Yeah. Fair enough. People in buildings . . . Whatever looks like a person, shoot?"

"Yeah."

"I'm trying to get some details about plans over here."

"They didn't give us no plans."

"Did they give you money?"

"No money."

"Guns?"

"Nope."

"Targets in the U.S.?" the agent asked again.

"I'll say they're going to tell us big buildings. I'll say that for sure."

"Here in Sacramento or San Francisco?"

"I'll say maybe in L.A. Maybe, ah, San Francisco."

"Your goal is to do jihad here?"

"Yeah."

"You have to go to America to fight jihad?"

"Yeah."

"Who was in charge of the camp? We're talking about someone you know very well."

"Maybe it's my uncle."

"Maybe it's your uncle?"

"Maybe my grandfather."

"Maybe your grandfather? You can't play dumb with me. It insults me and it . . ."

"Hurts me and hurts you. Yeah, I get that."

"Is Al Qaeda tied to this camp that you went to?"

"I'll say . . . they are."

"Al Qaeda? Al Qaeda runs?"

"I'll say they run the camp."

"Ah, all right," said the agent. "They're the supporters. You mean they provide instructors."

"Yeah, that's what I'll say."

"Yes, clearly, they want to do damage to us, the United States. Whether it is overseas or here."

"Anywhere."

"So a big part of your training was against the U.S.?"

"Um-hmm."

"Bush, Colin Powell, Rumsfeld. They put their faces on the dummies. Do you remember that?"

"Um-hmm."

"You're being trained to act against targets. What kind of buildings? Financial buildings? Private buildings? Commercial buildings?"

"I'll say finance and things like that."

"Hospitals? Did they say hospitals."

"Maybe. I'm sure."

"They plant ideas in your head?"

"Uh-huh."

What were the jurors thinking, Wedick wondered. If he wouldn't be able to tell them exactly what he thought—that this was the "most derelict and juvenile investigation" he had ever seen the FBI put its name to—he could at least take the stand and point out the gibberish in the interrogation. He could at least tell them about the care he took in Shrimpscam, how he had prepared a single year for one interview and got an informant to cooperate after he meticulously lined the interrogation room with giant surveillance photos of the guy accepting a sizable campaign check. Or how he brought in an FBI behavioral scientist from Washington to help him design a set of questions that fit the particular language and style of one of the suspects—all in the name of eliciting an accurate confession.

It was far from certain, though, that the court would agree to Wedick serving as an expert witness. Up until now, Judge Burrell had shown something akin to belligerence when it came to any requests from the defense side of the table. A small, frenetic man, Burrell gave the impression of feeling uneasy in his robes, and he seemed to compensate for this insecurity by playing bully. Ironically, he found his most convenient target in defense attorney Griffin, a black man like himself. Each time Burrell ruled against Griffin, he did so with an impatience that bordered on browbeating. On the matter of Wedick testifying, Assistant U.S. Attorney Deitch had filed nearly one hundred pages of motions to keep the former agent off the stand. He argued that Wedick had "grossly overstated" his experience in counterterrorism and that his musings would prejudice the jury and amount to "needless" cumulative evidence, the legal equivalent of piling on.

Griffin stood up to offer several reasons why Wedick's testimony was needed to illuminate serious flaws in the government's case, but he appeared intimidated, his articulations reduced to mutterings. Burrell ordered him to sit back down. "I know his proposed testimony," he snarled at Griffin. "You can go on to the next issue." To no one's surprise, the judge sided with the government and put a muzzle on Wedick.

Outside the courtroom, a dazed Wedick tried to fathom the ruling. He wondered how the prosecutors and agents could muster the gall to dismiss his credentials as if he had never worked for the FBI, much less achieved star status. These were the same prosecutors and agents who had failed to produce a single piece of corroborating evidence in four years of sleuthing that cost taxpayers millions of dollars and unearthed not bin Laden's right hand but a pair of immigrants, father and son, who canvassed the town of Lodi blaring "Pop Goes the Weasel." "To see the government's power from this side of the fence is a strange thing for me," Wedick conceded. "What we're doing to these Muslims is along the same lines of what we did to the Japanese in the 1940s. It comes from the same fear and the same overreaction. Instead of camps in the desert, we're deporting them on trumped up charges or sending them to prisons in Cuba or the Middle East." With Wedick silenced, the defense put on its final witness, a university scholar who testified that madrassas typically focused on teaching an orthodox brand of Islam, not churning out suicide bombers. Then both sides closed and the case went to two separate juries that had sat side by side for two months.

The Pakistani Muslims of Lodi watched and waited, old men huddled in the shade of the marigold mosque, young men with heads bowed down as they wheeled out forty-pound boxes of fresh kosher chicken from the Pak India market—the same store that the government's informant had placed at the center of a ring delivering funds to Al Qaeda. "This little place can't even support one goddamn family," storekeeper Mumtaz Khan said. "How can it support Al Qaeda?" He motioned to the fifteen brands of tea, the basmati rice from the Punjab, the red lentils, pickled mango, Islamic prayer clocks, and the small stick tree filled with Tootsie Rolls. "We are trying to raise our children to live in America but still keep a little faith and not become fully westernized." The storekeeper said a Muslim American no longer had the freedom to criticize the United States. So if asked his opinion, he would criticize his own. "Osama bin Laden has done more harm to the Muslim people throughout the world than anyone else in history," he said. "Everybody is scared. Everybody is scared."

At the yellow house, the kids were shooting hoops along a driveway lined with pomegranate, fig, and loquat trees, one child in traditional garb driving to the basket and his cousin in jeans trying to block him. They stopped playing as soon as they spotted the strange SUV parked across the street, not sure if the driver wearing sunglasses and taking notes, a journalist, might be a government agent. The ice cream truck sat idle, and the coop where father and son used to tend to their birds was empty. Hamid Hayat's uncle shuffled outside in his leather sandals and stood beneath a row of the freshly washed purple and gold cotton garments hanging from a cord strung across the porch. He lit a Marlboro cigarette and sighed. "We are sitting and waiting. We have been sitting and waiting for a year." Then a young man, a dead ringer for Hamid Hayat, only he was wearing a Tupac Shakir cap turned backward, baggy jeans slung low and Air Jordans, walked up the steps and into the house. This was Arslan Hayat, Hamid's teenage brother. "It's a lie," he said. "The whole world's a lie." He emerged a few minutes later pushing a wheelchair that carried his dying grandfather. He and four other relatives loaded the old man into a small truck to take him to the doctor. As they backed out of the driveway, the new ice cream man, also a Pakistani but playing a different tune on his musical box, made a left turn and blocked their path. They waited patiently as he sold popsicles in the colors of the U.S. flag to a gaggle of kids.

The verdicts came a day later. The jury deciding the fate of Umer Hayat was deadlocked, and the judge declared a mistrial, though the government vowed that it would try him again. As for young Hamid, he was found guilty on two counts of making false statements to the FBI and one count of providing "material support" to terrorists. He faced up to thirty-nine years in prison. "I hope it gets the message out," said juror Starr Scaccia, explaining why she and the others voted guilty. "Don't mess with the United States. It's not worth it."

Wedick had a difficult time looking the son in the eye. He had pledged to him months earlier that he was going to do everything he could to see injustice righted, even if it meant turning his back on the bureaucracy he had served for thirty-five years. "This kid could be my kid. My son boasts. My son does all sorts of things that drive me nuts. Hamid is a hapless character, but my God he isn't a terrorist. The government counted on hysteria, the thousand-pound gorilla, to be in the room. And it worked. Damn, it worked."

He saw one juror holding back tears, and the next day he tracked her down to an apartment in downtown Sacramento. She wouldn't let him in, preferring to talk through a crack in the door. For four hours, he stood on her front porch and tried to calm her fears. When she finally relented and opened the door, it took only a few minutes to tell him what he suspected.

No, she didn't believe the kid was guilty. The pressure to convict him from fellow jurors was so intense that she had to check herself into the hospital a few days earlier. Throughout the trial, she said, the foreman kept making the gesture of a noose hanging. "Lynch the Muslim," she took it to mean. Another juror, she said, had prepared a six-page analysis on her home computer to persuade the others to vote guilty—a direct violation of the judge's instructions. Wedick asked her to write it all down and sign it. Then he filed the affidavit with the federal court, hoping it might lead to a new trial.

The next day, he drove out to a field at the edge of a vineyard alongside Highway 99 and gazed down a long entrance road to a spot where four hundred men in skull caps and flowing robes had gathered after work. He drew close enough to see their faces burned by the sun and hands worn to the bone, the faces and hands of fruit pickers and truck drivers and machine operators who had left Pakistan years before to try a new life in California. He watched them unload a plain wood box from the back of a hearse and carry it over the graves of the other Muslims. Then they broke into twenty lines, side by side, facing east, toward Mecca, and began praying. They prayed the same supplication—"May Allah protect us from evil. May Allah destroy our enemies"—that the holy warrior prayed. Then in the distance, as the sun was setting, a half dozen men removed the body of Hamid Hayat's grandfather from the casket and placed it directly into the ground. What was left of the old immigrant had been wrapped in three linen sheets, all that would separate him from the earth of this unaccustomed land.

chapter three | Eyre of the Storm

This time, the center was holding. It was a country of record foreclosures and endless recalls of beef and nearly $5 a gallon gas and a presidency that had violated the most sacred pledge of our justice system—that the accused has the right to hear the evidence against him. It was a country that had lied itself into war and could not account for the billions of dollars that had gone to the subcontractors and greased the way for one corporate colossus to swallow the other and shrugged as 62,000 jobs vanished in a single month.

It was not a country on the verge of coming undone. It was not a country in the midst of open rebellion. It was the United States of America from the hot early summer of 2007 to the hot early summer of 2008, and the newspapers were dying and the streets were calm except for the occasional massing of very large women and men running over each other in the latest gadget stampede. "I don't know how I'm going to feed myself," remarked one customer at Best Buy, as he handed over his last dollar to clutch the Halo 3, Microsoft's newest video game.

The city of New Orleans, still ravaged three years after God's hurricane, wore its most placid face as the candidate for president rolled into town on his Forgotten Places of America bus tour. The county of Los Angeles, home to Countrywide Financial, did not tar and feather CEO Angelo Mozilo for turning the subprime loan into an instrument of countrywide swindle. The state of Virginia, still mourning the massacre of thirty-two college students, took no umbrage at the Supreme Court's ruling that no matter how anarchic the murder rate, guns belong to the people.

I found myself regarding the center and its holding with a kind of awe. Complacency certainly didn't explain it, not when so many parents were hitting the road in big towns and small to turn their children into blue-chip volleyball and softball and soccer and baseball prospects. What had changed between this United States and the one I grew up in the 1970s? Had Americans not toppled a president and ended a war? Had there not been a revelation, a Second Coming, a new order, in the 1960s? Surely we had watched it rise out of the social hemorrhaging of the summer of '67, as Joan Didion so masterfully drew it in *Slouching Towards Bethlehem*. So where had the ardor gone? Was it simply the military draft? We had one back then and didn't have one now, so that no college kid needed to lose sleep anymore over his lottery number. Or was it something deeper than the absence of shared vulnerability, shared sacrifice, something missing in the American soul?

And so it was that during the fortieth anniversary of the Summer of Love, I got into my car and steered west—west in the shadow of Didion. I was going to where else but San Francisco and the other side of the bridge to Berkeley, back to the old epicenter, to walk Haight-Ashbury and People's Park and sit on the steps of Sproul Hall and put my ear on whatever rumblings might still be heard.

I am apparently looking for someone called Redwood. Not Compost or Yogurt, who are standing on Piedmont Avenue in front of the football stadium where the Cal Golden Bears play, but Redwood, a well-built kid in his early twenties with long blond hair and a bushy red-tinged beard, who's temporarily in charge.

"Redwood," Compost shouts and then whistles. "Redwood." Beneath a canopy of coastal oak, I hear the sound of feet on bark. Down, down, down the tree it comes, lands soft.

"Hi, I'm Redwood."

I introduce myself, but there's no need for the usual song and dance. With a glance, he distills my purpose. Writer searching in a land of silence for the howl of protest, he says. Welcome to Berkeley, the new Berkeley, at least.

"We're not hippies, but you've come to the hippest, hippiest place on the planet. We aren't tree huggers. We're tree sitters."

He and a dozen mates, an ever revolving cast, have been living high up in the oaks for the past 207 days. They went in, militia like, at five in the morning on the day of the Big Game, Cal versus Stanford, and have held the ground ever since. On the surface, they're trying to block the university from mowing down the oak grove in Strawberry Canyon to make way for a $125 million athletic center.

The town of Berkeley appears to be split on the matter. Yes, there's much to admire in the throwback grit of the activists.

But there's also a football team that routinely ranks in the Top 20. A new training house, four stories tall with the latest high-tech devices for enhancing speed and agility, would be a recruiting marvel. Not to mention a big boost to the upgrading of Memorial Stadium itself. Built in 1923 with "dimensions that slightly exceed the great Coliseum of Rome," its 74,909 seats sit right atop the Hayward fault, where the next big earthquake awaits.

"We're trying to wake up the students," Redwood says. "We're trying to show them the old way."

Redwood isn't a student, at least not at Berkeley. He heard about the resistance six months ago and arrived from "somewhere else." Now he eats in the oaks, reads in the oaks, does his business in the oaks. His toilet is a five-gallon bucket filled with sawdust that he moves up and down the tree by rope. His waste, like all the rest, gets buried in the ground below.

A guy and girl approach, trying to score some weed. "I don't smoke pot anymore," Redwood tells them. "It's too expensive."

They turn around and leave, walking right over the message written on the sidewalk in brightly colored chalk:

All Life Is Sacred
Value Life Not Capital
Trees = Oxygen
Love Your Mother

Redwood no longer is in charge. Zachary Running Wolf, the candidate for mayor who won 6 percent of the vote last time out, has returned to duty. He introduces himself as a Native American, a descendant of three tribes but registered with only one, the Blackfoot out of Glacier National Park, Montana. He looks real enough, dark hair and suede vest and a bear claw hanging from his neck.

"I led this group in and seven months later it continues. Like I like to say, we're playing our own 'Big Game.' It's right here. Right here. You hit the heartbeat. And the best thing about it, it's indigenous. It's back to the land."

I ask about the group's makeup, since Running Wolf appears to be in his mid-forties and many of the others seem past the age of having parents willing to indulge such exuberance.

"They're hopping rails, following the anarchist trail west," he says. "We've had two hundred to three hundred of them come from all over the country, Great Britain and Canada too. Lately a few of the students on campus are starting to hop aboard."

On Naked Day, forty people showed up to commune with the oaks without wearing so much as a bandana. The cops arrested no one. Now they're hauling off fully clothed tree sitters for trespassing and dwelling in an illegal camp. A few even face deportation. Running Wolf is having a hard time keeping up, what with the restraining orders and lawsuits and three arrests of his own—one for threatening a cop and two for spray painting stop signs. He's posted a $40,000 bond and retained the services of J. Tony Serra, the dope-smoking, tax-dodging, vow-of-poverty defense lawyer made famous by the 1989 movie *True Believer.*

"I know what you're thinking," Running Wolf says. "There's a war going on, civil liberties being trounced, a crisis far worse than anything Richard Nixon ever cooked up. So why all this for twenty-six oak trees?"

I tell him that's exactly what I'm thinking.

"Well, this is Berkeley, the birth of the free speech movement, and things have been on ice for a long time. This university, its research arms, feed the war machine. UC has sold its soul to the military-corporate complex. We're quite literally standing in the belly of the beast. So this is about a lot more than a stand of trees."

Three girls, high school age, big fresh smiles, cell phones in hand, ask if they may snap a picture. They've never seen a real-life Blackfoot Indian before. There's Romene from Kenya and Sharon from Korea and Rei from Japan, though they've been in the States for some time now and all speak flawless, L.A.-wise English. They've come to Berkeley, or rather their parents have sent them to Berkeley, to take a weeklong SAT prep course. For four thousand bucks, they get to live in the dorms and eat in the cafeteria and listen to instructors blast them with how-to's on raising their math and English scores and writing a compelling personal essay.

"We heard about your protest from one of our teachers," Sharon says. "Cool. We've brought you some bottled water and food we ripped off from the cafeteria."

Running Wolf thanks them, explains why their gesture stands apart. So few Asian students on a campus that's 51 percent Asian could give a damn about the trees or the war. "They never look up," he says. "Their heads are down all the time."

"Especially Koreans," Sharon adds. "All they care about is straight A's. Their parents push and push. The best college. The best jobs. Lawyer and doctor. You never hear of them doing anything creative. They play some instrument but only to look good on their résumé."

She is talking, it turns out, about herself. "My parents pushed me from the age of five. Study, straight A's, play the piano. I hated it."

They take turns snapping pictures of each other with Running Wolf in the middle, and I figure it's a good time to leave. As I walk back to the car, I can see Redwood standing by himself off to the side of the grove. He's standing next to the giant statue of the Golden Bear. I notice he's barefoot and as grimy as the rest, but when he smiles, all you see is the white of perfect teeth.

"So where *are* you from?" I ask.

He nods and smiles. "My name is Nathaniel Hill. I come from upstate New York. My dad's a teacher. We drove out from Buffalo in an '87 Jetta."

"The dad-son version of *On the Road?*"

"No. I'm a professional lacrosse player. I played in high school and college and then for the Rattlers. They're a franchise out of Rochester. I came out here to continue my pro career. The Riptide in Los Angeles just released me last week."

I am staying in the upstairs apartment of a woman who's gone off to Mendocino, the friend of a friend of my aunt and uncle who earned their degrees from Berkeley and were there when the National Guard stormed People's Park and Mario Savio delivered his incandescent rants against the machine.

I pad from room to room, give in to the impulse of nosing around in the museum of someone else's life. Without a single photo on the wall, I try my best to conjure the woman who lets strangers stay at her apartment while she's away in Mendocino. I study the six varieties of green tea in the cupboard and the

business cards of tai chi and meditation masters tossed into a
basket. Inside the bathroom, she has written this note: "To any
guest: Be Sure to Pick Up All Your Hairs." I fall asleep on her
futon in full dress. The phone awakens me at eight sharp.

"Good morning, Dad."

"Hey Ash."

"You ready to go to the Gay Pride parade today?"

"I guess so . . . BART or bus?"

"Bus. Let's meet at the corner of Bancroft and Shattuck. In
one hour."

She's our oldest child, like one of those Korean kids never a
B. Dutiful daughter, she sends me dispatches now and then
from the Berkeley campus. They make me fret for our future.

I learn that John Yoo, Dr. Yes, the charming lawyer who
gave the Bush administration the legal nod to torture, white-
washing all inflictions of pain short of "death or organ failure,"
is teaching at Boalt Hall, with nary a peep of protest from the
law students.

I learn that several of my daughter's dorm mates, all boys,
have been placed on academic probation in their first year.
Each one is addicted to a video game.

I learn about kids whose fingers involuntarily twitch during
sleep because their brains are so programmed to text message.

I learn that my daughter and her friends are being followed.
If they use Google's email and happen to mention the BMW
that nearly ran them off the road, ads for luxury cars pop up on
their screens. If they refer to some boy as a "worm," they're
given a link to Uncle Jim's Worm Farm in Spring Grove,
Pennsylvania. I learn that Facebook, already a meet market for
perverts, is tracking, in real time, their online buying. If they
decide to shop for a book or movie, they're pursued store to

store by the Facebook stalker. Then their purchases are announced as "news" to hundreds of their Facebook friends.

I learn later that MoveOn.org, the Berkeley-based liberal
blowtorch, tries to rally youth against this spying by holding
the online equivalent of a protest march. Privacy, for the most
part, is too quaint a notion to draw much of a crowd anymore.
Yet enough Facebookers are perturbed by the idea of a birthday gift no longer being a surprise that 80,000 of them join in
on the march. Facebook has stopped the practice, at least until
it can fine-tune its snooping.

So now we're tramping up Market Street in downtown San
Francisco, besieged by tens of thousands of straight folks staring meth-eyed at the queer folks—a parade of dykes on bikes,
he/shes with beards and boobs, hairy gay men with saggy bottoms, hairless gay men with steroid pecks, dancers sprouting
wild-colored balloons from their heads like Rastafarian locks,
IMPEACH signs in pink, JESUS SAVE THEM signs in red,
queers on stilts, queers on skates, queers on floats, so many
corporate floats that I wonder for a moment if it's January 1 in
Pasadena. There's Tylenol PM, Comcast, Wells Fargo, Hare
Altoids, and, of course, the Google float, Starship Google, to
be exact, with George Takei, *Star Trek*'s gay Captain Sulu, riding shotgun.

"This isn't exactly what I expected," my daughter sighs. "I
thought it would be a lot more . . . untamed."

"I'm sure it was—back in the good old days."

"You ready to leave, Dad?"

I thought I might check out the Summer of Love fortieth
anniversary gathering at the Mission Delores school audito-
rium on Sixteenth and Church, so I place a call. The woman
who answers says it would be worth my while. The theme is a

night at the Avalon Ballroom, the city's legendary rock venue, now long gone. There will be a lecture on the art of the rock poster.

"You a survivor of '67?" she asks.

"No," I say, "my surviving came a few years later."

"Well, I am, and I encourage you to come. It's only five dollars at the door, and there's going to be a simulated joint rolling contest . . . oregano and basil."

Across the street from the Cheeseboard, on the sidewalk in front of Chez Panisse, I watch a young Greenpeace recruiter, patient and earnest, attempt to sign up a Berkeley student. She doesn't wave him off. Quite the opposite. She makes him work. Is it true, she asks, that Greenpeace has set fire to subdivisions built on wetlands? Is it true that Greenpeace has lied about the toxic dangers of Apple laptops? He does not dodge her questions. It takes twenty minutes, but he signs her up as a card-carrying member. She is Asian.

I walk in on the lunch crowd at Chez Panisse and try to see Alice Waters, but she's still smarting over a tepid rating in Michelin and busy with her book tour anyway. Back on the street, I pick up the *Daily Planet* and read the whopper of a headline: Mystery Surrounds Tilden Murder/Suicide.

A popular local physician, Mamiko Kawai, forty, and her two daughters, eight and six, had been shot to death in a se- cluded area of Tilden Park. The suspect was her husband and their father, Kevin Morrissey, fifty-one, who then used the .357 magnum to kill himself. Police surmised that Morrissey was distraught over financial problems that stemmed from his wife's struggling dermatology center. Botox and laser treatments, it seems, are a tougher go in Berkeley, though if your problems are psychological, it's the place to come—the shrink capital of the world, one psychologist for every hundred residents.

Then the newspaper story adds this: Morrissey had told friends he had been a CIA agent stationed in the Middle East. Before managing his wife's practice, he had served as the administrator of Medicine International, a physician group that provided medical training and care to mujahideen fighters in Afghanistan.

And then this: Morrissey's close friend, Dr. Mark Edward Stinson, executive director of Medicine International, had been found dead in his Oakland home just three months earlier. His body was so badly decomposed that the coroner could not determine the cause of death.

By the time I return to the apartment, the woman next door, Sally, the old hippie who is a friend of my aunt and uncle, has digested the story and methodically searched the web for clues. She hands me a stack of printouts.

"You google Medicine International," she says, "and it has no address, no phone number. Strange. It does list Dr. Mark Stinson and Kevin Morrissey as advisory board members. They both went to the University of Texas at Austin in the early 1980s. Strange."

On his résumé, Morrissey plainly states, "As a Foreign Service Officer in the U.S. Diplomatic Corps, I provided operational and technical expertise to senior U.S. officials worldwide. I supervised staffs of hundreds and managed budgets of more than fifteen million dollars during the collection and analysis of information that was disseminated throughout the U.S. Government."

"Strange," Sally says.

We hop into the car and drive over to the Morrissey-Kawai house, a simple California bungalow, wood siding, with an obvious add-on. Sally says the couple probably bought it for around $800,000, a decent starter house for north Berkeley. Out front, the communal mourners have erected one of those shrines that have become part of the ritual of tragedy in America. We all feel the grief. This one, though, is different. No fuzzy bears or Virgin Mary votives. There's a Buddhist shrine with a candle inside and a collection of children's books: *The Secrets of Droon, The Moon Dragon.* One mourner has written a note: "These were really special people, warm, loving and friendly. What's wrong with a society that leaves so little choice?"

We're about to leave when a car pulls up. It's Morrissey's brother, Jack, short cropped hair, pot belly, who has just arrived from Texas. Sally conveys her condolences. "He and Dr. Stinson were very good friends," she says. "Strange."

The brother's face could not be more grim. "Yes. It's been a very strange time."

We climb the hills above Berkeley on our way to Tilden Park, to the Mineral Springs parking lot near Inspiration Point where the bodies were found, the two girls slumped in the rear of the car, the husband and his physician wife sprawled on the asphalt. We get lost near Lake Anza, and I ask the park ranger for directions. He's a tall, big shouldered man who's followed the story in the paper.

"Everything points to a man in the depths of desperation. Right?" he says.

"Right."

"Then you go a few paragraphs deeper and find out he was a CIA agent and his friend and fellow agent was killed just a few months earlier, not far away. And your mind goes to where it doesn't want to go."

"The church of conspiracy," I smile. "One of the places I've done time."

"Hey, we live in an era where the emperor has no clothes. And this is Berkeley. Go get 'em."

A mile up the road, a picnic table sits on a flat spot in the hillside, beneath a gathering of eucalyptus and oak. At the far end of the parking lot, I come across an even stranger memorial. A pound of sugar has been poured onto the asphalt in the shape of a big heart. In the center there's an arrangement of flowers and a note: "Dearest Mamiko. I will never forget you. I love you. Dah."

Sally is too tired to accompany me to the memorial service that evening. The room at the hospital is packed tight and hot. Friends, family, the Kawai sisters on one side, the Morrissey brother and his wife lonely figures on the other side. After a nod to Buddha and Jesus, the speakers begin their litany of remembrance:

"Mamiko took care of my skin. I just wanted my skin to be beautiful for the holidays. You never know when someone is about to break or do something really sick."

"This is a shock. The entire situation only God knows. I'm feeling such anger. If you have to take another life, take someone terrible. There's plenty of them."

"Mamiko was a year behind me in residency. The first thing I noticed was how beautiful she was. It's so hard for me to move the negative energy in a positive way."

"Kevin was stressed. Two days before, he was trying to refinance and things weren't going right."

"Kevin was extra good with the kids. The kids are in a better place."

The brother keeps his hand to his lips the whole time. On the way out, I overhear a woman talking about the death of Dr. Stinson. "No one knows if Mark was killed or not. His body was so badly decomposed."

The next morning I call the lead detective on the case, Sergeant Tyrone Davis. He has never heard of Stinson, knows nothing about his death, even though it's been all over the papers for days. In any event, that death has nothing to do with this murder-suicide. "When something this unbelievable happens, people have a hard time believing that someone they know is responsible," Davis explains. "They want to believe that someone—something—they don't know is responsible. But we have to stick with the facts we found at the scene. And nothing indicates that anyone other than Kevin Morrissey did this."

I spend the rest of the afternoon fishing for old and new hippies in Haight-Ashbury and People's Park. I meet many vagrants and homeless men. They all have a story to tell about San Francisco and the summer of '67. "The Three M's," one old black man mutters. "The Three M's."

That night, on the other side of Altamont pass, racing down the grade into the valley back home, it hits me. The Three M's . . . The Giants . . . Mays, Marichal, McCovey.

<u>Where Other Conferences End, Conspiracy Con Begins</u>
Ten of the world's most controversial speakers to convene in the San Francisco Bay Area June 7–8, 2008.

The Nuclear Threat Scam
The 4th Reich in America
Cover-Ups: UFOs to 9-11
Chemtrails & Morgellons
9-11: An Inside Job
Vatican Assassins

I had missed the seventh annual Con Con the year before. For this one, I call Arlene, an old family friend in Berkeley, and we make a date. Arlene is the seventy-year-old daughter of Arisineh Nishigian, one of the Armenian lefties who was a comrade and lifelong friend to my grandparents. Remarkably, Arisineh is still alive and sharp at ninety-eight. Mother and daughter live together in a house in the Berkeley Hills. The plan is to spend the night there and drive in the morning to Santa Clara, the site of this year's Con Con.

Arlene needs to be explained. She is a conference regular, a believer in UFOs and past lives that she traces with the help of an applied kinesiologist who uses the means of regression. These sessions have enabled Arlene to discover that she is, or was, Mary Magdalene. In the past year, she has been to Belgium and a village in southern France chasing Mary's bones. When she finds them, she plans to submit them for DNA testing to prove her past. She is convinced that the FBI and CIA have been tracking her (this life) since she was ten, when her parents first came under Hoover's surveillance as subversives. As of late, the government has bombarded her house with microwaves, implanted an electronic chip in her ear, and seeded the sky above her with chemical trails, all in an effort to keep her from writing a book about what really happened on

9/11. The electronic barrage has caused her once knockout body to become plump. She has paid thousands of dollars for experts such as Roger Leir—author/lecturer, alien implant researcher, podiatrist—to find the government's fingerprints. She is committed to searching still.

And yet I refuse to believe that Arlene is crazy. She has managed to live in Spain, Costa Rica, and Mexico, picking through remote villages for antiques to bring back to the United States to sell. She is a dedicated mother, patient grandmother, a woman who has never smoked a joint or consumed an alcoholic beverage and started buying organic vegetables in 1969 when Berkeley had only one small market that sold them. She serves her family bowls of organic blueberries and organic cherries and prepares only free-range, antibiotic-clear chicken and buys the best European cheeses for her mother, whom she carries up and down the steep stairs, bedroom to living room, house to car, every day.

Thus I try to be patient when suspicion becomes a pathological state inside the house on La Vereda Lane.

"How I married my husband, I'll never know," Arlene says, her voice a kind of vibration. "I had no connection with him, nothing in common. He was Armenian, and I had never dated an Armenian. As it turned out, he beheaded me."

This sends her eleven-year-old granddaughter, one of three granddaughters who have come to the house to eat pizza—topped with nettles and clams and crooked-neck yellow squash—to the floor in robust laughter.

Not the head she's wearing, the granddaughter understands, but her head from two thousand years ago.

"They all see me as crazy," Arlene says.

"You're not crazy, Grandma," the youngest granddaughter pipes in.

Arlene's son, Yon, has heard enough. Tall and bony, a cyclist and martial artist, he stands over the kitchen table and taunts her.

"What about the electronic attack you're under, Mom?"

"Yes, absolutely."

"Tell him, Mom. Tell him."

"I paid a man $1,500 to measure the waves. He used to work for Howard Hughes, looking for bugs. He came over with all kinds of machines. He was here for hours."

"Tell him how the man found nothing, Mom."

"Well that's not exactly true, Yon. He did find . . ."

"The waves," sings the granddaughter on the floor. "The waves are making Great-Grandma shrink."

"Tell him, Mom, how your doctor couldn't find the implant, the one you swore was planted in your rib cage."

She shakes her head, but no words come out. Her son then turns to me, explaining his interrogation.

"This stuff has hijacked my mother. Something happened to her in the '60s or maybe the '50s. Something deep. She's right about one thing. It all stems from her previous life. But instead of going back to her childhood to find out what it is, she's going back to France to find her bones. Mary's bones."

"I should have known not to talk about this in front of you," she says.

"Mom, how is it that every one of your next door neighbors over the past twenty years has been a CIA or FBI agent? They keep sending them to spy on little ol' Arlene. You're the center of the world, Mom."

We talk until two in the morning about the antiwar protests she marched in and the five-year battle she waged in the 1970s to win custody of her son and daughter. She suspected her former husband, a physician, of making plans to kidnap the children and move to another country. So she beat him to it, whisking them away to a three-year exile on the island of Majorca. She returned to Berkeley in 1980 only to lose the kids when she joined a UFO cult called Solar Cross.

"It was at that point that I became catatonic, clinically psychotic," she says. "It's taken me years of dance and meditation and regression therapy to become healthy again. That healing, the CIA is doing its best to undo."

She gives up her front bedroom for me. I try to fall asleep but the whole room is humming, buzzing, the strangest vibration. For a second, I think it's an earthquake, but the shaking, like one of those massage loungers, never builds or dies. Its dullness plays on me like a soporific. The next thing I know, it's morning.

On our way to Con Con, we pick up Arlene's friend Barry, who takes a seat in the back. He's tall and sturdy with a thin nose and intense blue eyes, narrow set, that he keeps opening and closing, one eye at a time. I ask a few questions, but Barry isn't big on responses. He doesn't like sharing details of his life, at least not to anyone ever associated with the *Los Angeles Times*, which is affiliated with the Council on Foreign Relations. I do manage to glean this:

Barry left L.A. in 1964 or 1965. Drove up to Berkeley to hear Mario Savio speak in front of Sproul Hall and never returned. He eked out a living painting houses in town and would be homeless today if not for a kind liberal who lets him stay in her garage. He spends day and night poring over the two-thousand-page tome of a British conspiracy theorist named David Vaughan Icke. Barry is convinced that the world is ruled by a secret group known as the "Illuminati," a race of reptilian humanoids that includes Jacob Rothschild and George W. Bush and Queen Elizabeth II and Henry Kissinger.

Barry should come with a warning: Even if you regard the word "and" as one of the most important inventions in human communication, listening to Barry, absorbing his elaborate constructions, requires a particular forbearance for the word. "And" is mortar, and Barry uses lots of mortar.

"I have the membership list of the Council on Foreign Relations and the Trilateral Commission and the Bilderberg group, and it's a real eye-opener, a must-see if you've never beheld it before, and I have a list of the Committee of 300, and that's another eye-opener, and they seem to outrank the other lists that we've heard about so far, and do you know how much money there is in the world? There's supposed to be $300 trillion and a third of it is owned by the Rothschilds, and I've charted all this, and my chart incorporates all the charts I've ever seen, and I have the hierarchy of the Committee of 300, and above that I draw another square, and do you know what I label that square, the highest square on the chart? I label it the 'You Don't Want to Know' square. It's Satan."

Arlene jabs at the heavens with great excitement. "Look. Look. It's a chem trail."

I crane my neck. "Isn't that just the vapor from a jet?"

"No, vapor dissipates. A chem trail is thicker and last hours and hours."

"What's the purpose?"

"They're spraying the sky with these electromagnetic chemicals to change the density. By changing the density, it makes it easier to carry the beams of electricity they use for spying and mind control. Spray and zap. Spray and zap."

"I've seen some pretty dramatic ones," Barry adds. "One poured over Shattuck Avenue like Niagara Falls."

"People don't pay attention," Arlene says. "They need to look up and ask questions."

"Heck, Arlene," Barry snaps. "All these concentration camps are being built all over the country and people aren't speaking a word about them. When they start filling them up with millions of citizens, maybe people will wake up."

"Who's going into these camps?" I ask Barry.

"Dissidents, the homeless, so-called terrorists. Step by step, you can match it up with Hitler and Nazi Germany, right down to the phrase 'homeland security.' It's not about America anymore. It's about the world. They want to govern the world."

We pass under the giant beak of the Yahoo hatchery in Santa Clara, enter the Marriott Hotel, and walk the perimeter of the Con Con showroom. Barry turns to me. "You're should be feeling like a babe in the woods right now. If you don't have that sensation of 'Where have I been all my life?' then you're truly not discovering stuff."

It is a lot to take in.

A pyramid with the all-seeing eye—the same symbol of the Freemasons and the dollar bill and the Israeli Supreme Court building erected by Baron Rothschild—hangs from each attendee's neck.

There are booths for UFO/TV, magnetic jewelry, and psychic readings by Joseph Ernest Martin, winner of the Visionary Award of Excellence.

A large woman from the San Fernando Valley is shouting "It's all pieces on a chessboard" as she hawks hundreds of DVDs with titles such as "Mohammed Atta and the Venice Florida Flying Circus."

A stern-looking man with a Texas accent and a necktie in the design of the Don't Tread on Me flag sells memberships to the Free Enterprise Society, a Fresno-based group that advocates income tax evasion and a new theory on the Oklahoma City bombing, one that exonerates Timothy McVeigh.

A tall, striking woman from rural Pennsylvania with blonde hair past her waist explains the narrative threads that hold together her husband's thirteen-and-a-half-pound book, *Vatican Assassins*. He is elsewhere.

A makeshift bookstore along the back wall features titles such as *Phantom Flight 93*, *Sexual Encounters with Extra Terrestrials*, *The Secret History of Free Masonry*, and, for reasons I cannot determine because one of the booksellers, spooked by my note-taking, keeps snapping my picture, the Rwandan genocide classic, *We Wish to Inform You That Tomorrow We Will Be Killed with Our Families*, by Philip Gourevitch.

In the middle of the room, Jim Fetzer, distinguished professor of philosophy and computer science, founder of the 9/11 Scholars for Truth, is standing behind a table pushing his latest DVD, "9/11 and the Neo-Con Agenda." With heavy jowls and long gray sideburns, he looks like an elder of the Amish tribe. When he talks, his words topple from the side of his mouth. "It's all here. The fact that the FBI says there is no hard evidence connecting Osama bin Laden to 9/11. The thousand lies, according to the Center for Public Integrity, that induced us to support the war."

I had spent a week researching Fetzer and the various off-shoots of the belief that everything we've been told about 9/11 is a hoax. It wasn't the work of Al Qaeda and nineteen of its foot soldiers but an elaborate machine of far more sinister pro-portions laboring here and overseas in perfect synchronicity. An inner sanctum of our government—the exact combination of players could only be guessed at—had conspired to set up 9/11 as a pretext to grab oil, protect Israel, and remake the Middle East in our image.

Theirs wasn't a movement of the fringe. Polls showed that more than a third of Americans believed that federal officials had assisted in the attacks or knowingly let them happen. Hun-dreds of thousands of disciples were tuning in to YouTube to watch videos that poked holes in the official version. One clip showed Bush, three months after 9/11, making a fantastic blun-der. He told a town hall crowd that he learned of the attacks the same way they did. On the morning of 9/11, moments before he entered the Florida classroom to meet with kids, Bush re-called seeing the TV image of the plane striking the first tower. "I saw an airplane hit the tower—the TV was obviously on. And I said, 'Well, there's one terrible pilot. It must have been a horrible accident.'" Bush then recalled his chief of staff enter-ing the classroom and whispering into his ear about the other tower being struck. "America is under attack."

Problem was, this sequence of events could not have hap-pened. There were no live images televised on the morning of 9/11 that showed the first plane hitting the tower. The attack, after all, was a surprise. Only on 9/12 did such videos emerge. So this was either a confused retelling by the president or the slip of something darker. Guess which one the YouTube bloggers believed?

Fetzer can recite many such peculiarities. A professor emeritus at the University of Minnesota, author of more than twenty books, among them *The Evolution of Intelligence* and *The Great Zapruder Film Hoax: Deceit and Deception in the Death of JFK*, he is a man of considerable erudition. Yet he is not a scholar comfortable with the idea that stupid people, idle people, sad, hapless people who occupy society's margins can, in one simple act aided by a bit of planning and propelled by the tailwind of luck, alter the course of history. Thus no one such as Lee Harvey Oswald, using a mail order rifle, could have ever killed JFK.

In his 9/11 postulations, Fetzer begins with an indisputable premise: the attacks *were* a conspiracy. Whether you buy his version or the official government version, dozens of men were involved. Then he trots out a series of more or less confirmed facts:

- Bush-Cheney have used the Big Lie time and again to propagandize on behalf of the military and corporate complex. From altered scientific reports to mobilizing a small army of retired generals who sold the war on every TV news show, this presidency has institutionalized the Big Lie as the highest form of spin.

- A conspiracy of such magnitude is in keeping with the administration's hubris. Bush-Cheney had brought aboard a group of neocons who called themselves the Project for the New American Century—the same group that had been wishing aloud for a Pearl Harbor–like match to ignite America to the dangers of Islamic radicalism. Many of these neocons were Jewish and strongly pro-Israel.

- Israeli spies, tracking Al Qaeda on American soil, likely had prior knowledge of 9/11. Several Mossad agents, posing as employees of a phony company called Urban Moving Systems, were caught in Liberty State Park filming and jumping for joy as the Twin Towers came crashing down, according to the *New York Times* and several New Jersey newspapers, though the stories were all buried. After two months in custody—and numerous evasions and failed lie detector tests—the spies were flown back to Israel on the orders of Attorney General John Ashcroft.

- The corporations benefiting most from the war had close ties to Bush-Cheney. Halliburton, for one, had handed the vice president $35 million in stock.

For the Arlenes and Barrys of the world, this wasn't simply a set of disconnected facts but proof of a larger truth that led back to the crime scene, Ground Zero itself.

"Buildings struck by airplanes sway and buckle and then topple over," Barry says as we stand in line to meet Professor Fetzer. "They don't come down in a perfect free fall. Only a moron would believe it happened that way. It just so happens that we have a nation of imbeciles."

I ask what, if not those planes, brought the towers down.

"Controlled demolition," Barry says smugly. "Only controlled demolition makes a building come down in perfect pancake fashion."

He suggests that I read the work of Steven Jones, a professor of physics at BYU. "Jones has discovered traces of thermite
in the debris at Ground Zero."

"Thermite?" I ask.

The man in front of us jerks his head around. Bushy gray
beard, wild hair in a ponytail, splashy blue T-shirt decorated
with salamanders, he knows thermite.

"It's an explosive agent," he says. "Laced with sulfur, it can
do very powerful things. But I happen to believe that it wasn't
thermite but a new material, one even more powerful, that
brought down the Twin Towers."

He is a scientist, he says, an expert in "nano technology"
who once worked on lasers for the Star Wars program. This
gave him access to the innermost corridors at Los Alamos
and Lawrence Livermore labs. "I'm the guy who used to have
Q clearance," he says. "That's before I started wearing
salamanders."

"So you believe in this too?"

"It's not a matter of believing. It's a matter of science.
Those towers were built to withstand plane crashes. There was
a core and ring built around the core and crisscrossing lattice.
There's no way a plane spilling fuel and fire could bring it
down. It's not going to work. Sorry. This was something else.
This was prepositioned demolition charges."

"You mean in the days before, a team was sent in to salt
both buildings, all 160 stories, with high-tech gunpowder?"

"Yes, yes. Thank you, thank you." He bows at the waist
with Chinese deference. "He gets it. The man gets it."

"Three thousand of our own people expendable?"

"Trust me, my friend. Trust me. Death is nothing to these
men."

Fetzer is about to leave and I want to talk to him, but the bushy-bearded scientist is now speaking in acronyms about another building in the World Trade Center complex, a forty-seven-story steel-framed skyscraper known as Building Seven. It sat a block away and was never hit by a plane but fell instantly at 5:20 that evening, imploding in the exact manner of a professionally engineered demolition.

"This is the building that housed all the secret documents about spying and such," he says. "CIA, DIA, the whole shebang."

It occurs to me at this moment that he and the others aren't "gullible illiterates," as one blogger committed to the official line put it. They are, to the contrary, very smart people with minds as intricate as their theories. They gobble up impossible amounts of data, and the magnitude of the material, its accumulations and meanderings, becomes its own truth. That their theories are elaborate should come as no surprise. This is purely a function of their minds, the capacity to construct and hold such elaborations. Minds such as these cannot be contained to one sealed off theory. Minds such as these need to breathe and produce other offshoots. Theories grow into physical contraptions. UFOs suddenly have an integral role in the plan. Russia and China become bedfellows with Israel. The Rothschilds join up with the Bilderberg Group, and the faces of Satan are glimpsed in the smoke that billows down from the burning towers.

I want to ask Fetzer about his scholarship, how it is that he builds one piece of his case by citing the work of a strange website called Judicial Inc. It is full of anti-Semitic rants and *Protocols of the Elders of Zion*–type malarkey. But the professor has sold his last DVD and left the room.

People are heading to the speakers hall to hear Sean-David Morton talk about the Great Antichrist, the Indigo Children, and the 2012 apocalypse. I walk in the opposite direction and step outside. Under the canopy of the side entrance, I find Charles, an old moonshiner from the hills of Virginia who hasn't filed an income tax return since 1960.

This is his first Con Con. He's here to launch a new 911 phone system. Only this one is activated by hitting the numbers 119. "If a cop stops you, you dial 119, leave the cell phone open, and we tape everything that goes on. Get it all on record. This is the only way we're going to stop the criminals in uniforms from accosting the people."

I ask him if it feels funny setting up his table next to so many old hippies and dippies.

"You know what they say. The left goes west and the right goes east and at some point 'round the bend their roads meet. We're standing in the same place. Plum pissed off at the government."

On the bridge back to the East Bay, Arlene can see a sky full of chem trails. "They're going to be hitting Berkeley hard tonight," she frets. Already, she is feeling ill from the electrical assault on the exhibit hall. "Think about it," she says. "What more could the CIA ask for. All those activists under one roof."

She and Barry discuss the importance of taking lots of minerals and chelation flushes to ward off the vibrations. If all else fails, drink your own urine.

"People all over the world do it," Barry says. "It's the first medicine of man."

"Cured me of cancer," Arlene says.

I climb the hill to La Vereda Way. Arlene invites me inside for homemade organic lasagna, but my appetite isn't what it should be. I take the Earl Warren Parkway to the 580 east and steer straight into the searing heat. From Livermore to Los Banos, it's all a blur of Shane P. Donlon "Land for Sale" signs planted in the hog wallow. On Highway 152 past Red Top, where I once pulled weeds from sugar beet fields, I think back to those years I had spent covering local, state, and federal governments, all the stories and investigative pieces that made hay of bureaucracy's schemes and plots. I had found plenty of evil, yes, but it was stupid evil, blinkered evil that lacked the imagination to link up to the evil below or above it. No matter how involved I had imagined it to be—and it always seemed impossibly ornate from the outside looking in—once I broke through the design, it was a small man's chicanery at heart.

I think back to Watergate, the plots hatched in the White House basement, the deeds of Nixon's "plumbers" who possessed, in the words of *Time*'s Lance Morrow, "the low cunning of Daffy Duck thinking hard. An entire Administration brought down by an immense yet pissant doofusness, culminating in Nixon's inexplicable failure to burn the tapes." Now that was a government conspiracy.

I try to imagine the disappointments of Arlene and Barry and the others who traced their awakening to the summer of '67. All those years fighting Vietnam and Nixon, all their endeavors to change the system, and then to see it culminate two generations later, grandparents now, in the lies and war of George W. Bush. My psychologist cousin said it was textbook. Those who had tried so hard to change the social order and failed had retreated into their own psychic order. Protest turned into mysticism, and mysticism led to phantasmagoria and paranoia.

The social transformation of San Francisco and Berkeley, its ionic foot bath and organic tampon self-absorption, the inexhaustible consumption made possible by the ascent of the silicon chip, mirrored Arlene and Barry's own pilgrimage inward. And what about those who would stand in their place? Blame it on a lack of courage or the absence of a military draft or the submission to the dot-com or too much Ritalin or something missing in the nation's soul from way back. I only knew that when I strolled across People's Park and onto the Berkeley campus and finally found the steps of Sproul Hall, there wasn't one man raging to thousands about throwing his body onto the gears of the machine but thousands, en masse, heedless, staring into the iridescence of their cell phones.

| Legend of Zankou

In a mansion in the hills above Glendale, a man named Mardiros Iskenderian rose from bed one recent morning and put on a white silk suit he hadn't worn in twenty years. He stuffed a 9-millimeter handgun into his waistband and a .38-caliber revolver into his coat pocket and walked step by small step down the stairs. His wife, Rita, who had fallen in love with Mardiros when she was twelve, couldn't believe it was him. For a man who was so near death, cancer everywhere, he looked beautiful. It had been months since he had ventured outside by himself, months since he had driven one of his fancy cars, and she fretted that he was too weak to go anywhere. He told her not to worry. He was feeling much better now, and besides, he was only going to Zankou Chicken to see an old friend.

He had lived his life like one of those princes of Armenian fable, maybe Ara the Beautiful or Tigran the Great. The fable began in a tiny storefront in Beirut, where his mother wearing her apron hand-spooned the fluffy white garlic paste that would become their fortune. From Hollywood to Anaheim, he had opened a chain of fast-food rotisserie chicken restaurants that dazzled the food critics and turned customers into a cult. Poets wrote about his Zankou Chicken. Musicians sang about his Zankou Chicken. Now that he was dying, his dream of building an empire, one hundred Zankous across the land, a Zankou in every major city, would be his four sons' to pursue. In the days before, he had pulled them aside one by one—Dikran, Steve, Ara, Vartkes—and told them he had no regrets. He was only fifty-six years old, that was true, but life had not cheated him. Everything he had ever wanted to do, he had done. He did not tell them about the one piece of business that still remained.

There was one son, the second son, Steve, who always seemed to know what was on his father's mind. He was the son most like Mardiros: his smile, his temper, his heart. Had Steve been home that day, he might have sensed trouble or at least insisted that his father not go alone. But Mardiros had sent Steve off to the local mall to fetch him a slushy lemonade, the only thing he still had a taste for. By the time Steve got home, the lemonade still icy, his father was gone. The boy would forever question whether it was design or chance at work that January day. Was this errand a ruse, part of his father's last plan, or had he simply failed to hurry home fast enough?

"Steve, something bad has happened," his mother cried at the door. "There's been a shooting. At your Aunt Dzovig's."

"Where's Dad?"

"He's gone."

"What do you mean, he's gone?"

"He took the car. He said he was going to Zankou. But I don't believe him now. They heard shots at Dzovig's."

Dzovig was Mardiros's younger sister, as pretty as he was handsome. She lived in a big house on the other side of the Verdugo Hills with her husband and two sons. She managed a pair of Zankous for Mardiros and had taken on the chore of caring for their mother. Of course, everyone knew this was no chore at all because the mother, Margrit Iskenderian, the creator of the garlic paste and most every dish worth tasting at Zankou, was a woman who pulled her load and the load of three others.

The drive to Aunt Dzovig's house that winter day in 2003 was a winding seven miles. Steve ran every stop sign, racing down one side of the canyon and up the other. As he rounded the bend and the Oakmont Country Club came into view, he could see the TV news helicopters circling like vultures.

"No, Dad," he shouted. "Please, Dad, no."

Up the hill, where the canyon oak gave way to palm trees, neighbors were spilling out of their million-dollar estates. Police were everywhere, and his aunt's house, front to back, had been cordoned off. He jumped out of the car and made a dash for it. He could feel himself running with the lean of a man who had every right to whatever reality existed on the other side of the yellow tape. A detective halted him short.

"Who are you?"

"I am Steve Iskenderian."

"Who are you looking for?"

"Mardiros Iskenderian. I am his son. Is he inside?"

"Yes."

"Is he dead?"

The cop wasn't sure how to tell it to the son, so he told it straight, answering only the question posed to him. "Yes," he said. "He's dead."

For a moment, Steve felt a strange relief that only later would he attribute to his gratitude that his cancer-ridden father had finally found release from his suffering. Then, almost in the same instant, it occurred to him to ask the question that he already knew the answer to.

"My grandmother and aunt. Are they dead too?"

The cop stared into his eyes and nodded. "Yes, they're dead too."

The police had questions, and Steve tried his best to answer them. On the drive home, he had to forgive himself for allowing his mind, at such a moment, to consider the family business. Who would take over now that his father and grandmother, the heart and soul of Zankou Chicken, were gone? His mother, Rita, by design, had never worked a single day at Zankou. His older brother, Dikran, was a born-again evangelist whose fire took him to street corners, and a younger brother, Ara, was addled by drugs. And no one was more lost than Steve himself. Just three years earlier, he had been charged with shooting at a prostitute and her pimp and had faced a life sentence. The case, as luck would have it, ended in a mistrial. He did have two cousins, Aunt Dzovig's sons, who were capable enough. But how could they be expected to work beside the sons of the man who had murdered their mother and grandmother?

"My God, Dad," he said, climbing the hillside to give his mother the news. "What have you done?"

In the weeks and months and years to follow, five years to be exact, the Armenians of Glendale, Hollywood, Montebello, and Van Nuys, and their cousins up and over the mountains in Fresno, told and retold the story. "Let's sit crooked and talk straight," the old ladies clucked. There was no bigger shame, no bigger *ahmote*, than an Armenian son taking the life of his own mother. And who could explain such a shame from a man like Mardiros Iskenderian? He was the same son who had honored his mother on Mother's Day with lavish ceremonies at the church, celebrations in which Margrit Iskenderian, short and plump, her salt and pepper hair cut in a bob, was invariably crowned queen. Wherever they went as a family, he made his wife take a seat in the back so his mother could sit beside him. For twenty-five years, she had lived with Mardiros and Rita and their children, her bedroom the master bedroom, where a single photo, of her and her son in 1950s Lebanon, graced her dresser. Each day at 6:00 P.M., when Margrit returned home from her long shift cooking at Zankou, Rita was there to greet her at the door. So why, after all those years of devotion, did Margrit Iskenderian leave her son and move in with her daughter Dzovig, a breach so complete that mother and son would share words only one more time—the words that preceded the gunshots?

The old ladies gave answers, some less cruel than others. The cancer that filled Mardiros's body had gone to his brain. He was thinking like a crazy man. No, it wasn't cancer; it was the scars from growing up in Lebanon with a father who was the drunkard of Bourj Hamoud and a mother filled with bitterness. No, haven't you heard the talk about the Pepsi company offering the family $30 million for the Zankou chain and trademark? Greed, at last, split the family house in two.

Others insisted there was no sense to be made of it because life made no sense, death made no sense. Yes, we Armenians were the first people to accept Christianity as a nation, way back in 301 A.D., before the Romans, before the Greeks. But to answer this question of why Mardiros Iskenderian killed his mother and his sister and then himself, Armenians had to reach back to their pagan past, to a way of seeing older than the Bible itself. *Pakht*, they called it. Fate. *Jagadakeer*, it was muttered. Your destiny is etched into your forehead at birth. What is written no one can change.

Thus from Turkey to Beirut to Hollywood to Glendale, from the genocide to the garlic paste to the mansion to the murders, it was all foretold.

Rita was an Armenian Catholic schoolgirl growing up in the suburbs of Beirut in the late 1960s when she first set eyes on Mardiros Iskenderian, the bad boy gunning his banana yellow 442 Oldsmobile up and down the lane. When he blew the engine, he turned up the next week with a brand-new 442 Olds, this one burgundy. The pampered son of Zankou Chicken hardly noticed Rita Hovakimian, who was seven years younger. He kept a rooftop apartment across the ally from where she lived with her family. From balcony to balcony, she spied on him. She got her money's worth.

"There was no missing him. He always came and went with big noise," Rita said. "His reputation as a playboy was very bad. Arab girls, Maronite Christian girls, Armenian girls, single girls, married girls. For me, he was the most beautiful guy in the world. Nobody was like him. His smile was gorgeous. His hair was gorgeous. He wore the most beautiful perfume. He was always dressed in Pierre Cardin or something. And when he would open his mouth, out came the charm. What more did a young girl want?" Her parents had forbidden her from seeing any boy, much less a man with his associations. A few years earlier, Mardiros had been implicated in a notorious jewelry store heist and murder, an inside job by three Armenians who had killed the handsome scion of one of Beirut's wealthiest Arab families. Not knowing that his friend was one of the three robbers, Mardiros let him use his apartment. Only later did he discover the stash of jewels in the attic. His testimony ended up sending the trio to prison, and from that day on, alert to revenge, he carried two pistols wherever he went.

The gap in their ages seemed to narrow as Rita blossomed into a tall beauty with big round eyes. They began meeting on the sly, Mardiros tossing her messages in an empty cologne bottle from the roof. For three months, they kept their relationship hidden, until a nosy Armenian neighbor saw her riding in his car and told her mother. It became a big family scandal, with lots of threats back and forth. In the end, her parents knew they were deeply in love. She was nineteen; he was twenty-six. Their wedding came amid the fierce fighting of Lebanon's civil war. She wore a full white gown, but he wanted no part of a tuxedo. His Angels Flight pants touched so low to the ground you couldn't tell if he was wearing shoes or not.

They shared a two-bedroom walk-up in the crowded Armenian quarter of Bourj Hamoud with his parents, his two sisters, and his mother's mother, a survivor of the Armenian genocide. Right below was Zankou Chicken, the take-out they had named after a river in Armenia. There was no cash register, no table, no chairs. They used every square foot to clean and salt the chickens, roast them inside a pair of rotisserie ovens, and keep the golden brown wholes and halves piping hot. Customers parked on the one-way street, ran in, handed the cash to Mardiros's father, and ran out with their steaming birds and dollops of pungent garlic paste.

"It was a drive-thru before there were drive-thrus," recalled Garo Dekirmendjian, a Beiruti Armenian who befriended the family. "The mother would be standing in the mezzanine in her apron, cleaning the garlic cloves and whipping up her paste. And the father was a cash machine. All day long the same movement, his right hand stuffing wads of money into his left shirt pocket and pulling out the change. Mardiros was helping turn the chickens when he wasn't having fun."

Rita understood that Mardiros's position in the family— first child, only son—gave him an exalted status. *The prince. The pasha.* In time, it would shoulder him with a great burden. But she was confounded by the degree of devotion between mother and son. "Before we married, he told me, 'I am going to live with my parents my whole life. I will never leave my mother.' I figured this was my *pakht.* But it was too much. 'My mother. My mother.' She was the queen of the house, not me. Next to God, it was his mother."

Unraveling the family dynamic was not easy. Her father-in-law, a smart and generous man, disappeared on long bouts of drinking. Day and night, from bottom floor to top floor, her mother-in-law worked. Even if she was compensating for her husband, her capacity for labor bordered on the maniacal. Rita wondered if Mardiros simply felt sorry for his mother and sought to honor her service. Or maybe deep down he understood that no one worked so hard for free. He had watched her punish his father with the guilt of indebtedness. Maybe Mardiros feared that his own debt would be turned against him if he didn't pay her back with absolute allegiance. Whatever it was, Rita felt swallowed up by their world.

Stuck inside the apartment with baby Dikran, she could smell the aroma of Zankou floating through the cracks. This was as close as she would come to the business. Her job, set down by custom, was to raise her children and tend to her mother-in-law's mother. So each day, without complaint, Rita finished rocking the baby and listened as the old lady told her story of survival, of the Turks rounding up all the Armenians in her village of Hajin in the spring of 1915, and herding them on a death march to the Syrian desert. Was it *jagadakeer*? Her mother-in-law said she came upon the skull of a dead Armenian and picked it up. She looked at the forehead to see if any words had been written there, but there weren't any. "She said she learned that day that there were no words to read. For her, the only words were God's words."

The survivors had streamed into Beirut by the thousands and formed a new Armenia in the "Paris of the Middle East." They built sixty Armenian schools and published ten Armenian-language newspapers and held sway far beyond their numbers. Without them, the Muslim Arabs would have ruled the country. With them, the Christian Arabs kept a narrow edge. It stayed that way until 1975, when the civil war upended everything. The Iskenderians, like so many other Armenian merchants, didn't want to leave. Zankou was a gold mine, and they poured the profits into rental properties throughout the city.

Then one evening in 1979, the war struck home. Mardiros was sitting outside one of their empty storefronts, not a block from Zankou, when two men on motorcycles sped by. He had no reason to suspect that a dispute over rent with an Armenian tenant, a man connected to a political party, would turn violent. But the motorcycle drivers, wearing masks and clutching

AK-47s, circled back around. They fired dozens of rounds, hitting Mardiros with bullet after bullet, sixteen shots in all. They say it was a miracle he didn't die right there.

Mardiros had always been a student of maps, but what he found when he came to America was something else. "Rita," he shouted from a back room. "These Thomas brothers. What geniuses!" They had taken a city that made no sense to itself and given it a structure, a syntax, that even foreigners like him could fathom. Here was a whole bound guide of maps that divided up the sprawl of Southern California into perfect little squares with numbers that corresponded to pages inside. Turn to any page and you had the landscape of L.A. in bird's eye: parks in green, malls in yellow, cemeteries in olive, and freeways, the lifeblood, in red. He pored over the maps at night, reviewed them again in the morning, and then took off to find his new city. By car and foot, he logged hundreds of miles that first week, close to a thousand the next. He was looking for the right business in the right location and wasn't in any particular hurry. They had come with plenty of cash.

One thing was certain. His parents, looking for something easier, wanted no part of the food business. There would be no Zankous in America. They settled instead on a dry cleaning shop, only to find out that the chemicals made Mardiros sick. Father and son traveled to Hong Kong to explore the trade of men's suits, then decided the business wasn't practical. The deeper Mardiros journeyed into Los Angeles, the more he bumped up against the growing pockets of immigrants fresh from the Middle East. No restaurant seemed to be dedicated to their cuisine, at least none that served it fast and delicious and at a price that would bring customers back. So in 1983 he went to his parents and pitched the idea. His father resisted. His mother cried. They threatened to return to Beirut. In the end, sensing their son's resolve, they consented.

He picked a tiny place next to a laundromat on the corner of Sunset and Normandie—could there have been an uglier minimall in all of Hollywood?—and erected a sign with block letters in blue and red. ZANKOU CHICKEN. Before long, the Arabs and Persian Jews and Armenians found it. So did Mexican gang bangers and nurses from Kaiser Permanente and the flock from L. Ron Hubbard's church, who methodically polished off their plates of chicken shawarma, hummus, and pickled turnips and returned to their e-meters with a clearness that only Margrit's paste could bring.

This wasn't Beirut. Mardiros put in long hours. He tweaked the menu; his mother tinkered with the spices. It took a full year to find a groove. The first crowd of regulars brought in a second crowd, and a buzz began to grow among the network of foodies. How did they make the chicken so tender and juicy? The answer was a simple rub of salt and not trusting the rotisserie to do all the work but raising and lowering the heat and shifting each bird as it cooked. What made the garlic paste so fluffy and white and piercing? This was a secret the family intended to keep. Some customers swore it was potatoes, others mayonnaise. One fanatic stuck his container in the freezer and examined each part as it congealed. He pronounced the secret ingredient a special kind of olive oil. None guessed right. The ingredients were simple and fresh, Mardiros pledged, no shortcuts. The magic was in his mother's right hand.

Word of a new kind of fare, fast and tasty and light, spread to the critics. The *L.A. Times* called it "the best roast chicken in town at any price." Zagat anointed Zankou one of "America's best meal deals." No one was more breathless in his praise than Jonathan Gold, the guerrilla warrior of city chowhounds. Gold called the chicken "superb, golden, crispy skinned and juicy," but declared that nothing in heaven or on earth compared with the garlic paste. "A fierce, blinding-white paste that sears the back of your throat, and whose powerful aroma can stay in your head—also your car—for days. Go ahead, Ultra Brite; go ahead, Lavoris; go ahead, Car Freshener. My money's on the sauce."

The hole in the wall was raking in $2 million a year, half of it pure profit. In Mardiros's mind, the family was growing and the business needed to grow with it. This is America, he told his parents. We've got something good. Let's duplicate our success. His parents, hands full with one Zankou, were dead set against an expansion. Mardiros kept pushing, though, and in 1991 the family agreed to a split. Mardiros would take the Zankou concept and build a chain across the region. Any new restaurants he opened, success or failure, would belong to him. In return, he would sign over his stake in Hollywood to his parents and two sisters. The split was hardly a parting. The garlic paste still would be prepared by his mother and used by all the Zankous. And as a favor to sister Dzovig, he would pay her a salary to manage some of his new stores. Nothing, he assured them, would change at home.

After so many years playing the pampered son, Mardiros now saw himself as the patriarch, a role that became official after his father's death. Over and over, he preached the same: Success means nothing if we don't stay as one. Greed must never rear its head. There is plenty for all of us. He loved Dzovig's two boys like his own, and he knew she felt the same way about his sons. The boys were more like brothers than cousins. They lived only a few minutes apart in Glendale and attended the same private Armenian school. Dzovig would take them each morning, and Rita would pick them up. A gang of six, they climbed the hills, rode bikes, played video games. They had the coolest toys, the latest gadgets. If they were spoiled, and they were, it came with the turf. As the grandchildren of Margrit, each one was something of a food snob. No one's cooking could measure up to hers. She made the best lentil soups, the best raw meat and bulgur *che kufta*. She wasn't big on hugs or kisses; she could be downright stern, but she wanted her grandchildren to know what good food tasted like. When they turned up their noses at her sheep's brain soup, she bribed them with $20 bills just to get them to take one sip.

Mardiros didn't need to travel far to find his next spot. Glendale was a city made new by three successive waves of Armenian refugees, first from Iran, then from Beirut, and now from Armenia itself. He picked a less grimy minimall squeezed behind a gas station for Zankou number 2. As soon as it began turning a profit, he found a spot in Van Nuys for Zankou number 3. Then came Zankou number 4 in Anaheim and Zankou number 5 in Pasadena. His white house, way up in the Verdugo Hills, was now known as the home of the rotisserie chicken mogul. It sat higher than the mansions of doctors, lawyers, and investment bankers. Only a porn king looked down on him. He and Rita drove a Jaguar and a black Mercedes-Benz. They had live-in servants. Yet it wasn't the kind of wealth that let them lounge around playing golf or tennis. When Rita wasn't tending the boys, she was feeding and bathing Mardiros's ninety-seven-year-old grandmother. As for Mardiros's mother, Margrit, it was true she had high tastes and wasn't afraid to indulge them. She had her own seamstress and dressed in the finest silks and wools. But more often than not, Margrit's tailored clothes were covered by the apron she put on each morning at 7:30 sharp. When she finished preparing dishes for the customers, she began cooking delicacies for the employees.

As for Mardiros, he spent his days hopping from Zankou to Zankou. He did the payroll, made sure the food tasted right, and timed the customers from the second they walked in to the second they were served. When he wasn't working, he was cutting around with his gang of rich buddies. He went to Vegas with them, to Cabo with them. Every so often, he'd pile Rita and the kids into the Mercedes and take them to his favorite Chinese restaurant. This is what passed for family time. If he felt bad about neglecting his wife and children, he tried to make up for it by giving to the Armenian community. He gave to schools, dance troupes, and starving artists. He gave to orphans and widows and soup kitchens back in Armenia. He gave so often that a cartoon in one Armenian American newspaper showed two doors leading into Zankou. One was for food, the other for philanthropy. All in all, he had done what he had set out to do. At night, out on the balcony, he sat in his chair and could see all the way to Catalina Island. He'd take his telescope and look up at the stars and then look back down at the twinkling lights of Los Angeles. He belonged here. This was his place now. He and his Zankous had become part of the map.

He could feel the pain down below growing worse. He figured something terrible afflicted him. Next week, he told himself, next week. By the time he got to the doctor, he was told it was too late. The cancer in his bladder had spread to his rectum. Chemotherapy would buy only a little time. He broke the news to Rita and the boys the best he could, and then he gathered his mother and sisters in the living room to tell them. He was going to fight it, he said, but if he died, he wanted them to know this: his sons—Dikran, twenty-five, Steve, twenty-three, Ara, eighteen, and Vartkes, seventeen—would be taking over his Zankous. The room fell silent. His sisters, Dzovig and Haygan, seemed tongue-tied. His mother sat stone-faced. She didn't ask what kind of cancer he had or what kind of prognosis the doctors had given him. Instead, as she put down her demitasse of Turkish coffee, she blurted out in Armenian, "Your sons. The shadow they cast is not yours." Then she rose, walked up the stairs to her bedroom, and shut the door.

Each one of his boys, it was true, was struggling to find his place. Vartkes, the youngest and perhaps the brightest, was using his allowance to buy marijuana. Ara, pent up and quirky, was addicted to painkillers. Dikran, the oldest, had found the Lord and was preaching salvation during the day and telling his brothers at night, in bed, that they were all headed to hell. He had become a born-again after a scandal in 1997 that cost him his dream of being a lawyer. A top student at Woodbury University, Dikran had been caught in an elaborate scheme to cheat on the law school entrance exam. He paid a fine and served probation, but no credentialed law school would ever accept him.

For Steve, it was a different weakness. He had gone to the 777 motel in Sherman Oaks on a winter night in 2000 to meet a call girl. He didn't know she had a listening device broadcasting to a pimp, who then stole his money. Steve gave chase down a freeway, and shots were fired at the pimp and the prostitute, hitting their car. Steve was charged with two counts of attempted murder and bail was set at $1.4 million. If the verdict didn't go his way, he faced life in prison. As it turned out, the prosecutor made a small blunder during the trial, telling the jury about a prior crime that Steve had committed when, in fact, it was his brother Dikran. His attorney, Mark Geragos, objected, and the judge declared a mistrial. Steve pleaded guilty to a lesser crime, did a year of work furlough, and was let go.

In days that followed the news of his cancer, Mardiros couldn't help but notice that his mother's behavior toward him had changed. She would come home from work, Rita would greet her as usual at the front door, and she would walk right past him and into the kitchen without a word. No "How do you feel today? No "Are your treatments working?" She would pour a glass of water from the refrigerator, turn around, and walk upstairs to her room. He wouldn't see her again until the next day, when she would stage her silence all over again. His hair fell out, he lost sixty pounds, but not once did she seem to notice. It didn't occur to Rita that her mother-in-law might be miffed about Mardiros's desire for his sons to take over the business. After all, Margrit had opposed the expansion from day one, and Mardiros alone owned Zankous 2, 3, 4, and 5.

This went on for more than a year, not a word spoken between mother and son. Mardiros might have taken it upon himself to ask what offense he had committed to deserve such treatment. But all he had left was his pride. Then one day, while his mother was away at work, he walked into her bedroom and reached atop the dresser and grabbed the photo of him and her when he was a child back in Lebanon. He could see that she had the faintest smile on her lips as she was leaning over to hug him. *Her prince. Her pasha.* He took the photo out of its frame, tore off the side depicting his mother, lit a match, and watched it burn. Then he folded up his side of the photo and threw it away. A day or so later, as it happened, the house caught fire. Flames shot up from the maid's bedroom downstairs. He and Rita were stuck on the balcony, choking on smoke, when the fire fighters finally rescued them. They packed what they could and went to live at a hotel in Glendale while the house was being refurbished. It was the next to last time he would see his mother. She had taken all her possessions and moved in with Dzovig.

Over the following year, as he lay dying, his mother never once called him. Neither did his sisters or his nephews. His treatments had caused fluid to build up in his brain, and he was thinking all kinds of crazy thoughts. He told Steve about setting the image of his mother on fire, and how that image had come back to light the blaze that had burned the house. In more rational moments, he thought that a mother capable of disowning her son in the hour of his greatest need, a son who had dedicated his life to her, was capable of engineering great mischief when he was gone. Yes, the Zankous he had built belonged to him alone, and he believed the trademark was his too. But how could he be certain that his mother and sisters wouldn't challenge the inheritance of his wife and sons?

His head began to throb, the pain so severe that his sons had to take turns rubbing his skull with their knuckles. He told Steve he was certain that his mother and sisters were plotting against him. He could barely stand up, but each week he made Steve drive him to the two Zankous that Dzovig managed and open the safe so he could count the receipts. Steve, conflicted by his love for his grandmother, asked his father if he could ever find it in his heart to forgive her. "God will forgive the devil before I can forgive my mother," he said. "Because this is a mother, not the devil."

He rose from his bed on the morning of January 14, 2003, took a shower, and got dressed. His wife would recall his putting on a white silk suit that hadn't fit him in years. Only now, after losing so much weight, could he wear it again. He reached into the closet for his .38-caliber revolver and stuck it into his coat pocket. Then he jammed his 9-millimeter semi-automatic Browning into his waistband, next to his diaper. The gun held eleven rounds, and he scooped up nine extra bullets just in case. As he walked down the stairs and said good-bye to Rita, he had no intention of going to Zankou Chicken to see an old friend. He had telephoned his sister at work and arranged a meeting with her and his mother to discuss family affairs.

He maneuvered his black BMW down the steep canyon, looped along La Crescenta Avenue, and climbed the backside of the mountain until he reached the split-level brick and stucco house on Ayars Canyon Way. He parked out front, walked up to the tall entrance past two sago palms, and knocked on the door. He was now wearing a dark brown jacket with gray pants. Perhaps he had changed clothes on the way over, or maybe his wife's memory had played a trick, dressing him for a last time in white silk. The housekeeper led him into the dining room where his forty-five-year-old sister, Dzovig Marjik, was standing. She was wearing blue jeans and a long-sleeved brown sweater. Her hair was curly like his, as if she had just gotten out of the shower, and it was tinted an odd red. She asked him to take a seat at the dining table and poured him a glass of lemonade.

He chatted pleasantly with her for a half hour as he waited for their seventy-six-year-old mother to come home from work. When Margrit Iskenderian walked in a little after 2:00 P.M., she was carrying a big box of food. She set it down on the kitchen table, put on her white slippers, and greeted his sister and then him. The housekeeper poured his mother a glass of lemonade and topped off his glass and the glass of his sister. Then she walked downstairs to her bedroom to let the three of them—mother, son, and daughter—talk.

His sister sat across from him, and his mother to his right. His voice was calm. Their voices were calm. He waited about five minutes, for the conversation to go from nothing to something, and then he reached for the gun in his waistband. He grabbed the handle, put his finger on the trigger and extended his arm across the table and over the pitcher of lemonade. He fired once into his sister's brain. The bullet knocked her off the chair, and she fell face down on the granite floor. He then turned to his mother. She was screaming and running toward the door. He chased her down about fifteen feet short of it and stood in front of her. He raised the gun and waited long enough to hear her plead for her life. "Don't shoot. Please," she said in Armenian. "Please don't shoot." He fired once into her chest and she staggered backward, falling flat and face-up on the floor. He stood over her, straddling her body. She looked up at him and raised her right hand. He fired a second bullet, a third bullet, a fourth, fifth, sixth, seventh, and eighth. Each one he aimed straight into her heart. She was wearing a beautiful silk top, the color of eggplant, but he couldn't tell. She had died with her apron on.

As he looked around the room, he could see his twenty-three-year-old nephew, Hagop, trembling halfway up the

stairs. He didn't say a word to the young man he had once regarded as his fifth son. He turned away and walked a dozen
paces to the leather couch in the living room. Then he sat
down, pointed the gun at his right temple, and fired one time.

On an early winter afternoon not long ago, five years after that
day, the widow of Zankou Chicken sat in her little office in the
back of the Pasadena restaurant and stared into her computer
screen. Live images from each Zankou, the four her husband
had built and the two she had opened since, popped up with a
mouse click. Every car in the parking lot, every customer
standing in line, every worker taking an order or manning a
spit of meat, from Burbank to Anaheim, came under her gaze.

   She studied the movements the way she imagined her husband had scrutinized them from his perch inside each store,
looking for signs that the service wasn't fast enough, or the
food good enough, or that an employee, God forbid, might be
stealing. She had her cell phone at the ready in case her sons
needed to reach her to discuss business or some difficulty in
their lives. This had become Rita Iskenderian's vigil, watching
her stores and bird-dogging her sons for any sign of trouble. A
life-size photo of Mardiros, mustache drooping, middle-aged
body thick in a suit, handsome still, kept watch on her. She
looked up and shook her head.

   "I didn't have time to cry. I had to get out of bed. I buried
him and fifteen days later I was running this business. I was not
a working woman. I had no position. No ground. But I know
how important this business is. That is what my husband built.
I have to be on top of it. I am doing for him. Everything for
him." Her English was broken by the backward phrasing and
accent of a woman who carried Syria and Lebanon in her past.

The smoke from two packs of cigarettes a day had turned her voice husky, and her whole manner had the weight of weariness. When a smile did come, she'd catch herself and put it away before anyone could notice. And yet she had managed to keep a sense of humor, a kind of gallows giggle, that life, luck, had turned out the way it had. Only when you got to know her well enough did she betray a hint of the anger she felt toward Mardiros. Her disquiet was not only for what he had done to her and her children and the rest of the family but also for what he had done to himself, the stain across his name.

"It's a shame that a man of this value has left behind this thing. Because he was a man who gave all his soul. He never said no to anybody. What his mother did to him, I cannot explain. What his sister did to him, I cannot explain. Can jealousy explain this? Can foolish pride? Five years later, it is still a mystery to me."

She regretted not putting aside her own pride back then and visiting his mother and sister. Maybe she could have helped broker a peace and kept the whole thing from happening. What had taken place in those years since was its own crime. She and Mardiros's surviving sister, Haygan, had been best friends since childhood. After the deaths, they had met and consoled each other, and Rita continued to make gestures of reconciliation. But then the lawyers marched in, and a war between the two sides broke out. If Mardiros had intended to erase family entanglements and leave the business to the next generation, he had left behind an even bigger mess.

His registration of the Zankou trademark had lapsed in 2000. Rita believed the chain's good name belonged to her as part of the 1991 split. But during probate, she received a letter from lawyers representing Dzovig's two sons, who intended to challenge her claim. She filed suit and the matter went to trial. In late 2006, to the displeasure of everyone involved, the appellate court ruled that the trademark belonged to both sides. Rita's in-laws and one of her nephews then countered with a lawsuit of their own, alleging wrongful death and seeking tens of millions of dollars from Mardiros's estate. Their lawyers, however, had failed to file within the statute of limitations, and it was dismissed.

Rita didn't discourage her sons when they talked about the love they still felt for their cousins and the desire to be one family again. But she was sure the other side was thinking up ways to take the Zankous from them. Indeed, her two nephews and sister-in-law, who would not speak publicly about the matter, were preparing a new lawsuit to not only take full control of the trademark but to wrest away one of the two houses owned by Rita and her sons. "It never ends," she said. "It never ends."

She opened her office door and walked down a long hall to the front of the restaurant. A giant map of Los Angeles, lifted from the pages of a Thomas Bros. guide, shouted a welcome to customers. Two Armenian cashiers, smiles from the old Soviet Union, took orders. Rita poured herself a soda, parted the black plastic curtain, and entered the main kitchen for all six of her Zankous.

Mexican men in yellow T-shirts with ZANKOU written in red were cleaning chickens, slicing chickens, marinating chickens, skewering chickens. They sent to the ovens 48,000 pounds of Foster Farms roasters and fryers each week, 2.5 million pounds a year. Blood dripped off their knives, down a gutter, and into a drain. On a big black stove, twenty stainless steel pots filled with garbanzo beans—next week's hummus—

bubbled on the fire. Bins brimmed with tahini, the sesame seed paste, and *mutabbal*, the creamy roasted eggplant dip, and *tour-she*, the long thin slices of pickled purple turnips. The skewers, both horizontal and vertical, were piled thick with beef and chicken. From the inside out, the fat sizzled, dripped down, and coated the meat, turning the exterior into a delicate caramel. This was the dish that Mardiros had invented, the best seller they called *tarna*.

Against the far wall, a Formica table and chairs had been set up gin rummy–style. Four ladies, two from Mexico and two from Armenia, sat all day performing a kind of circumcision. They took every clove of garlic that came whole and peeled from Gilroy and excised the tiny stem at the tip. Bud by bud, they cleaned 1,500 pounds of garlic each week. "You would think they stink of garlic," Rita said, gesturing toward the women. "But get close and all you smell is soap."

Of all the possibilities, no one had thought that the widow who had never worked a day at Zankou would be the one to step into her husband's shadow. Her sons didn't think she could do it. She wasn't sure herself. Together, they had grown the chain by adding a store in west L.A. and one in Burbank, the fanciest of the bunch. For the most part, though, it was still a mom-and-pop. She took her workers into her extended family, for better and for worse. She paid them more than the minimum wage and provided free food for lunch. Many had stuck around for years; only a handful had left disgruntled.

She didn't apologize for being a hard driver, a stickler for quality. Indeed, her insistence on using only the best and freshest ingredients, and cooking everything from scratch, was cutting into profits. The cost of tahini alone had doubled in the past year. Back in Mardiros's time, profits from one store opened the next. In the case of Burbank and west L.A., Rita had to take out large loans on her house. She had no choice but to raise prices, so that a plate of chicken *tarna* now ran close to $10—the danger zone for fast food.

"Everybody thinks we are making millions," she said. "Would you believe it if I told you that the one Zankou in Beirut was making more money back then than all of the Zankous put together today?" At age twenty-four, Zankou was a survivor. Fending off challengers, some of them shameless in their imitation of Zankou, was nothing new. The Internet droned with foodies debating the chain's "overrated" chicken or lamenting how the garlic paste had somehow lost its zest. "Zankou Chicken, I don't get the hype," one wrote. Another declared, "Arax is the best falafel stand in Hollywood. The only reason I go to Zankou now is when Arax is closed." Zankou defenders shouted back, "What do you mean over-rated? It's better than ever."

Rita quieted down talk by sons Dikran and Steve about bringing in outside investors to triple the chain, or about selling Zankou nationwide as a franchise. Look around, she told them. Koo Koo Roo, Boston Market, Kenny Rogers—the street was littered with small chains that grew into bigger chains and imploded because they forgot what good food tastes like.

"They are smart boys and in many ways they know this business much better than me. But when they say, 'Mom, look at Starbucks. Mom, look at In and Out,' I tell them, 'Sure, okay. But these are places that are selling one basic item.' It's coffee. It's frozen meat and potatoes. We are not those places."

Dikran, the marketer who handled everything from menus to charity, seemed to understand. Steve took it personally. He

was twenty-eight now and knew more about the food operations than any of them. He had Mardiros's instinct for the business, Rita agreed, and his taste buds too. He could take one bite
of food and know immediately which spice was too much or
too little. But he also had the curse of his father's temper. Rita
worried that he might get into trouble again. And when it came
to managing people, she did not trust his judgment.

Five months earlier, Steve had insisted on hiring a supervisor for the Pasadena Zankou, a woman who had a long career
managing fast-food franchises such as McDonald's. After
much discussion, Rita gave in. The new manager wasted no
time making small changes (name tags) and big ones (hour-by-
hour sales tracking). Steve saw an operation evolving from un-
professional to professional. Rita saw it going from friendly to
sterile. It was a classic battle, pitting the virtues of smallness
against the efficiencies of bigness. It turned ugly. The manager
was fired.

Steve became furious with his aunt, Rita's sister, who
worked at the Pasadena Zankou and had complained bitterly
about the manager. He confronted her. She was ten years older
than his mother and blind in one eye. His mother wouldn't
speak of the details, but it was clear that Steve had gotten
physical with his aunt. Rita felt she had no choice but to fire
him and kick him out of the house.

"What Steve did to his aunt, I am too ashamed to talk
about," she said. "He is a good boy, and he's got a big heart.
But he has given me no choice. He has to learn how to control
his temper. His anger, we will not accept."

Steve knew the back streets of Los Angeles every bit as well as
his father had. Tooling from Glendale to Hollywood, cranking

the wheel from freeway to road, he could tell his global positioning system a thing or two about the best way to get there. He had been blaring Bob Marley for two days, ever since his mother had given him the boot. Now it was time to continue his education on "The 48 Laws of Power." He slipped the CD into his player, and a voice, eerily disembodied, began to intone:

> Power is more God-like than anything in the natural world. . . . Power's crucial foundation is the ability to master your emotions. . . . If you are trying to destroy an enemy who has hurt you, far better to keep him off guard by feigning friendliness than showing anger. . . . Make your face as malleable as an actor's. Practice luring people into traps. Mastering arts of deception are among the aesthetic pleasures of lying. They are also key components in the acquisition of power.

Law 1 seemed easy enough: "Never outshine the master." He was having more difficulty with Law 15: "Crush your enemy totally." It didn't occur to him that the tape, like his favorite movie, *Scarface*, was so over-the-top that another listener might find it comical. He wanted to believe in the message. Whether that message came down from Sun Tzu or Donald Trump or Tony Montana, he was willing to hand over his whole being to it. He saw himself as putty going in, a rich and beloved American tycoon coming out.

"My goal in life," he said, "is to have as many people at my funeral, to have affected as many lives in a good way, as I can. I want to live a great life. I want to be a great person. I really enjoy hanging out with different people, intellectual people, important people. I know I really can't do that unless I have power."

He seemed, in some fundamental way, far too sweet a kid to become truly adept in the art of ruthlessness. Among Armenians and beyond, people were awed by his generosity in the same way they had admired his father's. Zankou didn't deliver, but there was Steve, bags of spit-roasted goodies loaded in his Lexus, heading to a school or charity that needed free food for its function. He was paying the monthly rent on a building in Ontario that a black preacher, a friend, had converted into his first church. Steve was the one friends called when they were nearing bottom and needed a push into rehab. He drove them there, nursed them through the cold turkey, and then monitored their recoveries like a hawk.

As for his own life, it was a mess. He had dark circles under his eyes and was thirty pounds overweight. His younger brother Ara, whose addiction to Vicodin had morphed into an addiction to exercise, thanks in part to Steve, was trying to work him back into shape. He kept skipping sessions at the gym to gorge on lobster and crab at the Mariscos Colima restaurant in North Hollywood. After one monumental meal, he caressed his belly. "Bro," he said, eyes twinkling. "You wouldn't know it, but underneath these pounds I used to catch a lot of ladies." He was sure he was paying a price for all that softness. People saw him as an easy mark. The world played him for a sucker. No wonder his mother discounted his vision. "She thought the manager I hired was pulling the wool over my eyes. But she doesn't know what it takes to move this business forward. Don't get me wrong. My mother's been awesome. She surprised all of us with her work ethic. But she doesn't understand this business the way I understand it."

He had been at his father's side, watching and learning, since he was a kid. If only he were calling the shots now, the next move would be big. "I believe we can open a Zankou in every major city in America. But she doesn't want to hear it. I have to sugarcoat everything. I have to walk on eggshells."

Walk on eggshells? Had he been walking on eggshells a few days earlier, with his aunt?

"My aunt was totally provoking me the whole way," he said. "They are making it like I beat her up, but I didn't. They are insisting that I hurt her. And I didn't hurt her. I lost—I lost my control, bro. I was mad. You know?"

So he hit her?

"I slapped her on the hand. It didn't hurt, though, bro. I know it didn't hurt."

Now Steve wasn't sure what to do. Should he stay with friends? Get a place of his own? Leave town? He packed his bags and headed north, past Santa Clarita and Bakersfield, straight up Highway 99. The grape fields all around him were in winter slumber, and he felt his mind begin to race. One image after the other, his life over the past ten years, came back to him. He saw Dikran, the older brother he so admired, walk into the bedroom they shared and whisper at night. "Steve, you're going to hell if you don't change your ways." He saw the 777 motel and the call girl and her pimp. He saw the courtroom in Van Nuys and the prosecutor making the tiniest of blunders. He saw his father lying on the couch, a hat covering his bald head, and his grandmother home from work, walking past him as if he were already dead. He saw his father burning the photo and telling him he would never forgive her. "God will forgive the devil before I can forgive my mother. Because this is a mother, not the devil." He saw his father asking him for one of those slushy lemonades from the Muscle Beach shop at the Glendale Galleria. He saw himself coming back home, the lemonade still icy, his father gone.

He kept driving through the California farm fields until he reached Fresno. That night, sitting in a friend's backyard, he heard the story about the Armenian kid who had stolen a crate of raisins in the 1920s. Fifty years later, at the church picnic, the old ladies sitting in their lawn chairs pointed to a boy standing in the shish kebab line. "See that young man," one old lady said. "That's the raisin stealer's grandson." No one needed to tell him the moral. He was the son of the Zankou Chicken mogul who had murdered his mother and sister and then had the decency to kill himself. What struck him wasn't the story's lesson—that you can never escape the past—but what the storyteller had left out. Did those whispers reach the ears of the raisin stealer's grandson? Or was he lucky enough to be standing just outside their reach? Did he manage to live his life never knowing the peculiar bent of his patrimony? Steve wasn't so lucky. He had heard the whispers, and it made him think about the son he might have one day. Would the whispers follow him? Or would his son know the story because Steve had chosen to tell it from his own mouth?

For three days, Steve ate white bean and lamb stew, drank whiskey, and imagined living in a place such as Fresno, the land of Saroyan, far from Zankou, far from family. On the fourth day, he climbed back into his car and headed home.

This time, as the highway opened up, his mind fixed on a different image from the past. It was 2005, two years after the murders, and the grieving was finished. The family had decided it was time to honor Mardiros and open a new store in west L.A. Because he was the son most like his father, the job was given to him. You find the location, his mother told him. You find the contractor. One day, the store half done, he found himself unable to get out of bed. For ninety days, he lingered in a state of deep depression. Doctors prescribed pills, but he wouldn't take them. Nothing could reach him. Not food or drink or sex. His mother didn't know what to do. She was paying $15,000 a month in rent for a restaurant with no opening in sight. She finally persuaded him to see a psychiatrist, a Greek doctor who heard the story and could see where the problem was buried.

All his life, he had been told he was Mardiros's son. And all his life, good and bad, he had done his best to make that true. The girls, the outbursts, the devotion to business, the loyalty to family, it became his way of honoring the father. But what it meant to be Mardiros Iskenderian's son had changed irrevocably that day. It was one thing to be second coming of a patriarch beloved by family and community. It was another to know that all this legacy had been washed over by one act. Who was the father? Who was the son? How could Steve ever be expected to build a new Zankou in his father's name, without ever owning up to what his father had done?

Usually he did not plan his visits to Forest Lawn. He went only when the impulse seized him, and that was rare. Truth be known, he wasn't sure if he was strong enough. But that December day in 2007, as he barreled into Los Angeles, he decided he would do something different. Inside the cemetery gates, he visited the grave of his father, and then he headed to the opposite end of the grounds to locate the graves of his grandmother and aunt. He hadn't gone to their funerals. He had never said a proper good-bye. "I know it sounds stupid, but it wasn't until I was standing there, staring into their headstones, that it hit me for the first time. That my father had killed them. I never really looked at it like that before. He took two lives. He was going to die anyway, so I don't count his life. But he took two lives with him. And those lives belonged to my grandmother and my aunt. There was no turning away from it. This is what my father chose to do as his final deed."

He wanted to believe that none of it was truly planned, that his father, racked by rage and cancer, was not of sound mind. He wanted to believe that in the living room of his aunt's house, his father awoke to his crime and felt immense sadness. He could only hope that his father had asked for forgiveness as he sat down on the couch and raised the gun to his head. What he didn't know was that the coroner had checked for traces of salt beneath his father's eyes and found none. Mardiros Iskenderian had shed no tears.

The son left the cemetery that day with the same questions he had been lugging around for five years. They were questions, he now knew, that had no answers. How could a woman who cooked with such love disown her son on his deathbed? How could a man so intent on passing to his sons the good name of his life's work hand them this name, this act?

He drove up the canyon to the mansion that sat on a ledge in the Verdugo Hills. He parked his car and walked up the driveway past the koi pond in the entrance and knocked on the door. His mother and three brothers were waiting for him inside. There was Ara, who struck an impressive bodybuilder's pose, and Vartkes, the university student who was still trying to finish a condolence letter he had been writing to Dzovig's sons for five years. And there was Dikran, the uneasy patriarch, who felt the need to speak for them all.

"Dad wanted us brothers to love each other and always support each other no matter what. We are different, each of us, but we are one. We love each other, and we will die for each other. As his sons, we can never let money or outsiders tear us apart. To do less would be to dishonor Dad's memory."

Steve sat down on the couch next to his mother, leaned back, and closed his eyes. Rita took a puff of her cigarette and smiled. *Her prince. Her pasha.* Then she opened the family scrapbook to a page from Beirut, the year 1975, and she began to narrate. "To this day, I never see anybody as beautiful as your father was. I met him when I was twelve. Roof to roof, we passed each other notes. It was forbidden, but we fell in love."

chapter five

The Summer of
the Death of Hilario Guzman

This was the sum of Hilario Guzman's ledger as he walked
into the grape fields on the morning of his death:

$6,700 to the coyote who smuggled him and his family over
$2,000 to the bandits who robbed them along the border
$350 a month to rent a tin shack in the San Joaquin Valley
$400 a month to feed four children with another baby
on the way

He had a job that paid twenty cents for every tray of
Thompson grapes he picked and laid out in the 105-degree sun
to make raisins. In the two harvests since the family left Oaxaca
in the spring of 2003, he had never made the minimum wage,
never picked more than 250 trays, $50, in a ten-hour day.

That September morning, with a fruit tub in one hand and a sharp curved blade in the other, he cut enough bunches to make ten trays, and then he vanished. No one saw the Triqui Indian leave, not the crew boss who thought he saw everything or the men and women picking in their delirious states. He didn't tell them that his baby son, Geronimo, the one born on the right side of the border, had been sick for weeks. He didn't tell them he had been drinking all night and woke up drunk. Later they would hear the story that he had gone straight from the vineyard to a liquor store near Fresno and drank some more. He must have nodded off halfway home because on Jensen Avenue, just past the crematory where the dairies send their used-up Holsteins to become chicken feed, his '93 Ford Escort began to veer, first to the vineyard on his right and then to the alfalfa field on his left. He tried to slow down but the car hit a dirt embankment, bucked and flipped, and he flew out the window and through the air, landing on his head.

The police found his pregnant wife, Veronica, in a trailer deep in the vineyards. After they persuaded her that they had come not because of her complaints of wild dogs but because a man named Hilario Guzman, thirty-two, the same one in the photo, was dead, she tried to remember everything about the previous twenty-four hours. She could remember only that he had picked up medicine for the baby the night before and lingered strangely next to the child that morning. "Geronimo was feeling better, doing better, and Hilario stood over him and began to speak," she recalled. "He told him, 'You are going to be responsible someday. You are going to be the man of the house. The man of the house,' he said. Then he took his lunch and water and left for work."

Had Hilario Guzman died of heat stroke while laboring in the fields, the United Farm Workers would have sent an honor guard to stand over him. Instead, with a blood alcohol level twice the legal limit, his body lay in a funeral parlor in Selma, the raisin capital of the world, for the next ten days. It took that long for the Triqui, a community of migrants who had crossed the border illegally over the past five years and settled in rural California, Washington, and Oregon, to raise $2,600 to ship him back to their village of corn and beans and dust and fog high on the mountain. And so his body was returned to San Martin Concepcion but his soul remained trapped on that patch of alfalfa between Fresno and Kerman. That is where the tribe's transplanted elders and bad curse doctors would gather—without a single woman present—to erect a cross in cement and set down enough votive candles and cans of his favorite beer to send his soul back to Oaxaca.

By this time, his grieving wife had returned to the village as well. Only she was wearing a mark of shame on her forehead, put there by Hilario's mother. Veronica was the reason her son was dead, the old lady spit. Her greed, her selfishness, her constant belittling—all had caused him to venture north. Why was he drinking so heavily if not for her failings as a wife? Why was she not working beside him that morning like the other wives who had gone to America? Her tirade ended with Veronica's banishment from the village, from the house that belonged to Hilario and her. To see the mud adobe hut standing there was one thing. It had no running water, no toilet, and only a single bare bulb as light. But it became something else once you got to know their dreams. The plan had been to pour their savings from the California fields into a grand remodeling and to return there—in three or five years—with the children, maybe this time for good. Not one penny, though, had been saved in those eighteen months in the United States, and now he was buried next to his father in the cemetery on the knoll, and Veronica was left to wander back across the steep ridge road to her parents' village on the other side.

San Martin Intunyoso, the town of her birth, was bigger but just as sad. The cinderblock houses were all half finished, rebar sticking out the roofs, waiting for the next gracing of dollars from El Norte. Only the men too old or too addicted to their moonshine were left. All day they did nothing but drink and stumble about and defecate on the main road and in the river where the women went with buckets to draw the drinking water. The women, shouldering big axes, fetched the wood too, climbing the hillside with donkeys to where the corn and beans gave way to the pine trees. When they came back down, they bathed the children in wheelbarrows and kept them hidden from a pack of feral dogs that roamed through town, feasting on the men's droppings. As the women began to cook, the wall of fog washed in, swirling up from the valley and through the gorgeous canyon, sweeping the whole town of its filth and misery for the night.

For Veronica, the cloud became the way she understood her situation. "Everything is foggy. Everything is not clear. He was alive when we got to the other side. And now I have brought him back dead. Whatever hopes we had, that's where they ended." In her arms she carried Geronimo and by her side stood nine-year-old Rigoberto. The death of her husband had re-united her with her oldest son. Because of a strange growth on his chest, Rigoberto hadn't made the trek north in 2003, staying behind with Veronica's mother and father. But now both of them were dead too, her mother killed by a drunk driver in

Oaxaca a few months earlier and her father collapsing just a week after Hilario's funeral. "How could it be possible that all these things are happening?" she said. "I must act strong in front of the children, but I can't keep up with it much longer."

Like all the other crossings, this one had come with a steep price. Her two daughters, Yolanda, eleven, and Monica, six, had to be left behind with her sister and brother-in-law. They were living in a tarpaper and stucco shack planted on a stretch of alkali and tumbleweeds outside Fresno. All her thoughts were now focused on making the family one again. She knew it would not be in Oaxaca. The banishment from Hilario's village had made her choice clear. Their future, she was sure, lay in the United States, even if she had no idea how she would come up with the money to cross the border with her boys. And if a coyote did succeed in getting them over, how could they manage to live without a breadwinner? She had never worked a single day in the grape fields. To begin now would mean that she would have to find someone to watch over her children. The chance of finding another man to rescue them was as good as nil. In the Triqui culture, the men look for girls fifteen and sixteen years old to marry. No woman in her late twenties like her, saddled with four small children and already showing a fifth, could possibly expect to find a man to assume such a burden.

This was Veronica Diaz's life when the harvest in the faraway San Joaquin Valley ended. The fields, like a great heaving oven, exhaled their 265,000 tons of sun-baked raisins, and tens of thousands of peasant workers suddenly lost their jobs. The ranks of the unemployed included the sister and brother-in-law to whom she had entrusted her two daughters. She had been told that Yolanda and Monica were back in school and doing fine. They did enough chores around the house and ate so little that they presented almost no hardship for her sister, who had three children of her own. The truth, like so much else that photographer Matt Black and I would see over the next year as we followed the family from harvest to harvest, rested on what side of the border you grew up on or, more precisely, what deprivations your eyes had grown accustomed to.

The girls were attending school, all right, but they were showing up unwashed and without underpants. Yolanda was crying much of the day, her teachers and counselors unable to console her, in part because she could not speak English or Spanish and they had no way of understanding Triqui. The weight the two girls were pulling to lighten the load on their auntie and uncle must have seemed perfectly normal back in the village. Yet to come upon their labor fresh from my suburban Saturday was to be stopped cold by the understanding that rural Mexico—at its most remote and backward—is only a thirty-minute drive away. Hidden behind the blue-gray shack, next to a heap of burning trash puffing an acrid smoke, the two girls stood with bare feet in the mud. The ground all around was hard and dry, but in that one spot where they had been working all morning, soapy water trickled out from a wash basin and down the sides of a broken slab of concrete. The slab had been set atop four old tires, high enough so that they could stand with the proper leverage and scrub their clothes clean. Hanging from a barbed wire fence was every item they had finished—jeans and pink blouses and towels drip drying. Stacked in a pile were the shoes and socks still to go.

Monica, a pretty child with brown hair cut in a pixie and highlighted in red, had a runny nose and was coughing. She dipped a plastic cup from an old Barbie set into the water and wetted a sock. Then, with a bar of Zote laundry soap, she began to knead the sock with both hands. "How long have you been working?" she was asked in Spanish. "Do you and your sister wash only your own clothes or the rest of the family's too?" She looked up, but her face registered nothing. The question was repeated but she returned to her sock without attempting a word. It took her five minutes to pound the sock clean. All the while, her sister was scrubbing a pair of tennis shoes with a toothbrush. The door of the shack was half open, and the TV was showing a Mexican soap opera. Of all the indigenous peoples crossing the border, the Triqui may be the most tradition-bound, the most discriminated against, the most wary. As we moved from the back of the house to the front, we expected to be spotted and the door shut tight. Instead, a small, handsome man stepped out and greeted us with a handshake. Moises Merino, Veronica's brother-in-law, had a sweet, easy smile and, as luck would have it, spoke decent Spanish.

He was twenty-seven years old and first crossed the border to work the fields eight years before. After going it alone for two years, he brought his wife and son in 1998. His two younger daughters were born in California and his wife was expecting again—the third U.S. citizen in the Merino clan. He recalled that he was a child back in San Martin Concepcion when the first road linked his village to the outside world; Mexico's great rural push brought electricity and a cash economy to a place that had been penetrated only by the Catholic Church. His father grew corn and beans and pumpkins on a tiny plot that had no way of supporting nine children. Two of his brothers also had come north, one working beside him in the fields and the other taking a job at a tortilla factory in Phoenix. "We came here to work and to send money back to the village," he said. He earned in an hour what he had earned in a day in Mexico. And because each dollar was the equivalent of ten pesos, the dollars he sent home turned into gold as soon as they crossed the line.

Yet in the nine years since he'd come north, he had sent "almost nothing" back home. Rent, gas, food, and diapers, the idle times between harvests, the trips back to Oaxaca to bury fathers and mothers, the expense of hiring coyotes to ferry them back—it just never added up in his favor. All he had to show for those nine years was an old maroon Chevy van and a faded blue Chevy Cavalier parked in the dirt path that led from the vineyard to the three-room shack that cost him $400 a month to rent. The only thing keeping them afloat was the $110 a month in food stamps and the $160 a month in welfare they received for each citizen-child. And now there were two more mouths—Veronica's children—to feed and the uncertainty of when and if she would make it back.

"We're responsible now for the girls. I told her, 'We'll take care of them. Don't worry.' But it's hard. If she comes back, it will be even harder. How is she going to manage without a husband?"

"Do you ever think that it's not worth it, that when you add up all the pluses and minuses, it's best to have never come? To have stayed home?"

He grinned and shook his head no. The children's education alone was worth the upheaval and risk. Back in the village, he had been a bright child who had shown much promise, but like his brothers and sisters, he never got beyond the sixth grade. Whatever became of their lives here—whether they decided to stay or one day return—their crossing had changed the family's fate. Learning the language and history and ways of the United States was like a magic card that would always give his children passage to another world, if they so chose it.

To give them that choice, he was hopping from one grueling job to the other. If he was lucky, if he never stopped hustling and every break went his way, he could make the minimum wage and cobble together six to seven months of farmwork in a year. The movement and the math hadn't changed in nearly a decade: raisins in late summer, chili peppers and olives in fall, pruning vines in winter, picking tomatoes in late spring and berries in Oregon in early summer. If he was lucky, in a year's time, he could make $10,000 to $12,000.

Red fire ants swarmed over his bare feet, but he seemed not to notice as his eight-year-old son, Ramiro, joined him. He was a chubby kid with crooked teeth and a funny haircut whose role in the extended family was exaggerated because he was the only one who could speak English.

"The schools in Oaxaca are bad," he said. "You can't learn anything. And the teachers are all mean. Here, I love my teachers. We're learning about presidents and vice presidents and the secretary of . . ."

"The secretary of state?"

"Yeah, state."

"Has life become harder since your uncle died?" I asked.

"My cousins fight with my little sister. They cry and hit her. I have to do my homework and take care of my little baby brother. I don't got big hands to go over there and make them stop. I'm not like the Fantastic Four."

He ran into the house to fetch his journal, a notebook filled with poems and short stories written with such grace that they surely came from the pages of a children's book. He kept insisting, though, that he had written them himself, and in a sense he had. The words belonged to some author, yes, but only he had scrawled them in his pencil and pen. He drew the animals he

saw in the country—jackrabbits, herons, snakes, and spiders—
and chronicled how he went with his parents to the fields on
weekends, setting out the trays so that they could go faster. He
wrote down how many trays they completed each day and what
it meant in dollars. How long it took—what they made by the
hour—didn't concern him. The only thing that mattered to the
Triqui was how much they brought home at the end of the day.

"We don't have to get much money," he said in his most
earnest voice. "Because if we get lots of money, the robbers
will come."

The farm that has taken root on the vast plain between Los
Angeles and San Francisco surely qualifies as a miracle, 250
crops in all, agriculture buzzing at a size and speed never before seen by man. That it rose up where the rain hardly falls is
a matter of intricate plumbing, a system of dams and canals
that siphon the Sierra rivers. That it needs a constant supply of
fresh hands to keep the wages low becomes a matter of crossing oceans and border lines. As far back as the 1860s, when the
bonanza wheat empires began to yield to orchards, vineyards,
and vegetable fields, the call went out to the lowly farmers of
the world. It was answered first by the Chinese and then by the
Japanese, Filipinos, Volga River Germans, Armenians, Pun-
jabis, and Okies white and black.

No land, though, has bequeathed more of its people to these
fields or shared a more complicated relationship with California
agriculture than Mexico. Up through Sonora and Baja California, bands of farmworkers began arriving in the late 1800s and
except for brief spasms of restricted immigration here and there,
they have kept coming ever since. In its most rural reaches, the
valley always has been a Third World country, but more and

more it belongs to Mexico's dispossessed. The last of the 1930s Dust Bowl migrants who built towns such as Arvin and McFarland are dying, their numbers being replaced by Mixtec tribes fleeing their own fields turned to dust. "I look at them and I see us," says Earl Shelton, one of the few Oklahoma natives still left in Lamont, the town where John Steinbeck gathered his stories. "They're the new Okies, the brown Okies."

Communities of Mexican migrants, like the immigration debate itself, have popped up everywhere across America. But before they ever step foot in the hotels of Los Angeles or venture east to the slaughterhouses of Iowa or the construction projects of Florida, many of them begin their new lives here. Every peach, every plum, every grape, every orange, every fig, every pepper, every tomato and head of lettuce is picked by a brown hand. Even with the rise of mechanization in some crops, the valley finds itself reaching deeper and deeper into the rural heart of Mexico. Today it is the indigenous of Oaxaca, Guerrero, and Puebla who are answering the harvest call. The bands of Mixtec pickers and packers now number an estimated 75,000 strong in these fields. While their presence is still overshadowed by the traditional migrants from Michoacan and Jalisco, the Triqui and other tribes represent one out of every five farmworkers in the valley. Ask any farmer, even the one who insulates himself with a labor contractor, and he will tell you that his workers, indigenous or not, come bearing papers, but that those papers, in eight out of ten cases, are frauds. And so the ebb and flow of these illegal crossings, the grudging symbiosis between industrial agriculture and peasant labor, remains the epic story of this land.

Perhaps understandably, as each immigrant group has worked its way up and out of the fields, its children and

grandchildren have come to regard those fields with more distance, if not disdain. My own grandfather, an Armenian with
eyes set on Cal Berkeley, traveled seven thousand miles by ship
and train in the summer of 1920 to become a harvest gypsy.
He picked potatoes in Weed Patch, peaches in Kingsburg, and
grapes in Selma before saving enough cash to buy a farm. My
father grew up on that vineyard outside Fresno, but by the
time I was born, we had turned our last raisins and gone into
the grocery business. I was raised like any other kid in town,
lost in suburbia, dumb to the fields all around us. How many
times we drove Highway 99 on our way to Disneyland or
Candlestick Park and never once looked to our left or right
and saw the fields. If our eyes did happen to gaze upon them,
the men and women with faces swaddled in bandanas were in-
visible to us. The few times we were forced to see them, by
the protests of Cesar Chavez or the scandal of children found
working in the fields or the death of a farmworker, our awakening was an uneasy one.

Over the years, it would remain just this way. A few weeks
before the accident that killed Guzman, I learned that a fifty-
three-year-old farmworker had died a far different death in the
vineyards of Kern County. Asuncion Valdivia was a small, thin
man who worked like an ox, his family said, but he had a hard
time keeping up with the quotas imposed by Giumarra Vineyards. He had been picking table grapes for ten hours under
the 100-degree sun when he staggered and collapsed. The
crew boss's daughter called 9-1-1 for help. Deep in the hidden
zone of the fields, she was unable to provide paramedics with
the cross streets. So the crew boss stuck him in a car that had
been baking all day and told the man's son to drive him home.
Halfway there, his mouth turned to foam and he went limp.

In the days that followed, I gathered the facts of his death and placed a call to John Giumarra, a lawyer who served as the company vice president. He said this was the first death from heat stroke he could recall in the family's immense fields, and he denied having a quota for pickers or knowingly hiring illegal migrants—all duly noted in the story I did for the *Los Angeles Times*. And yet the day it appeared on the front page, he was angry enough to call me from his vacation spot in Italy. "I'm not talking to you now as a farmer," he said. "I'm calling you as an attorney. When I get back, you'd better be able to explain every *i* and *t* in that story. Because when I'm done, I'm going to own you and the *Los Angeles Times*."

He was peeved that I had referred to grape picking as "one of the most brutal jobs in America."

"What are you trying to write?" he shouted. "*The Grapes of Wrath?*"

A few days later, Matt Black and I boarded an old church bus at four in the morning and barreled into the heart of the barrio. Behind the wheel was Humberto Mota, a labor contractor in a white cowboy hat who played middle man between coyote and raisin grower. It was Mota who had given Hilario Guzman his job and helped raise a few hundred dollars to send his body back home. Now, a week after the funeral, Mota had ninety minutes to pick up a busload of workers in southeast Fresno and deliver them to a vineyard in Fowler. Past the El Sombrero bar and Tequila nightclub, he drove under a crescent moon, the stereo blasting Mexican cowboy crooner Vicente Fernandez. Each time El Rey hit a high note, a panel of jerry-built lights at the front of the bus came on like a Christmas display. It was a strange piece of accessory given the odds that anyone would be in the mood for a ranchera-music light show at five in the morning. For Mota, it might as well have been high noon the way he floored the big diesel through the dark and quiet streets, stopping with a screech at the entrance of each apartment complex. If the rumble didn't wake them, his horn did.

Out they came, bleary-eyed, in groups of two, three, and four, lugging gallon jugs of fruit punch and orange juice and buckets filled with burritos. Except for one boyfriend and girl-friend couple, the women took seats in the front and the men in back. Under the sweat-stained hats of the New York Yankees, the Texas Longhorns, the Michigan Wolverines, they tried to find sleep again. The drive, like everything else, didn't come free. Mota charged $3 one way, $6 round trip. His route, full of zigzags and backtracks, made no sense except that it conferred great privilege on those he picked up last. What these workers must have paid him for that extra hour of slumber. It was 5:35 A.M. by the time he merged onto Highway 99 and headed south past the golden domes of a Sikh temple. Only in the shooting headlights of the big rigs did their faces become visible. All were young except for one man with gray hair. By Mota's count, they ranged in age from eighteen to sixty. Fifteen had come from Puebla, seven from Oaxaca, four from Michoacan, three from Guerrero, the rest from Sinaloa and Vera Cruz. Inside this one bus were six of the Indian languages of Mexico. One man spoke in the tongue of the Aztecs.

They had left villages of slash-and-burn farming for the most technologically advanced agriculture in the world, a leap of 150 years. Yet in the raisin fields of Fowler, a town built wholly on the wrinkled grape, the work could not have been more primitive. They attacked the quarter-mile rows at first light as if struck by some frenzy. Into the vine's thick curtain they dove on hands and knees, gnats flying in their faces and sulfur dust choking their lungs. Had a stranger come upon the field just then, he would have seen the vines shaking violently, but by what sustained force he wouldn't be able to tell. Not until he walked right in, bent low, and stuck his nostrils in the ferment would he know that it was a farmworker, no more than five and a half feet tall, slashing inside the green canopy. Baked earth, dried leaves, black widow webs, and mildewed berries stuck to the sugar juice splattered on his skin. He said his name was Eladio Mendoza, and he was eighteen years old and six months removed from his village in Oaxaca, where "the land had gone dead" from overfarming. He already knew the difference between picking table grapes, a job that places a premium on aesthetics, and this mad snapping of amber bunches that he let plop into a bucket below, a job that cares only about speed. When the tub was filled with forty pounds of Thompsons, he carried it from the vine to the middle row and spread out the bunches on a piece of butcher paper—the tray. The row had been sloped so that the high end caught the sun at its strongest, and if the sun turned to rain, the drops would trickle off the bunches and slide down into the silky powder of dust. It took eighteen days of valley sun to blister a grape into a raisin.

"Me and my friend said, 'Let's go north and sweep the dollars off the fields,'" Mendoza said. "I don't know yet how much they pay. I owe the coyote $3,000."

Two rows away, working at the same pace, was Alberto Cruz, a thirty-four-year-old Nahuatl who had left a wife and three children in Puebla. He had crossed the border only twenty days earlier but already had a backup plan. If the wages proved too low to send any real money home, he would leave the fields and join his nephew working construction in Atlanta. "I worked ten hours yesterday and made $40. That sounds like a lot in pesos. But I have to work one whole day to pay for the bus rides each week."

Marino Leon, forty-four, who was blazing down his row, had spent half his life traveling between Oaxaca and the grape fields. The back-and-forth, in fact, was written into tribal law. Every few years, he had to return to his village and give several months of community service or else the town elders would confiscate his acre of land. He said three of his sons and a nephew had joined him here, and they were among the fastest pickers in the crew, each averaging five hundred trays a day. They pooled the $2,500 a week they earned in the month-long raisin harvest and did the same with other crops. They stayed away from alcohol and spent wisely at the swap meets and slept side by side on the same living room floor. By year's end, they had saved a few thousand dollars. "I go home every November and take $3,000 or $5,000 with me," he said. "But it isn't enough to maintain my family and our land."

Mota, the labor contractor, stood in the vineyard clearing, warning the more knavish among them to stop "shorting the trays" with too few grapes. The field, he said, was its own world. It had its own law, madness, and philosophy. There was a man picking in his bare feet, and an old guy who grabbed a soda during a break, but before taking one sip, he tipped over the can and gave two sips to the earth. "The soil," he explained, "it's thirsty too." There was the modern woman from Oaxaca who had left farmwork to join the California Rural Legal Assistance, the one watchdog that still made routine checks on the fields. As she talked to the pickers, she fretted about a curse that had been put on her sick uncle, a spell that required the family to give three live roosters and $900 over nine consecutive nights to a *curandero*, or witch doctor. And there was the grower himself, not some ogre sitting in an air-conditioned truck but the grandson of an immigrant, a genocide survivor, standing in the 105-degree sun with a cotton ball stuffed into his ear and another one in his nose. His was the wince of a farmer battling a bad sinus infection and a flood of cheap raisins from overseas. "The air is rotten," he muttered, "and the prices are only a little better."

He had given us access to his fields on the condition that his name not be used. His workers, after all, were illegal. He explained that the raisin industry in California, even after yanking out 40,000 acres of Thompsons, was mired in a glut made worse by imports from Turkey, where workers are paid next to nothing. I asked if he knew that some of his fastest pickers were earning $10 and $12 an hour while many others were not even making $30 a day—somewhere between $2 and $3 an hour. It was unfortunate, he said, but most of the workers at the front end of the harvest were green. He expected, as in years past, that they would become more facile each day and end up earning a decent wage. Still, he conceded, a good many would never get the hang of it, never make the minimum wage. This was his bind. If he paid the minimum wage instead of piece rate, he'd go broke paying $6.75 an hour to workers who barely filled one hundred trays. If he stayed with the piece rate but fired all those who didn't tally $6.75 an hour, he'd have to let go dozens of them. How would they survive? Wasn't a job that paid $30 or $40 a day better than nothing?

He knew growers who used Mexico's poverty to excuse their treatment of the workers. "Sure they got it bad, but it's a helluva lot better than that village they come from," he'd hear them say. He wasn't one of them. He watched them move like machines up and down his fields and told himself that no people worked harder. But he was dealing with a harvest, a race that came and went in a few short weeks. Didn't city folks understand that a perishable grape gave him no chance to erase mistakes, no chance to do it over again? Yes, the whole mess was brutal, combustible, arcane, intolerable. But what more could he do? He put out plenty of toilets in the fields. He put out cold water and umbrellas and made sure they got every break the law required. He stood in the vineyard beside them, but he couldn't afford to understand too much about their lives. The cell phone was ringing in his ear. There were bins to stack, poly-paper trays to restock, and a truck that had broken down from the field to the packing house. In between, he kept the radio tuned to the weather to see if the rain threatening two days before was still on its way. He didn't have the luxury to memorize their names, what village they came from, how many children they had. Maybe they weren't so different from his grandfather, but he had no time to ponder the conditions that brought them to his field. The harvest, as much as he hated to hear himself say it, just didn't allow for a human-to-human exchange.

The shift ended nine hours after it began. There was no town whistle as in the old days, just the rumble of the Baptist bus as Mota turned the key. They came off the field with every reason in the world to hang their heads. The distance from family, the debt of their journey, the shame of their wages, the smell of their labor. They had every reason to be defeated except one. They were coming back the next day to do it over again. So they walked, like conquerors, off the field.

Summer had picked clean the vineyards and orchards on both sides of Highway 99, and the three-hundred-mile-long valley, bled of its green, fell quiet. The harvest left Moises Merino dog tired, but unlike the fields, he had no chance to rest. He had been promised six weeks of labor picking peppers on the Central Coast, so he said good-bye to his wife, three children, and two nieces and headed west to a new harvest.

If there was a low man on the totem pole, it was the indigenous of Oaxaca. They were the peasant's peasants back in Mexico, and nothing had changed here. They gave even the poorest Mexican a target for his ridicule. They spoke the "language of dogs," it was said. They did the work that no one else would do. And they did it, without complaint, for the lowest wages.

For two weeks, Merino made the long drive back and forth to Hollister, earning $35 a day minus the cost of gas. Counting travel time, this worked out to $2.50 an hour. Even so, he was grateful to have any work in the fall months. But when the pepper harvest ended four weeks early, he was left scrambling again. He had heard about apples in Stockton and drove two hours only to find a long line of workers in front of him. The labor contractor felt so bad that he told him to take home a tub of fruit. When we pulled up to their house on that October evening, Fuji apples spilled everywhere. His wife, Jacinta, a younger sister to Veronica, said we had just missed him. He had gone north to a place called Orland, where he was living in a field and climbing ladders and stuffing olives into a big canvas pouch.

The Triqui women were as shy as they were superstitious. When they laughed, they covered their teeth to keep from conjuring the image of a skeleton. We were about to turn around and leave when little Ramiro invited us inside. He wanted to show us the homework he was doing. He wanted to tell us about his field trip to the Big Fresno Fair that day, the glittering crystals he admired in the rock exhibit, the gigantic pumpkins and watermelons he gazed at in the farm exhibit. He asked his mother if it would be okay if we came in, and she nodded yes.

It was dark inside, and he was doing math by the TV light. His eyes moved back and forth between the equations and the soap opera, and it seemed a tough juggle. Yet he finished in a snap, and not a single answer was wrong. "See, I can do two things at once," he said, smiling through those crooked teeth. "Addition and subtraction is way easy. I want to be a teacher someday." His homework assignment, an hour's worth of math, reading, and writing, required a parent's signature when he finished. It was part of what the school called its Parents as Teachers program. But his mother was illiterate. She didn't know how old she was, much less the letters it took to scribble her name. So when his father was gone and he needed someone to sign his homework, his mother signed it with an X.

The inside of the house was warped and painted a strange turquoise. Adorning the walls was a set of nails from which the children hung their backpacks—Ninja Turtles, Spider Man, Scooby-Do. The kitchen ceiling was slanted, barely five feet tall at the low end. No halls connected the three rooms, so it felt like the inside of a cave. So many little pieces of plywood, cardboard, and stucco had been added here and there—to catch the rain, to keep out the smoke that blew in from the garbage fire—that the whole thing brought to mind a swallow's mud nest.

Yolanda, Veronica's oldest daughter, sat on a bed that took up half the main room. She appeared to be reading, highlighting words in the book *Holes* with great enthusiasm. "She's just underlining," Ramiro said. "She can't read. All she knows is Triqui." Her sister Monica, who sat beside her, spoke a little Spanish but still had not grasped the basics of kindergarten. She couldn't count to thirty, and her recitation of the ABCs stopped at F. Their principal and teachers would later explain that they didn't know which way to turn with the Triqui. Should they immerse them in English or assign them to a teacher who spoke Spanish? They went back and forth trying to find the best fit for the girls. Then their father died and their mother journeyed thousands of miles away, and it was enough just to keep them from breaking down in class.

With her sister and husband gone, Jacinta found her hands full. She cooked for her nieces but bathing them was a more difficult task, mostly because the hot water had to be carried over in buckets from a neighboring shack. All her energy was swallowed up by her eighteen-month-old daughter, who had been crying since we walked in the door. Of all the children, she said, this one was the most attached to her father. Each evening the little girl would stand by the garbage fire and wait for Moises Merino's return from the fields. He'd drive up the dirt path, take her in his arms, and wipe her nose first thing. She was crying, Jacinta said, because she thought our car might be him. She went from room to room calling out "daddy." Jacinta tried sticking a bottle of apple juice in her mouth, but she gagged. She fed her a pink marshmallow cookie, but she spat it up.

"She misses my father too much," Ramiro said. "She won't eat because he's gone."

I asked him if it was all right if I peeked in the refrigerator. It was the middle of the month, two weeks shy of the next government check, two weeks before Moises would return with his wages. Inside were a few dozen eggs, a package of frozen beef, and a couple of watermelons that Ramiro had taken from the patch at the end of the road. They were nothing like the watermelons at the fair. Off to the side sat a ten-pound bag of rice, a twenty-pound bag of beans, and a bucket of apples.

Jacinta giggled nervously as I surveyed the slim pickings. The accident that killed her brother-in-law had been a double whammy. Not only were there two more children to feed but there was no one to baby-sit now that Veronica was gone. Without those extra adult eyes, Jacinta could no longer join Moises in the fields. "I work next to him. I pick peppers. I've done raisins," she said in the singsong of Triqui, which Ramiro translated to English. "But after the accident, I stay home with the children."

The official mourning period—twenty-nine days from the day of Hilario's death—was now over. Yet if there was a plan to smuggle her sister and two nephews back across the border, she didn't know about it.

"If the plan was to work," Veronica said, "I had to think another way. It couldn't be only me and my two children crossing the border. I had to bring my youngest sister, Catarina, with me. That was the plan. If we crossed, she would watch the children while I worked in the fields. Or she would work in the fields while I watched the children. It was the only way. I had no man. So I chose my youngest sister. She would become my Hilario. We had to pay the coyote $2,700. Our brother who works in the city helped us with the money. We took a bus from Oaxaca to a town in Sonora. It took us two days and two nights to get there. It was a dangerous town. Lots of thieves and bandits yelling at people to get into cars. We spent three nights there in a hotel.

"On the second night, the bandits came. We were sleeping on the floor. Me and my two children and my sister and some others from our village. They burst in and pointed a pistol right at us. There was screaming, but I didn't scream. I didn't want to frighten the baby. But I was scared inside. The same thing happened the time before. But my husband was with me then. This time, it was scarier. They pointed guns and knives at the men's heads to rob them. If they refused to give their money, they were beaten. The coyote was not there right then. The bandits took about $1,000 from each person. But they never found my money. I kept it on the baby. I had put it in Geronimo's diaper.

"The coyote came the next morning. Twelve of us got into his truck. We drove for four hours to a hill looking over the border. Around seven at night we began to walk. We crossed the border on Christmas Eve. For three days and nights we walked across the desert in Arizona. During this time, we ate nothing. No food. The children were crying from hunger and the cold. The nights were very cold. I kept the baby warm with a jacket. And then I ran out of diapers and had to use the jacket as a diaper. We never stopped to rest. No sleep. Nothing. All we had was three little bottles of water. We walked through cactus and needles. No towns, no lights, no Border Patrol. Nothing. The full moon was the only light for walking. The baby soiled the jacket, and I had to throw it away. It was cold and he began to shiver. The coyote was a young man. It seemed to be his first time as a coyote. He was scared too. He was a nice man. He saw the baby shivering and put him inside his jacket. For the children, he offered to walk slower. I was afraid the baby was going to die. There was nothing for him to eat. He was crying all the time. The group was angry and yelling about the crying children, especially Geronimo.

"And then the water ran out. I was so tired and so weak that I began seeing things. I began hearing things. I don't know how we didn't die. I don't know how we kept walking. Was it the voice of Hilario I heard? I met him when I was fifteen. I liked his smile. His eyes. He was a really good man. He cared about his children. He wanted the best for them. He loved the baby a lot. The coyote carried the baby in his jacket the rest of the way. We walked on December 24, 25, 26, and then we came to a house near Phoenix. My feet were bleeding in my tennis shoes. I had to throw them away and buy new ones. We had dinner at the house. The baby was sick and wouldn't eat.

"Then we got in the car and drove to California. It was still daylight when we came to Kerman. My two girls were waiting for me in the house. I walked in and hugged them. There was a Christmas tree in the corner. Their teachers had bought them clothes and other presents. We are living now with Jacinta and Moises. We are sleeping in this one room. Me and my children, Rigoberto, Yolanda, Monica, and Geronimo, and my sister Catarina in this one bed. It is hard to sleep. The breathing and coughing, the bodies twisting. I am seven months pregnant so I am not working. It's winter so Catarina is working only a little, pruning the vines. What happens when my baby is born? I haven't thought of that yet."

The new sons of the Triqui tribe were born two days apart in mid-March. Jacinta's eight-pound baby arrived first, and then came Veronica's seven-and-a-half pound boy. By one calculation, Veronica's fifth child had traveled a lifetime before ever taking a breath. Conceived in the United States and returned to Oaxaca for the funeral of a father he would never know, he had crossed the border as one of a multitude of illegal aliens suspended in the womb. By another calculation, as soon as the umbilical cord was severed, he had become something else. Without equivocation, without a past, he was simply Luis Diaz Guzman, U.S. citizen.

Moises had been picking lemons on the east side when he got the calls and rushed his wife and then his sister-in-law to the same hospital in Fresno. They each stayed for two days, and then he took them back to a household that could not have been stretched any further. One man's toil in the fields was now supporting three women and nine children.

I waited a week and then drove out to Kerman. The tule fog of winter had lifted for good and in the vineyards beyond the new housing tracts, the canes strapped to wires already were budding. Mile after mile, they shot a perfect green across the horizon. Here and there, a field of Thompsons had been leveled to ease the raisin glut. Stacked into huge piles awaiting a match, the gnarled trunks somehow knew this was spring. Without earth, they were still sprouting new tendrils. The highway became road and the road became dirt path and the dirt path a quarter mile in became a junkyard of old tractors and pesticide spray rigs. This is where the knot of trailers and shacks sat hidden in the smolder of a fire lit once a week to burn the garbage of six families. What didn't turn to ash was a roost for the chickens. This is where Ramiro and his sisters and brothers and cousins chased the chickens and rode bikes and kicked soccer balls and invented games out of sticks, where poverty proved no match for the carefree joy of childhood. This is where I pulled up late that afternoon and found Moises sitting in a plastic chair outside a neighbor's trailer, too drunk to get up.

If there was a curse upon the Oaxacans, it was the abuse of alcohol by the men. Friday through Sunday they drank themselves into a stupor, and these were merely the weekend drunks. And yet I had never seen Moises with so much as a beer in his hand. I understood right then that my visit was ill timed. I called for Ramiro, but he pretended not to hear. Jacinta was sitting on the porch but wouldn't make eye contact. She took out her breast and began to feed the baby. The side door was ajar, and in a last-ditch effort I stuck in my hand and waved. Veronica was lying on the bed next to baby Luis, her eyes swollen and red.

Moises had been drinking for two days straight, she said. One job after the other had come up short, and there was no money to pay the rent. Her sister Catarina was trying her best to stand in for Hilario, but she was earning a novice's wage. They had begun rationing the meat, and Moises, Jacinta, and their children naturally had first dibs. Except for some leftover chunks of stew that Jacinta had given them a week earlier, they were subsisting on rice and beans. And now even those two staples were running low. The last time she went to the market, it came down to a choice between diapers and chicken meat. She chose the diapers. To stretch the supply, she washed and dried them and stuck them back on as best she could.

"This is the hardest it's been," she said, sobbing. "No work. No money. My part of the rent is $200. I don't know how I'm going to pay it. I keep borrowing from family."

Tending to the baby left little time for Geronimo. When he cried for his mother, more and more it was his twelve-year-old sister Yolanda who stepped in. She carried him in her arms as if she knew what she was doing, stroking his hair and pinching his cheeks until he stopped crying. As much as Veronica wanted her daughter to continue with school, learning did not come easy for Yolanda. And now she was fast approaching thirteen, the cusp of Triqui womanhood. Though Veronica's answer to the question of her daughter's fate was always vague, I got the idea that life here for the child would turn out no different than the life of any young girl in rural Mexico. She would marry young, give birth young, watch her dreams die young making the choices her mother made.

Before I left that day, I drove Veronica and Yolanda to the grocery store and bought them chicken and diapers. Halfway down Jensen Avenue, past the crematory where a Holstein had been dumped at the gate, stiff legs skyward, we came to the spot in the road where Hilario had died. The metal cross erected in winter by tribal elders was no longer standing. It had been plowed under by a Mexican man who tended to the field and believed the Triquis had put a curse on the land. The cross lay in the dirt, twisted and broken, his name and dates (July 28, 1972–September 1, 2004) split in two. We stood there less than a minute, the cars and trucks whooshing by, and I thought of an old line from a Saroyan short story. *We didn't say anything because there was such an awful lot to say, and no language to say it in.*

Heading home that night, I wondered how long I could keep separate what I was seeing in the fields from what I was hearing on the TV and reading in the papers. I had told myself to keep my head down, document the family's existence, and leave the opinions to the pundits and politicians. I was quite sure the experts on Fox and CNN couldn't tell a peach tree from a plum tree, though I wasn't sure it mattered. I imagined what a fool I'd appear going on TV and trying to put everything I had seen into a thirty-second sound bite. But more and more, the nation's debate on immigration seemed to exist in a universe separate from the one I was traveling through. And so that night I began to puzzle out an answer, to shape a point of view that at least seemed to fit this family and the rest of the migrants we had followed in a year of harvests. They had come from thousands of miles away, risked life and limb to get here, paid thousands of dollars to coyotes and bandits who worked in concert, and our hospitals had filled with their pregnant women, and our schools had filled with their illiterate children, and all this social upheaval was taking place so they could walk into a field that in ten or twenty or thirty years would be leveled for tract houses and pick a bunch of grapes and lay them in the sun to make raisins. Raisins. We had imported a whole peasant class, paid them $5 an hour if they were lucky, absorbed their poverty and pathology, and out the other end of the grinder came another ton of shriveled Thompson seedless grapes.

I knew it was more complicated than that. I knew that their labor had helped build the most productive and diverse farm region in the world. We were a lot more than raisins. And yet this valley was luring people to its fields with a promise it could no longer fulfill. My grandfather, working alongside his mother, brother, and sister, had gone from a fruit tramp to a farmer in four seasons. There was no way that even the most efficient farmworker family pinching pennies in the most severe way could ever hope to do that today. Instead, what brought a pregnant mother from the depths of Mexico to the doorstep of a coyote was a very simple calculation. If she got to the other side and gave birth, she suddenly had privilege. She had a free stay in a hospital, a monthly allotment of food stamps, and a monthly government check. And the schools provided free breakfast, free lunch, and a free education to every one of her children, legal or not.

I had read and digested all the think tank reports that, depending on the think tank, either found that the migrants were a great boon to the United States or a great drain. The reports came to represent for me the contradiction at the core of our country when it comes to the question of *the illegals*. We tremble at what they are costing us, but when it is time to trim the backyard tree or mend the backyard fence we go searching for the nearest Mexican. We can afford that iPod and new computer for the kids because we are paying $7 an hour to a Guatemalan nanny who knows more about their needs than we do. We are more than happy to buy a bag of plums for the same $5 we paid in the 1990s but give no thought to how that trickles down to the farmer and his field hand. And this contradiction extends to the farmer himself, who votes for the politician who wants to bar the Mexicans and then complains that his fruit is rotting on the vine because of a shortage of Mexicans.

We aren't taking in these people out of some shared humanitarian principle. By underwriting the relocation of Mexico's most desperate, we are giving a giant handout to farmers, meat packers, home builders, hotel chains, and big box retail outlets. Taxpayers are picking up the front-end costs of cheap labor the same way we are subsidizing cotton and oil and home mortgages. If we want to be honest, we need to stop framing the migrants as old-line immigrants, who left their country for good to start new lives here. Not only are farmworkers returning for funerals, weddings, and reunions but the Oaxacans go back for yearlong stints to perform the community service needed to keep their land. Only because this back-and-forth traffic has been declared illegal do they pay thousands of dollars to cross, creating the very indebtedness that allows them to be exploited.

If nothing else, their ordeal shows that most of their wages are being spent on this side of the border to sustain the families they bring with them. Yes, money makes its way back to the village, but just think what that flow of cash might be if the workers came and went without the women and children. And so I ask myself what kind of guest worker program would improve this situation? Not the bracero program that Latino activists still rail against as if we couldn't improve on a model sixty years old, but a version more efficient and less brutal.

Such a program would be premised on the notion that families remain behind as anchors to build rural Mexico. This would gut the underground of coyotes and illicit document purveyors. It would lead to a more predictable flow of workers so that employers know what skills they are hiring and workers know up front what they are earning. No more starting their journey here as indentured servants $7,000 in the hole. No more desperation of the kind that makes $2.50 an hour an acceptable wage. We could take some of the saved costs from food stamps and welfare and apply it to housing and transporting the men. At harvest's end, they would return home for five months and give their labor to their own land. If their villages hadn't been sufficiently built at the end of ten years and their families still wanted out, we'd put them on a fast track to U.S. citizenship.

As I poured my crazy logic into a tape recorder, I looked over at the young Oaxacan translator who was sitting in the passenger seat next to me: an eighteen-year-old migrant named Norma Ventura who had come to the San Joaquin Valley as a child and saw much of herself in ten-year-old Ramiro. She had grown up following the same harvests, lived through the same deprivations, and now was the valedictorian of her senior class at Kerman High.

"What do you make of my ramblings?" I asked. "They sound good in the abstract."

"I have one question," she said. "If such a program existed back then, would it have kept a child like me from coming here?"

"Yes."

"Stuck in Oaxaca," she said, considering the notion. "I wouldn't have the opportunities I have now. I wouldn't be the same person."

"It's about making the village better, not emptying it out," I said. "Someone like you, with your drive and smarts, would make it to a university in Mexico."

She shook her head, explaining the logic of the village. "When you're twelve or thirteen, you're old enough to marry, wash dishes, cook food. You don't need to go to school."

"Let me ask you this, Norma. How many of the Mixteco migrants you grew up with here graduated from high school."

"Not many."

"How many of the girls got pregnant?"

"Several."

"How many of the boys dropped out to work in the fields or join gangs."

"Maybe 40 percent or more."

"I know it sounds cruel, but do we make immigration policy based on the exceptions, based on the Normas and Ramiros of the world? Or should those exceptions become the exceptions of the village, the children who stay behind and build Oaxaca? At least that's the hope."

She smiled and nodded, but she didn't buy it. Yes, a part of her would always look back to Oaxaca, she said. And maybe when she got older she would live a two-world life. But for now, she was following the footsteps of her sister and heading to college at UC San Diego.

I waited two months before returning to Kerman, only to discover that Moises had packed the whole family into the van and left for a six-week berry harvest in Oregon. The landlord wanted me to know that their lives had grown even more bleak of late. All three sisters had begun working in the fields, entrusting the babies to the care of Yolanda and Romero. Even with the added wages, the family had left California owing a month's rent.

Matt Black and I made the 650-mile drive to Portland and spent a day searching the fields along the Tulatin River for any sight of them. It was a gorgeous valley where the farms were small and nestled amid rolling bluffs, and the tourists were invited to pick baskets of the sweetest raspberries and blackberries, a task made pleasant by the cool breeze drifting through the Douglas firs. What farmworkers hadn't been replaced by mechanical pickers were kept hidden behind the hedgerows and wildflowers. We were told about an old wino labor camp at the end of Rainbow Road near the town of Hillsboro and came upon three dozen cabins still standing in a berry field. Deep in, we found their van and a pile of tennis shoes with the bottoms stained purple and red. All thirteen family members were living in a one-room clabber board shack with a tin roof that hadn't kept out the late spring rains. It measured 12 x 16, just big enough for four bunk beds and a two-burner hotplate.

Ramiro couldn't stop gabbing. He talked about the night of July 4 and the fireworks that ended with a man in the nearby cabin getting stabbed by a drunken farmworker from a rival camp. "He sliced him in the gut and made a big red thing." He talked about the migrant services bus that picked him up each morning and took him to a school where they were reading a book called the *Bridge to Terabithia*. It was about a boy with too many siblings who loves art and wants to escape and meets a girl just as lonely and bright and together they create a magical kingdom on the other side of a creek. "They grab a rope and swing over," he said. "The shooting star leads them to Rainbow Canyon, and they become invincible."

Moises was sober and smiling, but the women weren't pleased to see us. Veronica, in particular, seemed to have grown weary of the whole exercise. Don't you have enough information already? Haven't I answered every one of your questions? What are you going to do for me and my children? She was standing over a skillet of eggs when Geronimo began to wail and then the baby started wailing too. Her eyes were glazed, as if she had taken a blow to the head, and the cabin seemed on the verge of some explosion. I stepped outside and walked toward the river and heard a cry directed at Matt. "I'm not mad at you," she said. "I'm mad at my situation."

Maybe we had pushed things too far by following them there, but it was only by visiting Oregon that I understood this: Even in this benign and beautiful place, a valley so much different from the San Joaquin, the math in Ramiro's journal hadn't changed. Dad and Mom, working side by side, were bringing home $400 a week. Before we hurried off that evening, they handed us a big bowl of blackberries sprinkled with salt and said good-bye.

We would see them one more time, on the west side of Fresno, almost a year to the day that Hilario Guzman picked enough grapes to make ten trays of raisins, put down his curved blade, and walked away. They were harvesting a vineyard near Kearney Park, but it wasn't clear what family members—Moises or some combination of the women—were part of the crew. So we decided to see for ourselves. Without telling them or the farmer, we drove to the vineyard early one September morning and joined the line of battered old farmworker vans that were once part of the army of suburban soccer moms. The sun came up and we went searching row to row. Moises was nowhere to be found. Neither was his wife. Then we spotted Catarina, the youngest sister, and followed a set of tangled footsteps to a spot halfway down row 68. There, inside the vine's curtain, we could see a woman hacking and slashing with a curved blade in her hand. A red bandana covered her features, but it was easy to see that it was Veronica. Whether her face registered surprise or anger or shame or resignation, the bandana hid everything. It hid everything except the seven-year-old daughter with pink tennis shoes and an old lady's cough standing to her left, and the nine-year-old son with baggy jeans and a strange lump on his chest standing to her right. It took me a moment to understand what was happening. I had seen kids in the field before, but always playing on the sidelines or baby-sitting a sibling or handing their parents a bucket—the way a child might help mom or dad during a visit to the office. This was different. Every few feet, Monica set down another paper tray to make raisins. Rigoberto, clutching his own curved blade, cut the bunches straight from the vine into the tub. It took the three of them to keep up with the rest of the crew. Yolanda was at home taking care of the two babies. With the labor of her children, Veronica had found a way. This is how the summer of the death of Hilario Guzman ended: with a new summer, a new ledger.

| Highlands of Humboldt

Back in the summer of 1994, when the marijuana growers of California were still outlaws, my mother-in-law, struck with real estate fever, invited us to spend a week in a place called Shelter Cove. Deep in the highlands of Humboldt County, something of a boom was at hand, and she had persuaded her husband, a man of considerable parsimony, to cough up twenty grand to buy three lots situated in the hills above the so-called Lost Coast. Each subdivided property had a view both north and south to the Pacific Ocean, and the sands that washed down from the rivers of the King range were not white but black. The mountainside gave rise to the primeval glory of redwood trees twenty centuries old and thirty stories high, and the tide pools teemed with immense crabs, and the seabed held vast fields of abalone. Along the shore, the resort's developer, a syndicate from Southern California, had built an airport with a 3,200-foot-long runway and a nine-hole golf course in the custom of a Scottish links.

My mother-in-law, exercising her pitchman's neglect, did not talk about the drive there, except to inform us that it was long and best divided by a short respite in the town of Ukiah. By map, Shelter Cove sat 250 miles north of San Francisco, a straight shot up Highway 101 through the vineyards of Napa and Sonoma and then past the redwood curtain until you reached the outpost of Garberville. From there, only one road connected the world to the Lost Coast, and it appeared in the mapmaker's pen to be almost benign. I thought much later that there should have been a way to draw that road to give some sense of the terror it inflicts on the first-time driver. But it did not wind, it did not climb, it did not fall, at least not by the conventions of every other road from mountain to sea that wound and climbed and fell. As a kid, I needed only one ride on the roller coaster at the Santa Cruz boardwalk to know that I would never ride a roller coaster again. This was the Giant Dipper on broken asphalt. It took a full hour to cover the twenty-five miles from Garberville to Shelter Cove. We arrived at nightfall, too dark to see "the mighty canyons and great mountain peaks and long stretches of thundering coast" that writer Bret Harte had called "America's uttermost west." As we pulled up to the rental house, my father-in-law kindly advised us to not park in the weeds. Our brakes, he said, were hot enough to start a fire.

The next morning I looked out the window to get my bearings. Where exactly was this resort of Shelter Cove? From one side of the mountain to the other, the world's tallest trees had been plucked clean. In stretches where the old forest wasn't bare, a ravenous scrub had taken hold. The developer had done his work too, platting an entire town of streets and cul-de-sacs. That afternoon, I set out on foot and traced the subdivision's insistent path up and down the hillside. Lindley Loop. Higgins Court. Shaller Lane. No matter which way I turned, each road, each cul-de-sac, led to nothing. Thirty years before, supervisor Elwyn Lindley and planning director Harvey Higgins and public works director Charles Shaller had stood in the sun with the "blue suede shoe boys from Los Angeles" and imagined four thousand cottages overlooking the ocean, the single biggest residential development in California. Thirty years later, the county men were gone and the roads bearing their names had faded into ghost trails.

The ocean down below was visible—in some cases the views were quite stunning—but many of the parcels were pitched so precariously on the ledge that no house could ever be built there. For the would-be retirees in Texas and Michigan and the military men stationed overseas who had bought the lots sight unseen, Shelter Cove became an epic swindle. Not even the black sand beach was for real, unless, of course, one considered rocks and pebbles, some more crushed than others, to be sand. If the developers had made good on the 3,200-foot airstrip, it was only because their con job depended on it. Investors from all over the state were flown in to catch a glimpse of the Scottish links and Victorian houses taking shape along the beachfront and then were flown out.

This was the play on the afternoon of June 27, 1971, when a DC3 owned by the syndicate landed at the airport with two dozen real estate salesmen and potential buyers aboard. After the customary tour, which avoided the roads washed out by the last big storm, the flight departed. As it lifted off from the runway, the plane clipped the top of the sewage treatment plant and plunged into the sea, smashing into a huge rock and breaking in two. Sixteen passengers died. Shelter Cove as a resort never recovered. The following year, with the land scam as Exhibit A, the citizens of California voted to change the state constitution to establish a coastal commission that would place unprecedented restrictions on ocean front development.

By the summer of 1994, my in-laws were standing at the edge of a new boom. They had already pulled permits for one house and had talked their son, a framer, into leaving Alaska and moving to Humboldt County. It didn't matter that Shelter Cove had no economy to speak of. It didn't matter that its forty miles of chuck-holed roads led to one restaurant, one bar, one motel. The yap of hammers and saws never ceased, and it was nearly impossible to find anyone in town who wasn't a builder, and the construction workers were not exactly hippies and not exactly hillbillies but a weird amalgam of the two, and what commerce existed was all done in cash, and the cash carried the strangest odor, something between fresh-ground coffee and skunk, although no one except the outlander seemed to be able to smell it.

After having spent the month of September examining your valleys, hills and table lands; consulting your oldest settlers, ranchers and fruit growers; examining fruits in the old orchards and vineyards that have had but little care, I am even more optimistic than I was last year when I told you that Humboldt County was the most perfect garden spot in America, and that your soil and climate under proper direction would yield millions to future generations, where your redwoods have yielded thousands to the present. (George E. Rowe, vice president of the American Pomological Society, September, 1913)

Rumors of a massive raid on the ganja gardens of Humboldt and Mendocino counties—the famed Emerald Triangle—lit up the Internet in the early summer of 2008. "THIS JUST IN: Up to 60 FBI agents may have recently rented houses in Eureka. No confirmation whether it's connected to the planned DEA actions."

Marijuana bloggers were nothing if not vigilant, a chatter that seemed to gush out of a mania that hit its stride at three in the morning. Dozens of hotlines had surfaced to share the secrets of plant breeding, hype new strains with holy properties, and alert the flock to the stirrings of the drug cops. Fear that the narcs were about to pounce was pretty much a constant state, a buzz that took on more and more paranoiac adornments as summer turned to fall and the buds evolved into musty fruit. These rumors, though, weren't tied to harvest anxiety. The whispers had begun months before the camouflaged warriors of CAMP (the state's Campaign Against Marijuana Production) were scheduled to launch their annual raids from the whoop-whoop of military helicopters. These rumors, it turned out, concerned an action that elicited a far deeper fear in a culture whose psyche had been reduced to six words on a bumper sticker: U.S. OUT OF HUMBOLDT COUNTY.

Word had somehow leaked that an FBI agent based in the old logging town of Fortuna was tracking an unusual real estate development known as Buddhaville. A fat Filipino named Robert Juan (a.k.a. Buddha) had put together a syndicate, the Lost Paradise Land Corporation, that had amassed two thousand acres of timber company land along the border of southern Humboldt and northern Mendocino counties. Juan's designs, it seemed, had nothing to do with condos in the redwood forest.

He had subdivided the land into dozens of smaller lots and was selling off the parcels as part of a gated community for the purposes of growing indoor and outdoor marijuana. Phase 1 had already broken ground. By the end of phase 2, dozens of fifty- to one-hundred-acre gardens would be cultivating the most exotic strains in the classic ideal of a collective.

Because the feds play by different rules, no grower took the threat of a U.S. raid lightly. The DEA doesn't answer to Proposition 215, the California ballot initiative that allows marijuana to be grown and distributed for "compassionate" medical purposes. Voters may have been thinking about the ravages of cancer and AIDS when the law was enacted in 1996, but in the decade since, 215 had been stretched and pulled in so many different directions that it had lost all meaning, or rather it meant whatever folks in Garberville and Arcata wanted it to mean.

It meant that half the weed grown under the license of health care wasn't really medical marijuana at all, but the bud of choice for you, me, and the world. It meant that marijuana was the single biggest cash crop in all of California, dwarfing the $10 billion a year agricultural bounty of Fresno and Kern— the number one and number two farm counties in the country. It meant that the geographic top of California—7,081 square miles, 215,000 people, 85 percent of them white—operated as a separate nation. The land had been ceded to the children of the old loggers and salmon fishermen and cattle ranchers and the hippies, who couldn't afford the rents in San Francisco after the summer of '67 and flocked to the hills two hours north, grafting cannabis onto redwood country. It meant that nearly every standing thing in a two-hundred-mile stretch from Ukiah to McKinleyville—hydroponic stores, garden shops, irrigation supply houses, fertilizer companies, hardware stores, sushi restaurants, Toyota 4 x 4 dealers, banks, hotels, glassblowers, T-shirt makers, realtors, concert promoters—was almost wholly reliant on the unfettered cultivation of marijuana. It also meant that at any given time, the federal government, desiring a piece of the action, could shut the whole mountain down.

To the grower, the risk weighed out simply. If you furnished more than three pounds of marijuana a year to a patient—a technical violation of California law—you maybe faced a few hundred dollars fine. The very same operation, busted by the feds, could land you three years in the U.S. pen. Thus the fear of a federal raid, even though such raids rarely occurred more than once a decade, stayed long in the air. "The DEA is on its way!" a blogger blared. "Hundreds of federal agents have booked rooms at the Red Lion."

By mid-June 2008, a state of alert had fallen over the Emerald Triangle. Residents began calling police with reports of unusual movements in the still of the night. Their neighbors—whose names they did not know—were clearing out garages and hauling off irrigation pipes and box lights. Brokers too were heading below ground, refusing to sell their turkey-roasting bags stuffed with purple Kush to any buyer they hadn't done business with before. The city council in Arcata, the first town in the United States to hand out medical marijuana user cards, a place that routinely out-liberaled Berkeley, issued a moratorium on new warehouses seeking to dispense medical pot.

The whispers and warnings and movements, both subterranean and official, continued into the early morning hours of June 24, when residents awoke to a convoy of 450 federal, state, and local police—cars, trucks, all-terrain vehicles, three-wheelers, a mobile communications center, portable toilets—roaring up the hillside. The shock and awe of U.S. Operation Southern Sweep was in full deploy. "It was amazing," a coffee roaster in Redway remarked. "I've seen some convoys go by, but never anything like that." Such was the timing that his first thought was the federal government had come not to raid the marijuana fields but to help put out the fires that were burning California.

It was late July, a full month after the federal bust, and I was sitting in a backyard in Ukiah around midnight, surrounded by a Zinfandel vineyard and, closer in, a small orchard of marijuana. If you didn't know better—and I didn't—the bushes all looked the same: lush and overdosed on nitrogen and forced upright by the will of bamboo stakes. Some of the plants were Maui and others were Sour Diesel, two distinct varieties that had come to cultivation after years of selective breeding. Inside the farmhouse, one of the growers and brokers I had hoped to meet was negotiating a major sell with two customers who had journeyed all the way up from Bakersfield. Understandably, the mood was jumpy, and so I waited on the porch, drinking a beer with another grower and broker named John Heath (a nom de guerre, as it turned out), who had agreed to act as my tour guide.

I had traveled north to see for myself how brazen the culture of marijuana had become in the decade since Prop 215 was passed and, if lucky, catch the tensions that seemed to be growing between the old hippies and new hippies. The back-to-the-earth disciples who had brought marijuana to these hills in the early 1970s were now rising up against the "diesel dope" factories that were polluting the salmon rivers and ravaging what was left of the redwood forests. In the days after the federal raid, I had called Bob Ornelas, the ponytailed former mayor of Arcata who once bragged to *Time* magazine that he ran his marathon races high on Humboldt bud. Ornelas was so thoroughly disgusted with the way the younger generation had perverted pot that he found himself applauding the federal agents as they ransacked the house across the street.

"For a while, I thought my neighbor was a high-class whore because she had so many young men coming and going at night. Then I realized she had turned the inside of her house into a pot farm, and the guys were coming to check on the lights and thin the leaves and make sure the acidity in the hydroponics was right," he said. "Hang out here for a few days and you'll see young people, twenty-five to thirty years old, spending their marijuana riches like mad. We call them 'The Tribe.' They try to put a hippie spin on it, but it's all bullshit."

I had taken a room a few miles outside Ukiah at the Vichy Springs Resort, founded in 1854. Though the inn had served a long and distinguished line of guests, including Mark Twain, Gentleman Jim Corbett, and presidents Roosevelt (Teddy), Harrison, and Grant, it billed itself simply as "Jack London's favorite resting spot." The two guests in front of me had pulled up in a mud-caked 4 x 4. The young man had the beak of Frank Zappa, and his dreadlocked girlfriend wore no makeup on her sunburned face. I imagined they were campers coming down from a long hike, needing a room with clean sheets and a place to shower. Angela, the front desk clerk, recognized them as something else.

"Welcome to the famous champagne baths," she said. "This is the only place in North America where the mineral waters are both warm and carbonated. Millions of little champagne bubbles will cling to your skin." She then ran down the list of available cabins. The boyfriend kept shaking his head until she came to the most expensive one. He pulled out three $100 bills from his wallet and off he and his girlfriend went in the direction of Little Grizzly Creek. Angela then turned to me. "Their money always stinks, but I don't smell it anymore."

Now huddled outside the farmhouse with the young grower John Heath, I tried to describe the couple. Rasta redneck was the best I could come up with. He knew the type well, he said. More than likely, they lived up the road, north of the county line, in southern Humboldt. So Hum, he called it. A geography and a psychology that existed on the far side of Laytonville, one of California's cultural divides.

"Laytonville is a fascinating place. It's where the organic hippie movement with its small-scale marijuana gardens meets the industrial grower," he said. "To the south is us. Mendo. Weed is a spiritual experience here. We grow it in a sustainable way. We grow it in backyards using the sun. To the north is hill country. They do it big, out in the middle of nowhere. They build these huge indoor grow houses and use diesel generators to keep the lights burning. They're grease monkeys. Their four-wheel drives are beat to shit because they actually use them. They're hard-core. They listen to reggae. Their girlfriends have dreadlocks. They pride themselves on the weapons they carry and the motorcycles they ride.

"We're town people, the sons and daughters of the professionals and hippies. They're hill people, the sons and daughters of the old lumbermen and fishermen."

When it came time to do business, the town people in this case went to the vineyard people to rent a rural farmhouse, converting the backyard into a pot orchard and the den into a showroom for Mendo's most extreme weed—up to four grand a pound. Every few minutes, the backdoor creaked open and out came somebody different, wearing the same "I need to exhale" face. They wandered about the six-foot bushes planted in giant plastic containers under a towering redwood. A few deep breaths later, they stumbled back to the drug deal inside.

John's partner, his old high school buddy Dennis, was negotiating the transaction. He had shown up at the farmhouse that evening completely high. Instead of "couch lock," the paralysis that some varieties of herb were said to induce, Dennis had the opposite problem. He couldn't stop moving or talking. His friends figured it was some strange amphetamine. Instead of closing the deal, Dennis kept digressing. The two buyers from Bakersfield, a sawed-off Mexican and a USC linebacker-size black man, had driven up in a Camry. The deal was taking so long because they were sampling each stashed pound, and Dennis was insisting they write testimonials to appear in his online promotions.

Indulging Dennis, the linebacker wrote this: "Purple smoke is no joke. Especially when it is real purple. The smell, taste, and high is easily one of the best in the world. One bowl of some purple Kush, and I'm done for a couple of hours . . . B-man, from Central Cal."

John was running out of patience. A straightforward dope deal that should have taken twenty minutes was dragging on for three hours. The air outside was turning chilly, but he didn't seem to notice. He wore cargo shorts and a T-shirt and nothing on his feet. He was a tall, good-looking kid with short blond hair, clipped goatee, and a paunch that had crept up on him in his late twenties. The farmhouse where he now lived, he said, was just a few miles from the house on a fancy hill in Ukiah where he grew up. His mother was a librarian and his father a CPA who had never been a hippie but played the electric guitar and smoked a little weed and leaned in his politics to the left. Then his mother died and his dad remarried, this new wife an evangelical Christian. Now his father was spearheading the local effort to change Mendocino's cannabis law, slashing the legal limit of plants from twenty-five to six.

"My dad thinks the loopholes in the law have been completely exploited. He's right, of course. You ask him if he wants marijuana to be legalized and he'll tell you yes. But if it can't be legalized, he wants it controlled. The accountant in him hates that so much of it is unaccounted for."

John was fifteen when he raised his first three plants from clones and stuck them in the backyard where the tomatoes and beans grew. By his senior year, he was farming two dozen plants that his mother watered while he studied abroad in France. The day before he came home, the cops busted a meth lab down the block, and his mom panicked. She hacked down all the plants, the flowers yet to bloom. "That was my first introduction to the heartbreak of this business," he said. He tried to get away from it—as a college student working part-time for the U.S. Geological Survey, as the French teacher at the local high school—but the money and the rush ("It's addictive, dude") always brought him back.

"People have this vague understanding that the Emerald Triangle is the marijuana growing capital of the nation, if not the world. But dude, unless you live here or work in the biz, it's hard to fathom just how big this business is.

"The lumber mills are closing and the salmon runs have died. They kept this place running for 150 years. Now it's weed. Easily, it's 80 percent of the economy. How many billions, no one can really say, but it's billions and billions, trust me."

Come early October, this little backyard, all by itself, would employ eight to ten young women. They would trim the leaves, nip the buds off the main stalks, hang them out to dry, and cure the final product in plastic containers. No worker would earn less than $40 an hour, likely the highest piece rate in all of American agriculture. When it was all said and done, the twenty-two plants would yield an average of two and a half pounds each. John and Dennis would walk away with 160 grand. And that didn't count the three grand a month that John made brokering weed for other growers.

"We do everything local. We buy our fertilizers and soil amendments down the street. All our supplies and tools, we buy at Friedman's. I go out to dinner, buy clothes. All local. And because we're producing something real that sells across the country, we're bringing in real dollars from the outside. Walk downtown, look what's popped up. It's amazing. That's all pot, directly and indirectly."

Not unlike the fruit and nut farmers of the San Joaquin Valley, a handful of growers, perhaps 5 percent, were making millions, they estimated. But with the higher profile of those millions came the higher risk of a raid. A much larger slice of growers, not unlike themselves, were quietly earning what good lawyers in a midsize town earned. Even so, John and his girlfriend, Annie, American consumers that they were, had no savings to lean on.

"At one point, Annie and I had $50,000 saved up," John said. "We tried really hard to hold on to that."

"We tried hard," Annie said, in a little girl's voice.

"And we're not high, dude. We spend no money on drugs. Just smoke a little of our own stuff. Our biggest vacation was going to Disneyland. But shit, that fifty grand was gone in six months."

"Paying rent, paying bills, paying insurance," Annie said.

Sitting across from John and Annie was a grower named Kyle, who believed it is less about making money than following a dream. He had come out from Montana two years earlier, a skinny farm boy sensing his destiny wasn't raising cattle on the Billings range but cultivating the finest Razzmatazz in Mendo.

"I fell in love with bud when I was thirteen," he explained. "Going to California. Going to California. That's all I thought about. When I got here, I didn't look back. This is where I belong."

If he still dressed in farmer's cap and Wrangler jeans, it only enhanced his lone wolf status. "You're looking at one of the two or three best indoor marijuana growers in the Emerald Triangle," John said. "The man's got a serious case of OCD. Imagine walking into a grow house and there's not a speck of dirt anywhere. Spotless. That's Montana."

Two students from Humboldt State, who had grown weary of the drama inside, joined us on the porch. The anthropology major said he had observed in growers an emotional stunting that might best be described as "the psychic guilt of marijuana ambivalence." Yes, by virtue of medical cards signed by friendly doctors, you could grow pot quite freely in these parts. But the law was confused. On one hand, it allowed you to grow twenty-five plants, which equates to fifty to sixty pounds of finished product. On the other hand, it was illegal to store more than two pounds at a time. This institutional confusion simply grew out of a much bigger societal confusion. Thus you spent a good part of each day hiding from the cops and your neighbors what you did for a living.

"As righteous as you might feel growing and selling this as a crop," the anthropologist said, "at the end of the day it's not corn or cotton or grapes or almonds. You're still a criminal, and you know it."

"I want to view myself as a good person," Kyle said. "I pay my share of taxes."

"A lot of this backlash," Annie said, "comes from pissed off people who have to work nine to five and are barely making it. They hate us."

"My inclination," John said, "is to be out front. But the impulse of this business is to retreat, and with that retreat comes isolation. In too many of us, it leads to depression and drug abuse. It leads to unhealthy spending habits. We spend to prove that we're for real. But the dough can only do so much to mask the isolation."

I wondered if any of them had found a measure of engagement in the political process, if the war on terror and the assault on civil liberties and the surrender to a deregulated Wall Street had been seen as a call to arms.

"Look, let me tell you this," John said. "Conceptual thinking is dead. The hippies might have done a great job of doing it themselves. But they forgot to pass that thinking on. Their children don't know what they're doing. They don't know what they want to do. And whatever they're doing, it has nothing to do with politics."

They pointed to Dennis, still haggling inside the den with the Bakersfield duo. His parents had left New York and journeyed to California in the '60s. They raised Dennis and three other children and then split up over different versions of what true radicalism meant. His father still lived in a nearby commune called Round Mountain. His mother had moved to Baltimore to join Father Berrigan at the collective known as

Jonah House. In and out of jail, she was still trying to beat nuclear arms into ploughshares.

"If you want to understand what became of the hippies and their children, tonight probably isn't the night," John said. "Come back tomorrow, and I'll take you to Dennis's place."

The two-story redwood chalet sat back in the woods on a clearing of meadow so sublime that air and light changed the moment we crossed the gate. The chalet looked out to a pond, grape vines, a vegetable garden, and a small fruit orchard, so much simple beauty that my eye nearly missed the jungle-thick bushes, twenty-five in all, that a man was watering with a hose in the dappled sunlight. "That's Dennis," John said. His combed-back hair was flawlessly cut, and he wore Dior sunglasses and no shirt and his shorts slung low enough to show off the top of his green boxers. On the deck, standing in the full sun, was a tall redhead with giant breasts in a purple halter dress. In the sky, atop a tree limb for a pole, flapped the rainbow-colored peace flag of his mother's Jonah House. "Welcome to my farm," he said in a voice that gave each word a waver.

Whatever happened the night before hadn't stopped him from a full morning dressing the topsoil of his marijuana with a mocha mix of bat guano. "Weeks ago, during the vegetative stage, I used a high-nitrogen bat guano to pack on the leaves. This stuff is more mellow, slower on release, and heavier on the potassium. Perfect for the blooming stage. You can have the fattest bush in town, but without the flowers, it's just rank green."

The apple, pear, cherry, and walnut trees, the tomatoes, squash, cucumbers, and corn, the Maui erupting from hundred-gallon nylon mesh planters—all of it was proudly organic. He let pennyroyal run wild because it snatched nitrogen from the air and stuck it back into the soil. Whatever dropped down from the blue and valley oak, he welcomed for its microbial matter.

"It's all about the soil. Pests, mold, poor production—it all goes back to weak soil," he said. "I spend most of my time building up the soil's profile. I use really strong chicken shit. And all the watering I do is by hand. Drip doesn't work with herb. It wants too much water."

Unlike indoor pot, where the lighting is manipulated to produce more bud than leaf, outdoor marijuana grows like koi in a pond—as big as the space you give it. Indoor plants are harvested once every two months. Outdoor plants are harvested once a year. Indoor plants, done right, yield one pound for every halogen light that shines on them. Outdoor plants, using the sun, yield two and half pounds each. As far as quality goes, indoor plants produce more resin and a stronger buzz and thus sell for a premium.

For John and Dennis, the choice wasn't theirs. The microclimates of the Emerald Triangle dictated the method of growing. If you lived in Salmon Creek or Arcata, fighting the cold mists of the coast, you grew indoors using diesel or electricity. If you lived in the hot and dry of Mendo, the garden you grew was outdoors.

"We get one shot at it," Dennis said.

"One harvest," John said.

"So if you get popped, you're done for the year," I said.

They looked at each other and snickered.

"So how much at risk are you guys really running?" I asked.

"Zero," Dennis said.

"Zero," John said.

"We always work within the guidelines," Dennis said.

"We've got the required paperwork for two dozen plants," John said. "But if we wanted to push the guidelines, we're allowed five times more."

"That's 125 plants," I said. "You're talking more than three hundred pounds a year. That's a million dollars."

The calculation was a long way from the commune in San Francisco where his parents took their vows against the war machine. Dennis said he and his three siblings lived in buses and in the back of a shop in Ukiah, where his father did graphic design between protests. For a long time, he tried to carry their causes. He left high school to live with peasant workers in Central America. In college, he learned how to gin up a pirate radio station from the father of Berkeley Free Radio, and he and John, pals since the eighth grade, ran the hottest station in town—102.9 FM, no commercials, uncensored tunes—until the FCC shut them down.

"My parents gave me this wider view of the world, and for that I'm grateful," Dennis said. "I'm even glad for the experience of growing up in buses and in other illegal arrangements. But I never wanted to live my life the same way."

He had finished watering, and we were sitting on the back porch, the sun straight up, glinting off his Diors.

"So how do your parents feel about this?" I asked.

"I'd be lying if I said they're happy. For them, pot is just another way of selling out. But my dad is beginning to realize that there's more to it here. There's a movement inside."

"I guess one thing has stayed the same," I said. "The feds are still big and bad."

"Can you believe their little field trip? In the middle of the worst fires ever in California, 450 drug agents ride to the rescue," he said. "And when the smoke clears, all they've got to show for it is ten thousand plants and not a single arrest."

No one in Mendo was exactly crying over the demise of Buddhaville, the planned pot community that would sprawl across the two county lines. The project was classic So Hum— big and brazen and contemptuous of the environment. The feds did manage to seize $10 million in land and houses. And indictments by the federal grand jury were expected to follow.

So far, John and Dennis had managed to fly under the radar. John had designed a more efficient distribution network to increase the pounds trafficked between Northern and Southern California. Dennis was taking the profits from one backyard and pouring them into another. In a matter of three seasons, he had realized his own Shangri-La for the price of 450 grand. Anywhere else in California, the meadow by itself was worth $2 million. This, though, was Mendo, where the living was cheap and the only economy that counted was the underground economy.

"Here we've got a code," Dennis said. "You don't get too big, you donate to political campaigns, and you treat your neighbors with respect. You give back to the soil."

His girlfriend's parents were coming to see the place, and he had to cut our visit short. "You're welcome back anytime," he said. As he headed up the garden path, he stopped and pointed at his mother's flag flying over the Maui. "It looks beautiful up there, doesn't it?" he said.

Only after Dennis disappeared into the lush canopy did John make a confession. Not everything in his best pal's garden was organic. This girlfriend, the last girlfriend, the girlfriend before that. "They come to him flat and always end up with these enormous plastic tits," he said. "Like everything else, they've got marijuana to thank."

I was headed to a meeting in So Hum, but John had a few more places he wanted to show me first. We stopped at a grow house called Hydro Pacific where shelf after shelf was stacked with bone meal, fish meal, folic acid, and live soil inoculants from Hawaii and Amsterdam. John and the clerk swapped cultivation tips for five minutes without ever once uttering the words "marijuana" or "pot" or "ganja" or "herb." There wasn't even a wink. The indoor garden display, complete with oscillating fans and exhaust ducts and CO_2 emitters and lights on a motorized rail, was all set up to go. The plants serving as props were a tomato, a bell pepper, and an eggplant. In the parking lot, a fork lift driver was pushing loads of soil amendment bagged in camouflage, as if destined for a war front.

"That's for the guerrilla growers in the mountains," John said. "They plant straight into the bag, and the bag is already camo-ed so you don't have to worry about a CAMP helicopter spotting you from the air."

We made our way to Friedman's, the local hardware store. Built on the scale of a Home Depot, it operates with a completely different sensibility. The aisles of the Home Depot in Ukiah are no different than the aisles of the Home Depot, say, in San Diego. Friedman's, on the other hand, knows exactly who its customers are. There likely isn't another hardware store on the West Coast that carries this many brands of irrigation timers, this many stacks of rigid wallboard insulation, this many bins filled with high-end trimming scissors. For Benny Friedman, who had died that month at the age of ninety and whose obituary was plastered across the front and back doors, it was all about serving a demographic.

"Friedman's stocks oscillating fans in the middle of winter," John said. "Who else in their right mind would do that?"

We drove through downtown past the house on the hill where he grew his first plants and then out on Orr Springs Road, which runs all the way from Highway 101 to the coast. In the hills of pine and oak where the asphalt turns to dust, he stopped his truck on a crest and gazed into the last of the sun. "This raw, beautiful territory is one of the earliest spots," he said. We had come to the gate of the Greenfield Ranch, the first, or at least the longest running, marijuana collective in California.

"This entire swath extends about ten miles. This is where the hippies from the Summer of Love came as part of the whole back to the land movement. Can you believe that they bought this hillside for a hundred bucks an acre?"

"How many families?"

"Somewhere around thirty. Think about how many of their friends came up to visit from San Francisco and latched onto this idea of a marijuana kibbutz. This is where it began. And the original settlers are still here."

We drove back to his place in Redwood Valley and shook hands good-bye. As I got into my car, he pointed me north in the direction of So Hum.

"There's something you need to know about where you're going. Garberville, per capita, has the finest women in the world. Girls with facial features that are unbelievable on bodies that are unbelievable. 'Dude, where am I? I'm in Garberville? Why is there like five of the most beautiful girls I've ever seen in my life working in the local coffee stop?'"

He had been an excellent tour guide and a fine backyard sociologist and historian to boot, and so I asked him if he had a theory to explain it. He did, of course.

"In the days before Prop 215, you could make four grand a pound for crap weed. And these guerrilla growers were doing it big. They drove Ferraris and built million dollar estates. They did wild world traveling and brought home the finest trophy wives they could find. So you have all these hot-looking fifty-year-old mothers and their even hotter-looking daughters. Tall and thin and super built with exotic faces and names like Chia."

This wasn't the California I learned as a kid. Father Junipero Serra didn't journey this far north, not by a long shot. There were no missions here, no padres with rawhide whips, no neo-phyte natives planting the first vineyards and wheat fields and digging the first irrigation canals, no Spanish land grants seized through wholesale scam by the European industrialists of San Francisco, no Chinese or Japanese or Mexicans brought in to build levees and railroads and harvest vineyards and orchards and vegetable fields. This was a land too rugged for even the most rugged of the fur trappers. There was a harbor, yes, but its opening was so treacherously narrow that it frightened off the captains of the discovery ships. The approach by land was even more of a bludgeon, coastal mountains that extended some 150 miles beyond the beach. Not until the Gold Rush, almost a century after Serra and his band of Franciscan friars began the taming of the American West, was the silence of the north broken. The first white man to colonize these parts carried timber in his blood. "Her pioneers were men of brawn, largely from Maine and Nova Scotia," reads the *History of Humboldt County, California*, published in 1915. "While the sturdy pioneers were carving their fortunes from the primeval forests, the red men were not strangers to the war dance and the poisoned arrow."

Such was the state of isolation that by 1854, four years after California joined the Union, the natives of the Whitethorn Valley still had not seen a white man. Such was the fever of conquest that by 1864, just ten years later, the entire society of Sinkyone, Yurok, and Karok had been destroyed. What was the wiping clean of one culture and the planting of another if not the prosecution of an American holocaust? The execution may have been more haphazard than the genocides and Holocaust to come, but it was no less efficient for the means available at the time. "The people of the county are driven to madness by the red-skin scourge that has long been preying upon their lives and property. They are impatient to have the county rid of it," read one of the first editions of the *Humboldt Times*.

They got rid of it by exacting a revenge that held to the calculus that for every white man killed by an Indian, 150 Indians needed to die in return. This is what happened in Weaverville in 1852 and again on the night of February 25, 1860, when "a secret society of settlers" crept ashore Indian Island in Humboldt Bay and proceeded to massacre "every man, woman and child they could find," wrote Humboldt historian Ray Raphael. They did not stop until nearly three hundred natives had been slaughtered. Bret Harte penned an angry editorial and was run out of town. The grand jury convened but failed to turn up a single clue identifying the offenders.

It made sense that a place so cut off would be accountable only to itself, exile begetting lawlessness. Once the settlers got accustomed to taking, it didn't matter if it was the Indians or the U.S. government they were taking from. Out West, through the Homestead Act, land could be purchased for $2.50 an acre, as long as the buyer swore off speculating or turning over his deed to a third party. The law somehow didn't apply to the California Redwood Company in San Francisco, controlled by a wealthy syndicate out of Edinburgh, Scotland. The company scoured the streets and signed up hobos and sailors who were paid anywhere from five to fifty dollars to file a claim for cheap land. As soon as the deed became theirs, they handed over the land to the syndicate. In this way (the same way it was being done with great stretches of farmland in the Central Valley) 64,000 acres of virgin redwood timberland became the domain of a handful of robber barons.

California had already witnessed the forty-niners turn its northern rivers into great scours for gold and eight thousand Chinese coolies tear through the granite of the High Sierra—some days progressing no more than ten inches with steel drills that bent like licorice—to lay the tracks of the Central Pacific. Extracting red gold from the Humboldt mountains was no less an act of rapacity. Early on, there were no train tracks and no roads through the redwoods, and each piece of equipment for the mill towns that rose up on the Eel and Elk and Mattole rivers had to be carried in by mule. The trees were felled in summer so that by early fall the riverbeds were piled high with huge timbers. To move such a mass to the mill, the loggers built dams along the rivers and waited for the autumn rains to fall. As the dams were brimming with water, they lit dynamite and blew open a crater, sending an awesome wave of water and mud and timber down the canyon. To harvest the groves beyond the river, the loggers built "skid roads" out of small timbers that were then slathered with grease to make it easier for the oxen, yoked and harnessed, to pull the haul. These miners, with their honky-tonks and stills and outhouses situated directly over the streams, lived no lighter on the land. When they wanted fish to eat, they simply drained the millponds of all but the most shallow pools of water; so many salmon and steelhead got mired in the mud that even their dogs gathered at river's edge to feast. The few natives hired to help, men called Indian Ike and Big Charlie, had to turn away their eyes.

The industrialization of the redwood forest kept up this way for the better part of a century, small mills gobbled up by bigger mills until the mountainside was owned by Georgia Pacific and Louisiana Pacific and Sierra Pacific. Then, one by one, thanks to deforestation and poor management and tree huggers turned tree sitters, the mills began to slow and shutter, so that by the time I arrived in Garberville in late July 2008, the headline shouting from the front page told of the last day of the venerable Pacific Lumber. A contentious bankruptcy battle was sending the 150-year-old company into new hands: the Humboldt Redwood Company, owned by the Fisher family of Gap stores fame.

"Even though the last few years have not been the best, I hope you will always be proud of having been a part of this great company," President George A. O'Brien wrote to employees that day. "If you stay with Humboldt Redwood or the Town, I know you will give it your all, because that is what you have always done. So good luck."

If you didn't count the twenty-year reign of Charles Hurwitz, who leveraged Michael Milken's junk bonds to harvest the old-growth groves, Pacific Lumber was much loved here. Locals said the pain of its slowdown would have been more widely felt had the economy not shifted years ago. Consider Alderpoint, the tiny town outside Garberville, where thirteen mills once followed the Eel River up the canyon. The last of those mills, owned by

Louisiana Pacific, shut down in 1982. "We've been without a mill for twenty-five years," said Ed Denson, an Alderpoint resident since 1980, when he moved his mail-order record company from the Bay Area. The former manager of Country Joe and the Fish, the opening band at Woodstock, Denson was now one of the most successful marijuana defense attorneys in the state. His one-man office, an old chicken coop, sat crooked on thirty acres of rolling hills that looked out to Pratt Mountain.

"The loggers denuded the mountain and then the cattlemen and sheep men came in behind them, and everyone who could get out got out," he said. "That's when the hippies moved in and started growing pot. The rednecks hated them until they figured out that they could make money too. Then a funny thing happened. The children of the rednecks and the children of the hippies married. Now all you've got growing on this mountain is marijuana."

The blending of the two was far from complete, it seemed. That evening, in the old Veteran's Hall in downtown Garberville, residents were holding a community meeting on the growing problem of "diesel dope." I got there early enough to meet the half dozen organizers who were setting up. The first to arrive was a man in a cream yellow 1953 Chevy pickup, sweetly restored, with a bumper sticker that read, "Diesel Dope: Pollution Pot." He was in his late sixties, skinny, clad in sandals and jeans. The locks of his blond hair flowed into the immense gray of his beard. It was the head of a lion on the body of a grasshopper. I introduced myself and asked his name.

"Hardy," he said.

"First or last?"

"Hardy Har."

He said he had been on the run since 1971 when he was a campus leader of Students for a Democratic Society and shouted "motherfucking pig" at Governor Ronald Reagan during a speech at Cal State Fullerton. From that moment on, the cops were on his case. Facing a stiff jail term for selling hash, he jumped bail and fled to Humboldt County, where he joined a commune of pot smokers. "Now, thirty-seven years later, we're rising up in protest against the industrial marijuana grower," he said.

For a long time, Hardy and his friends couldn't decide what, if anything, to do. Here was a collision of two of their most cherished values: the freedom to grow pot and the obligation to save the environment. The first value had led them to build a marijuana society here; the second had propelled them to fight Hurwitz and the other clear-cutters of the forest. Now a series of diesel spills were contaminating Salmon Creek and other streams, and the old hippies were printing out fact sheets and bumper stickers. The time had come to confront the growers of diesel dope.

"There's a way to grow marijuana that doesn't degrade the drinking water and kill off the salmon," he said. "That's why we're here tonight, though I'm not sure any of the diesel boys are going to show."

A professional facilitator had written a set of admonishments on a large piece of butcher paper: "Be Respectful. Be Open to Different Points of View. Expect Unfinished Business." The lawn chairs started to fill, fifty in all, many of the men looking just like Hardy Har, many of the women wearing clogs and long skirts and clutching hemp bags. There were no Chias here.

The basic facts were quickly agreed upon:

Most of the cannabis grown in the Emerald Triangle is now produced by sophisticated indoor grow houses powered by large diesel generators.

It takes seventy-five gallons of fuel to produce one pound of indoor pot. That is the same as the average car making one trip from California to Texas.

The particulates in diesel exhaust are the most significant source of air toxins in California.

A high percentage of rural fires are caused by indoor grow houses.

Officials from the DA to the sheriff to the county judge to the local building inspector are turning a blind eye.

Many indoor gardens are infested with pests that have to be sprayed. Those chemicals are in your pot.

Then the discussion began, a little tentative at first with several speakers looking in my direction as I took notes. A tarot card reader named Juna Berry informed me later that the whisper working through the hall was that I was a DEA agent. Maybe this explained why a number of folks chose not to identify themselves.

Young man with goatee and baseball hat: No one wants to talk about how we've been silenced by political correctness. It's sad that I'm one of the few young people in this room. We've lost our voice. A lot of the old-timers don't want to speak out either because they'll be accused of being hypocrites. "You grew, and now you don't want us to grow."

Middle-aged man with scraggly beard: It's not about growing marijuana. It's about the kind of marijuana they're growing.

The problem goes back to a spiritual tear in our society. It goes back to mammon.

Francis Ford Coppola look-alike: We're talking about preserving what's left of the forest and watershed. Think of the great horned owl perched out there trying to listen for the sound of mice in the grass. That owl can hear nothing but the din of the diesel motor. MMMMMMMM.

Middle-aged man with ponytail: There's a huge blaring sun outdoors. Why go inside? It boggles the mind.

Tall woman vegetarian: Because the marketplace demands indoor pot. There used to be honor among thieves, but Prop 215 made people mad with greed.

Woman who grew up on farm: We live in an enlightened community, and I expect we can come up with our own plan to solve this problem. I don't want to use the word "regulation," but we need to apply gentle peer pressure to change this behavior.

Smart lady: We need to kick around the idea of a public education campaign. Pitch stories to *High Times* magazine about the environmental harm this dope is doing. We need to reach the young.

Coppola look-alike: We've got an ecological disaster on our hands. We need to stop these greedy assholes with a lawsuit.

It was past eight when I made it back to Garberville's main drag and finally caught the vision in John Heath's eyes: the tall, tanned trophy wives and daughters of the OGs flocked in front of Flavors coffeehouse. I smiled at the dead-on of his adjectives, but I was too tired to linger. I stuck a Swisher Sweet in my mouth and tried to locate the adrenaline for the long drive to Arcata. Word on the street was that the uproar over indoor dope had aroused vigilantism in the college town on the other side of the Humboldt Bay.

"They say I'm on a crusade. I'm not on a crusade. What I'm doing is fully consistent with trying to report a story. All I do is come out, take notes, and take pictures. Old-fashioned community journalism."

Kevin Hoover, editor in chief of the weekly *Arcata Eye*, was feeling a little defensive. He had been under attack from the marijuana faithful for the past six months, ever since he began compiling a list of suspected grow houses in town. "Weed Nazi," they called him, though the label didn't fit. Hoover had dope smoked his way through community college and was the kind of journalist who saw too much ambiguity to be a genuine muckraker. His bent for irony was on full display in his local police log, where he took the noise complaints and hit-and-runs and public drunkenness of a small town and turned them into limerick.

But now Arcata, the town he had grown to love, was under siege. Residential tracts were being converted into factories of marijuana. Whole blocks were being industrialized. Dope growers, he believed, made the worst neighbors. Like opossums, they kept to themselves and moved furtively at night. Lights in their eyes, they hissed and bared their teeth. With four and five grow houses on every block, neighborhoods were being hollowed out. College students and working-class families could no longer afford the rents. And then the house fires. Who, if not the editor of the local rag, needed to awaken the citizenry?

"I don't give a flying fuck that they're growing marijuana. I'm as much a 'U.S.-out-of-Humboldt-County' guy as the rest of them," he said. "But when I see neighborhoods going dead, that's when I get riled up. Don't grow in the middle of town. Don't gut perfectly fine houses."

He was an overweight man in his mid-fifties who wore a cap over his balding head and a beard on his double chin. He was giving me the same grow house tour he had given to the *New York Times* a month before. Every week, another neighbor or jogger or old lady walker sent him a new address to target. If the suspect house was a rental, he'd write a letter to the out-of-town owner. Your house shows the telltale marks of a marijuana grow: darkened windows, funny smell, PGE meter whirling like a Frisbee. You may want to pay a little visit to the renters. If the house was occupied by the owner, he'd knock on the door and ask a few questions—all very polite, nothing beyond the pale of journalism.

"I say, 'Hi, I'm Kevin from the *Arcata Eye*. I'd like to talk to you about growing. Is this part of a medical marijuana club? Or are you selling in the open market, which the law doesn't allow?'"

We were headed to Beverly Drive, the epicenter. "I don't turn them in. I'm not a cop. But the exploiters of 215 have done their best to conflate a wonderful hippie heritage and tolerance for smoking recreationally and medically with a cynical money-making enterprise. And that's a story."

We parked in front of a house with a detached garage and a new eight-foot fence. "This is a grow house all armored up. You can make a quarter million dollars a year off a garage like this."

In a middle-income neighborhood known as Sunny Brae, he asked me to stop the car alongside a redwood house. He dashed out, sneaked a peak at the PG&E meter, and ran back. He was out of breath. "Grow house for sure. Full tilt boogie. You can smell it. You can hear the ventilation system. And the meter was spinning nuts."

On A Street, he pointed out the house that a few months earlier had been tagged by an angry citizen with the word "GROW." Hoover had left his card, asking the renter to call him. A week later, the house was raided by the local drug task force. He headlined the story, "Tagged Grow House Turns Out to Be Just That."

"Some residents are advocating vigilante campaigns. They're pissed off because when the cops do go inside, often they find shotguns and meth. We're all about having a barbecue in the backyard with our neighbors, playing the Grateful Dead, and sharing a joint. An armed enclave next door? What kind of shit is that?"

We drove west of town to a section called Pacific Union, the home of Sun Valley Floral Farms, the biggest industrial enterprise in Arcata if you excluded marijuana. Martha Stewart had once visited to inspect the farm's world-famous floral bulbs.

"We're coming up to the house that was rented out to these slob growers. Total idiots. They were knocking holes in the walls with hammers to run wires and ducting. Of course a fire started. They had thirty cases of butane inside. Lucky the whole thing didn't blow up."

A crew was putting the final touches on a $55,000 repair job. The contractor saw us parked out front and walked over to chat. Most of the year, he said, he worked for General Electric. During the summer months, he did carpentry.

"There's not a construction worker in this county who hasn't helped build an indoor grow," he said. "I've helped build some of the damnedest houses. Designed to look like a home, but on the inside there was nothing. Just a shell. No floor. No sheetrock. Stand out front and you swore it was a house. They even put a swing set out front. But there were no kids inside. Just a million-dollar pot garden."

The Arcata city council, struggling to find a way to regulate while not really regulating the mess, was holding its weekly meeting. On the way over, I stopped by the local branch of the Bank of America to deposit a check. As I stood in line, my ear began to pick up a sound I had not heard before, at least not in a bank. *Ch-chut, ch-chut, ch-chut, ch-chut, ch-chut, ch-chut.* From one teller's station to the other, I could see little machines humping to keep up with a cascade of cash. Customer upon customer, satchel after satchel, the washing of redolent twenties, fifties, and hundreds. When I made it up front, the teller could see the out-of-towner's bemused smile on my face.

"Nine thousand, nine hundred, and ninety-nine dollars," he said. It was the magic number, a dollar shy of the bank having to notify the federal government of a "suspicious deposit."

Inside the council chambers, which gave the distinct impression of being inside the belly of a whale, five council members sat in perfect embodiment of the town: all white, all well-spoken, all very liberal except for one vanilla Republican. The youngest council member, the favorite of the pro-cannabis crowd, was actually named Harmony Groves. She had grown up down south in El Monte, watching her father die an agonizing death from cancer, wondering why the palliative of pot was not an option.

"I don't deny that indoor grow houses are a problem here," she told me over dinner at Tomo Japanese Restaurant. "But if you listen to Kevin Hoover, you'd think the whole town was overrun with them. He says one in five houses are grow houses. But I've walked two campaigns door to door. To me, it's more like one in fifteen."

This didn't mean the council was sitting on its hands, she said. She and her colleagues were seriously considering curtailing the local law that allowed one hundred square feet of marijuana plants for every medical card. Fifty square feet per card sounded like a more rational number. And she, like Kevin Hoover, was pinning her hopes on a new marijuana dispensary in town operated by Eric Heimstadt, a drug counselor who had once served time at San Quentin.

"You ought to go see what he's building," she said. "It's a state-of-the-art dispensary that will help ensure that only true patients are getting medical marijuana."

The next morning, I managed to finagle a tour of the facility, an old Quonset hut off the quaint main square of Arcata. Heimstadt, another child of the Summer of Love, had been inspired by a recent reading of the *King of the Castle*, a history of the Bronfman dynasty. Led by ruthless Sam Bronfman, the family had risen from bootleggers to the founders of the Seagram's empire, in part by using the cover of medical licenses to dispense illegal booze.

"Like Sam, I want to work with the authorities," Heimstadt said. "I want to take the illicitness out of pot."

He then outlined an audacious plan that began with his becoming an official Medi-Cal provider, a status that would allow him to build dozens of greenhouses along the Santa Barbara coast, the perfect clime to produce tens of thousands of pounds of high-grade cannabis. Then, like McDonalds, he would corner the distribution market by franchising hundreds of dispensaries up and down the state.

"We'd have completely transparent books," he vowed. "The state of California could look at every inch of our operations. I'd be the good guy of pot."

Deep in the interior of the hut, he had something to show me. Past the nurse's office, past the patient's room, through one door and then another, the air grew thick and began to hum. He hit a few numbers on a coded pad and opened the last door. There, in the middle of the room, under twenty shoe-box-size lights, were the lean but powerful plants of an indoor marijuana grow, a secret garden that only his closest advisers had seen. Forty-eight plants produced twelve pounds of bud every eight weeks. For the time being, until the city lifted its ban on dispensaries growing their own product, it was illegal.

"This is the model I'd take from Crescent City to San Diego. I wouldn't be a greedy bastard. With the economy of scale, I'd be able to undercut everybody else." He stopped there, letting the image sink it. Not Sam of Seagram's but Sam of Wal-Mart.

"Medical marijuana would be mine. Maniacal laughter would peal across the land."

> I came to the redwood forest
> Off Highway 101
> Going to a Reggae concert
> Where all the Humboldt hippies come
> I bought some Rasta jewelry, I bought some Rasta clothes
> I even showed up this year with a ring right through my nose
> Those Reggae songs they make me cry
> The people fight and the people die
> While I just sit here and get high
> I think Bob Marley's really grand
> I've got a snow cone in my hand
> And to the Reggae groove I move my feet
> Just as long as I stay out of the heat
> This revolution can't be beat
> —Darryl Cherney

On the way down the mountain, I hustled a ticket to Reggae Rising, the biggest outdoor reggae festival in the West, I was told. For three days, with the cops locked outside, tens of thousands of redneck hippies, tie-dyed hippies, Stanford hippies, Jamaican hippies camped out along a bend in the Eel River to smoke dope and eat Greek food and listen to the four-bars-then-a-drum-snare-then-a-verse descendants of Marley. I arrived as the sun was setting on a Friday night. On the shuttle in, I sat across from one of the diesel dope growers, a giant of a young man with the face of Yurok Indian, who was too stoned, too belligerent to give me much. "We look kind of like hippies, but we're not. Dude, how many drugs are we going to do down here? I fucking popped a bunch of Ecstasy and puked all over the carpet." He wore stitches over one eye and carried a pillow and sleeping bag and held hands with a girlfriend who seemed to have lost all patience. The family in front and the family in back started to cough, and then the whole bus began to cough, and I was sure we were headed to a convention of consumptives.

The colors of Jamaica were everywhere, and girls in bikinis were swaying to the music and children in dreadlocks were running from booth to booth. So much smoke was swirling up from the little round valley in the canyon that I thought it must have appeared from high above as one big bowl lit with Kush. I had a pass to the back stage where bartenders were serving drinks to the connected people. I sat down by myself and lit another Swisher, and up walked a woman in her late twenties, sloppy in every way. She said she was a student at Humboldt State and then asked if I believed in God.

"Here at Reggae?" I asked.

"Tell me why I should believe in him? Why shouldn't I live as if he didn't exist because if he existed I wouldn't be living the way I'm living."

It was a curious piece of logic, not so different from the self-regarding logic of the believer.

"Down the road, I'll have a change of opinion and all this excess will be forgiven, right? Isn't that what the born agains do?"

I stayed for two hours. On the shuttle back to the Benbow Inn, a Jewish hippy from New Jersey, who had flunked out of chef school and come west to find something new, saw me taking notes.

"Are you a writer?"

"Yeah."

"Would you mind critiquing this?"

From his backpack, he pulled out a two-page essay titled "Not Your Same Old Reading" and began to read:

"We are the robot generation. All aspects of our lives consumed by technology." It went like that for four long paragraphs, but he stopped after the first. The next morning, as I loaded up my bags, I read the rest:

"I'm to embark on a spiritual quest tomorrow afternoon. I'm going to separate myself from society for three to four days in the woods of northern California. This is to do some very important things. First to separate myself from cigarettes and daily consumption of alcohol. Second is to disconnect from my cell phone and everything robotic. Third, and lastly, is to deepen my connection with Mother Earth. I, Daniel Leiber, do not recommend going out in the woods or any unknown territory for any period of time, if not properly prepared. But please know that I am taking the necessary precautions."

I missed my children and thought about going to see them in Shelter Cove, where they were vacationing for two weeks at the house their grandparents had built on the hillside. But there was that hellish drive and at the end of it was their mother, who didn't want me there. I barreled down the mountain to the strains of Elvis Costello, past the Little Leaguers of Willits, past the Red Tail of Hopland, past the cellars of Healdsburg, past the Golden Gate Bridge. I thought back to a scene in Eureka a few days earlier in the basement of the sheriff's department. I was talking to Sergeant Wayne Hanson (Mad Dog to the growers of Humboldt), and after recounting twenty years of forest battles with the guerrilla white boys and now the Mexican cartels, he made a sad confession. "I hate to say this because it sounds like I'm throwing in the towel, but they need to legalize marijuana. Because we've lost the battle."

I asked how he and his crew kept on in the face of such futility. Easy, he said. Two years ago, they seized 130,000 plants and last year they seized 350,000 plants. This year's helicopter raids, which would kick off the first week of August, would surely bring in another record haul. If it was never more than 5 percent of what was growing in the hills, if their success was its own indictment, it didn't matter to the powers that be. They had their game to play just like the marijuana boys. Call it risk management or bureaucracy's need to self-preserve, but the cops weren't going anywhere. In the highlands of Humboldt, they were stuck chasing their tails. The more pot they seized, the more pot they needed to seize.

| Last Okie of Lamont

Most times, he could tell by just glancing at their picture. The flattop haircut, the squinty eyes, the cheekbones high on a face. If the picture didn't give it away, their names surely did. J. C. "Curly" Taylor, Ina L. Weeks, Claude "Grizz" Bess, Wayne Augustus Fenderson. Children of Tuttle, Oilton, Hoxie, and McAlester, Oklahoma. Born in 1920, 1928, 1931, 1934. Came to California in 1935, 1939, 1940, 1941. Truck driver, beautician, ditch tender, M.D. There wasn't a day that Earl Shelton didn't pick up his *Bakersfield Californian*, turn to the obituary page, and find one more Okie face, one more Okie name, staring back at him. Now and then, the next of kin whose job it was to write the notice would make some allusion to the history the deceased had lived through. Most times, it was never mentioned. Earl figured the kids were too ashamed or uninformed or maybe couldn't afford the extra newsprint it would have taken. How to keep the dates straight anyway?

How to sum up a journey that wasn't just one migration but a whole lifetime of crisscrossing?

He never intended to be a voice for anyone, much less the voice that journalists and historians, some from as far away as Japan, would seek out to tell the story of the dying children of the Dust Bowl. "Chewy," as his friends knew him, wasn't much of a talker. He certainly didn't feel proper enough to speak on behalf of a generation and its epoch, what the *New York Times* called "the largest peacetime migration in the nation's history." His wife, Norma, the one who read all the books, could go on forever. Earl, head down, simply lived it, leaving Scipio in March 1941, at the age of seven, not "because of dust, but because of hard times." He arrived in Lamont with no mother and a drunkard father and lived twelve years at the government camp on the outskirts of town—the labor camp John Steinbeck immortalized in *The Grapes of Wrath*. The community hall, the library, and the post office still stood in the same spot, now listed on the National Register of Historic Places. Earl stood there too, Okie relic, surrounded by families from Michoacán and Jalisco and Oaxaca. They were digging their knees into the same farm fields where he had picked cotton and unearthed potatoes some sixty-five years ago. Up and down Weedpatch Highway, as it shot through town, there was no other way for Earl to put it. Mexico had come north. Holy Roller white churches had turned to Holy Roller brown. Tops Café was no longer serving chicken fried steak. It was now the El Pueblo. He and Norma had to find another place to shop after Bibey's Market became the Maricos Las Islitas pool hall. No place in California had been more thoroughly emptied and restocked than Lamont. Once back then. A second time now. And so it became the province of the town's last Okie to remind people of the rhythms of the West, how the shifts never ended, how one migration simply became the next, a passing in the big night. "We crossed the Colorado, and they crossed the Rio Grande" is how Earl put it. "Other than that, I don't see much difference."

Earl watched his Okie buds depart long before they landed on the obituary pages, selling houses and farms in Lamont and Arvin and moving to nearby Bakersfield or all the way back to the aching earth they had come from. He understood the forces of white flight. He understood the hold that Oklahoma still had on its sons and daughters; many of them had floated back and forth all their lives. But he loved California, loved Lamont, and couldn't see trading in his fruit trees and giant pecan in the backyard for some box in the suburban city, be it Bakersfield or Tulsa. So he stayed behind until everything familiar to him took on a different hue, a different smell, a different sound. Lamont became someplace exotic. His new neighbors didn't speak English, and he felt no need to learn Spanish, not even when his daughter brought home Martin Escobedo for good. He had his routine. Once a week he put on his Levis and Pendleton, size 12 Red Wing boots, and a white Ranger cowboy hat and headed to the Veteran's Hall in Bakersfield to square-dance. Six foot two, pole thin, a big horseshoe belt buckle with "Earl" written in silver—it wasn't hard picking him out from other seniors turning allemande left across the scuffed floor. When the fish derby arrived in April, he and an old friend packed their gear and snaked up the big boulder gorge of the Kern River to Lake Isabella. When all else failed, he had his funerals, one a month sometimes. He was no professional mourner, not like some of them, but he did count on death to keep him in touch with the living. For a man who never made it past the tenth grade, the gatherings at Hillcrest Mortuary were about as close to a high school reunion as he got.

"There were five of us boys who grew up together in the Sunset Camp, the Weedpatch Camp as Steinbeck called it. When you saw the one of us, you saw us all. I was Chewy 'cause I chewed tobacco. There was Donnie Billingsley and Wayne Gibson, who we called Legs 'cause he was all legs, and George Sutton, Suttee, and Gerald Blankenship. We called him Cotton 'cause he had white hair. Now Donnie is dead, and Wayne he's dead, and George is back in Mississippi with Alzheimer's. It's just me and Cotton left, and he don't live in Lamont anymore."

A few months earlier, he had said good-bye to Bill Noble, and then it was Shirley Gibson, Legs's younger sister. On this day, April 17, 2008, he happened to be reading a story in the local section about the Orozco family of Buttonwillow, fined $11,000 by the air district for setting ablaze hundreds of dead cattle and sheep on their farm, when he noticed a familiar smile a few columns to the right. The photo had been taken a long time ago, but it was Rowdy, all right, William Lafayette Dobson, a cousin on his father's and mother's side and one of the older boys who had watched over him at the government camp. They had last seen each other at Shirley Gibson's funeral, and he never spoke a word about being ill. Earl read the eight column inches of type: William "Rowdy" Dobson, born in Scipio on October 6, 1929, operated a Shell service station in Lamont next door to his sister-in-law's coffee shop, moved to Bakersfield in 1981, raised prized sago palms, and hung out with his coffee drinking buddies at Zingos. There wasn't a word about Rowdy's family coming west in 1942, chasing crops from Mettler to Tule Lake, more than a dozen Dobsons, "piece work babies," born in the fields. The obit had left out an entire decade, making it seem as if Rowdy had landed, fat and happy, in Lamont in 1953, fresh from the Army and his marriage to Jean. "I guess they just chose to skip over that part," Earl explained.

He understood, deeper than most men, the desire to forget, even to erase. For all the writing he had done in the annual *Dust Bowl Journal* about his family and their rising in the West, he had never told the story of his father and brothers, the drinking and gambling and busted-up dreams that became their lives in California. He surely never wrote a word about the way it all ended, how his dad and two brothers took their own lives and his third brother, dying of cancer, tried to do the same. They weren't young men but they weren't old men, either, leaving Earl all by himself to ponder the family bent. He had always chalked up the suicides to some smirch in the blood, a strain that by the time it got to him, the fourth son, was diluted just enough to cause no foul. But he couldn't be sure. When asked to explain his exemption, he had no good answer, or maybe the best answer of all. "I guess I like life too much," he said.

That afternoon and evening, after he clipped out Rowdy's obituary, he kept turning over the dates, and the memories attached to those dates, in his mind. A whole decade missing, he thought, the decade Rowdy's people rose up and tore loose from their poverty, the decade a child became a man. The next morning, he and Norma climbed into their Odyssey van—license plate "An Epic," her little joke on Homer—and set out for Hillcrest Memorial Park. Gliding along Weedpatch Highway, through farmland and oil fields, Earl saw a country that hadn't much changed since that overloaded Hudson, lugging the Joads, came tat-tat-tatting down the mountain into the forever valley. Of course, most of the cotton had gone to other crops, and there were no more stick-and-card Hoovervilles flung up on the edge of rivers, the lips of canals. No more Ditch Bank Okies. As for the epithet itself, it stuck to the soil like the spores of some fungus, alive in the same ground where Steinbeck had found it in the winter of 1938. "Well, Okie use'ta mean you was from Oklahoma. Now it means you're a dirty son-of-a-bitch." Earl never forgot that line, or much else about *The Grapes of Wrath*. It was the only book, Bible included, he ever read. He read it thinking he might find in its pages some piece of the sad, stripped to the core man he knew as his father. As it turned out, Tom Shelton and Tom Joad, for all the fate they shared, were different men.

"My dad was Thomas Reuben Shelton, but no one ever called him that. He was Tokay Tom 'cause he liked that Tokay wine, and Weedpatch Blackie 'cause his skin was so dark. His color came from his mother. Grannie Shelton was half Chero-kee. She tried to register as an Indian, get that number and those benefits, but Grandpa Shelton wouldn't let her. He said, 'I don't want my people to know I'm married to a blanket ass.' Hey, Grannie could tell stories about the land rush of 1898. That's what brought them from Texas to Oklahoma, got them their eighty acres."

He was four years old, the youngest of four boys, when he lost his mother to cancer. His father put their log cabin on skids and by horse and mule dragged it ten miles across the prairie to his Grandpa and Grannie's yard. He never did take it off those skids, and Earl would look back at that cabin levitating a foot in the air and figure he had good reason for feeling as a child that nothing much about their lives was fastened and his father, unplanted, was a living threat to pull up stakes at any time. Most of the extended family, sixteen of them, ended up living on those eighty acres. His grandmother couldn't say no to any of her kin. Earl had cousins coming out of every corner. One of his aunts shot her husband because he gave her syphilis, and she and her five children moved in. "She truly did it with a gun," Earl said. "They had no medication for it. We all watched her go nuts."

The land was worn out, not a crop to speak of. His father kept a pack of twenty-seven dogs and hunted at night. Skunk and possum and, if he was lucky, coon. The country was rough rock, and the dogs would come back each morning with tongues lolling out their heads and paws chewed up and bleeding. His father made ten cents a hide, and the meat left behind from the skinning didn't go to waste. "Oh man, when you're hungry," Earl said. "Grannie made a mash with corn meal and fried it, so you almost couldn't taste that possum."

They weren't among the first or even second wave of Okies and Arkies, Texans and Louisianans, to come west. The movement began in the 1920s, before the Depression, before the dust. Some 350,000 migrants already had landed in California by the time the Sheltons came upon the billboard on Route 66, on the road between Tulsa and Oklahoma City. "NO JOBS in California," it shouted. "If YOU are looking for work—Keep Out." His father knew this to be a lie. He knew that at least one California farmer, a Sicilian by the name of Joseph A. Di Giorgio, who grew more fruit than any other man in the world and ran the towns of Arvin and Lamont with the malice and charity of some feudal lord, was hiring men, women, and children. So they kept pushing west, at poverty's pace. In Seligman, Arizona, they ran out of tire tread and money and were stranded for eight weeks until his father earned enough part-time dough to return them to the road. In the pitch dark desert outside Needles, California, a wheel came spinning off their '36 Auburn, and they burned all the pages of a Sears catalog trying to find it. When they finally reached Tehachapi's top and made eyes with the valley below, spring 1941 was in full bloom. "There was nothing like it," Earl said. "End to end, you could see every orchard, every orange grove, every vineyard. Beautiful alfalfa. This was my dad's dream come true. He was a farmer at heart. Hey, it was paradise. We all thought we had landed in paradise."

Paradise paid a penny and a half for every fifty-six-pound bag of potatoes they dug. It paid a dollar and a half for every hundred pounds of cotton they picked. They worked as a crew, the four boys, Charlie, 15, Herb, 13, Ray, 10, Earl, 7, and their father. He was five foot seven, more or less 185 pounds, big barrel chest and a head that sat right on his shoulders. He was a hoss. Pure hoss. Earl couldn't recall him ever getting sick or going to the doctor, but he drank plenty of P. Rooney, 38 percent alcohol, and he carried a thick slice of an Irish potato in his back pocket. Some kind of remedy for rheumatoid. He had been wearing it on the hip for so long that it had petrified. He went to work every morning, that's what he owed them, but how he spent his nights he owed to no one. If they were motherless, there was no feeling sorry. The Weedpatch Camp was full of motherly eyes watching over them. Miss Pitney, who ran the cafeteria, made sure the Shelton boys got one square meal a day. Earl always believed that the only kind of poverty a kid with his belly satisfied really noticed was a want of friends.

And all his friends lived right beside him in a circle of tents and tin cabins. They were like brothers, that pack of five, and it was a good thing because his own brothers grew up too fast. They were so busy making wages—for that first car, first date—that none of them bothered much with school. Herb was married before he was sixteen, Charlie and Ray not long after. "One by one, they left until it was just Dad and me. He'd work all day and hit the bars all night. He'd elbow me at four in the morning. 'Get up and make me a pot of coffee.' After a cup, he'd turn to me and say, 'Please, Earl, don't ever let me do that again.' Eventually he met a woman and got married. But her work ethic was a little shy, and boy did they fight."

Earl met Norma, his one and only, in the cotton fields. It was September 1952, and she was sick with valley fever. Her college plans on hold, she was helping her mother sell sodas and snacks to the cotton pickers. "Oh I caught sight of her, and Lord knows that's the most beautiful woman I'd ever seen." She was a whole lot smarter than Earl and wasn't afraid to work. She could pick cotton with any man. The most cotton Earl ever picked in his life was 629 pounds, her chasing him. Still recuperating from the fever, she could pick 500 pounds a day, if she could pick one. Of course, Earl would die before he ever let her beat him. "We went together for eight months," he said, "and it was the best courtship there ever was."

Earl wound up at the Hilltop oil refinery outside Lamont. They hired him for two weeks, and he stayed forty years. He was a machinist but did just about everything. The rascals never did offer him a salary job. He figured they had him right where they wanted him, working for wages. "When they said 'Frog,' I'd say 'How high?'" His brother Charlie, who had an eighth grade education but one of the keenest minds you'd find, bought the neighborhood grocery store in Weedpatch. Brothers Herb and Ray went into business with their father, contracting equipment and field workers to farmers. They started with a single potato digger and an old tractor, and before long they had twenty-nine cotton pickers—double and triple row machines—and all kinds of cotton trailers. Herb would have made a fortune had he bothered to patent the contraptions he invented. A hay loader twenty years before its time. A new way for the mechanical picker to blow the leaves off the cotton.

His dad and brothers made money and wasted money galore. Drank it down. Gambled it away. Ray was stealing his father blind. One day, Earl looked out the window and there was his father. He never came by the house. Norma was pregnant with their youngest boy, Trent. "How you kids doing?" he asked. "Hey, you know we claimed bankruptcy?" His father talked about it as if it was the most dishonorable thing there was. "I never beat a man out of a nickel in my life," he said. "And I ain't gonna start now." He went home that day and told his wife he was going to kill himself. She tried to reason with him, but he took that .38 and fired a bullet straight over her head. "Get out of here," he told her. She walked out of the bedroom, and there came a second shot, this one in his right temple. He was fifty-eight years old.

Charlie had been keeping three sets of books at his store. One for his wife, one for his bookkeeper, and one for himself. He'd take the cash out of the register and go drink and gamble. Poker at the Smokehouse. His wife finally decided she couldn't take it any longer and divorced him. Charlie would get drunk and break into her house at night. One day, he went by his daughter's place and grabbed a rubber hose from the yard. She asked him, "Dad, what are you gonna do with that hose?" And Charlie said, "I'm gonna water the yard." Three days later, an irrigator found him in an orange grove. About a half mile in. He had stuck the hose into the exhaust pipe, blocked off all the windows with towels, started the car and let it idle. He'd take a sip of wine and then a sip of exhaust. "Knew exactly what he was doing," Earl said. "This was ten years after Dad." Charlie was forty-nine years old.

Ray never stopped being a big shot, cigar in mouth, playing poker and buying the house a drink. One day, when he was still in business with their father, he went to pick up a check from a farmer. It was for $800. Only the farmer had made a mistake and added an extra zero. Ray took that extra zero and caught a plane to Las Vegas. He was gone for eight days, vanished. His wife got so worried she turned him in to missing persons. When he showed back up, the $8,000 was gone. That's the way he did his life, Earl said. He waited long enough for emphysema to get a hold of him. His wife was disabled, and he had no one but Earl and Norma to take him to the doctor. "It was Norma's forty-fifth high school reunion, and we couldn't take him that day," Earl recalled. "And he got mad as hell, a real fit. He took a shotgun and pressed it to his chest and pulled the trigger." Ray was sixty-six years old.

Herb was living in Arizona, retired, when he learned he had stomach cancer. He wanted to do the same, begged Earl to bring him a shotgun so he could do the same. He said, "Buck, if you bring me something, I'll do what the other boys have done." Earl told him, "I can't do that, Herb." The disease ended up killing him. He was fifty-four years old.

And now here was Earl again, walking up the steps of Hillcrest, this time Rowdy's turn. "He was four years older than me. I remember the first time I got drunk. I was thirteen and me and Roscoe and Donnie Billingsley stole Mr. Moore's homemade wine. A gallon of it stashed away under the standpipe. We got to drinking, seeing who could guzzle the most, and I passed out on the lawn of the camp. Ol' Rowdy saw me and dragged me to our tin cabin and put me in my own bed. He was a real person, a hard worker. Well liked. They'll be quite a few Okies inside." He recalled the time when Rowdy and he were standing on the camp lawn, and a real fine-looking girl came walking by. Rowdy said hi, but she just upped her head and walked on, swinging her hips side to side. Then Rowdy shouted, "Speak ass, mouth won't." The girl went home and told her father, and he came looking for Rowdy with a ballpeen hammer. "You bet, he would have killed ol' Rowdy if he'd found him." Earl could still see Rowdy's first car, a '46 Club Coupe Mercury. They had gone down to Figueroa Street in Los Angeles, and the car salesman came right out of the lot and pulled them in from the street. Rowdy drove that car to Tule Lake, up near the Oregon border, in the summer of 1951, to pick potatoes. They lived together in a tent. Earl and Rowdy and a cousin named Jeb Monroe. "Jeb, he's dead also," Earl said. "So many of them gone, I can't even count 'em anymore."

The pews were filled front to back, about 150 people. Small bouquets, big sprays, all in the colors red, white, and blue, lined the chapel's stage. Earl and Norma, to the twang of Alan Jackson's "A Small Town Southern Man," took a seat in the rear. The casket, draped in a U.S. flag, was half open, and there was Rowdy, head all pretty, like he was napping. Earl removed his white cowboy hat and let it rest on the knee of his jeans. He listened intently to the words of the Baptist preacher, a doughy man named Larry Wood, from Scipio himself, who knew nothing, really, about Rowdy or his life. He had gleaned from Rowdy's next of kin a few particulars—his fishing for strikers at Lake Isabella, his raising of sago palms in his backyard, his collection of one hundred Griswold Iron Skillets in his garage—and tried to knit together a remembrance. "Rowdy was honest and very loyal," the preacher said. "He never changed. Since he was a kid, Rowdy was always the same. 'What kind of brother was he?' I asked his brother Sam. 'A good one,' Sam said. 'A good one.'" When it was over, Earl walked up to the pulpit and whispered to the preacher that he had gotten it wrong. Rowdy didn't come to California in 1953. He came a decade earlier, in that caravan of seekers, brave men and women, scared men and women who were bereft of everything but the one thing that made them more brave and more scared, their children, clutching so many snot-nosed children and, shall we say, a dream, the dream of a dream. "The cars of the migrant people crawled out of the side roads onto the great cross-country highway, and they took the migrant way to the West. In the daylight they scuttled like bugs to the westward; and as the dark caught them, they clustered like bugs near to shelter and to water. And because they were lonely and perplexed, because they had all come from a place of sadness and worry and defeat, and because they were all going to a new mysterious place, they huddled together; they talked together; they shared their lives, their food, and the things they hoped for in the new country." The preacher Wood looked perplexed. If he had gotten it wrong, he whispered back to Earl, he meant no harm to history. He had merely taken the facts from the death notice, the obituary written by Rowdy's family.

Earl didn't stick around for the burial. He took Norma to lunch at the Westchester Lanes—the valley's best fish and chips. He told her, as if he had never told her before, that the happiest day of his life was April 11, 1953, the day they became man and wife. He was already making plans to attend the big square dance in Fresno at month's end. After more than fifty years, the club there didn't have enough members left. This would be the last dance. Down the middle, forward and back, circle left, circle right, do-si-do, so many of them gone now, never coming back.

chapter eight | The Great Microbe Hunt

In the weeks and months of the great *E. coli* hunt, as the nation waged a mass purging of leafy greens from its gut, a handful of salad growers from the Salinas Valley, squinting against the light, trudged out of their fields and into the open to share their befuddlement with the world. Coast to coast, hundreds of people had been hospitalized and three were dead after munching on California produce. The contrite farmers facing TV news crews could not explain how the *Escherichia coli* bacterium known as O157:H7 had managed to strike the perfect rows of spinach and iceberg lettuce. Whether by water or wind or compost or wild swine, the vector was as much a mystery to them as it was to the scores of state and federal investigators now ransacking their fields. They vowed not to rest, though, until they personally tracked down the pathogen's source and wiped it clean from the Salinas Valley.

Then one late summer evening in 2006, as the spinach scare was receding and the nation's salad bars began to fill up again, a new threat was found lurking in the refrigerator. This time, a farmer with a far different demeanor showed up on TV. He hadn't shaved in a week, and he wore the look of a man with two hands squeezed around his throat. His name was Mark McAfee, and he grew almonds and ran a dairy in the San Joaquin Valley, one hundred miles south of the spinach fields. Only days before, the state of California had linked five distinct cases of *E. coli* poisoning to his raw organic milk and shut down his operation. All of the victims were children. A seven-year-old boy from Riverside County and a ten-year-old girl from San Bernardino County were fighting for their lives inside the same intensive care unit at Loma Linda University Medical Center. This substrain of O157:H7, investigators determined, was intricately different from the substrain carried by the spinach. In fact, this incarnation of *E. coli* had never been seen in the United States.

Yet rather than dump the milk, the hard-core among McAfee's 15,000 customers in California, who regarded the state's recall as nothing more than a government conspiracy to deny them "living food," raced to pick up the last bottles from health food market shelves. McAfee, the biggest producer of raw milk in the nation—milk not pasteurized or homogenized, milk straight from the cow's udder to a child's mouth with only a cotton sock filter in between—did nothing to discourage them. Before he could bring himself to believe that his cows had sickened anyone, the state would have to find the fingerprints of the O157:H7 subtype in his milk or on his dairy— no different from what investigators had done during the spinach hunt. And that hadn't happened, at least not yet.

"I told the state, 'Have at it. Take your probes and poke into every crevice and crack on these four hundred acres.' The next thing I knew, sixteen state inspectors in their little plastic space suits were taking hundreds of samples. I lifted my kilt for full inspection and they did every test in the book. They tested the milk, the drains, the bottling machines, the milkers, the rear ends of cows, the fresh manure in the pasture, the fresh manure off the udders. Not a pathogen anywhere. No O157:H7. No salmonella. No Listeria. So why am I still shut down?" he glared. "Because they're afraid of the revolution."

In normal times, when food moved from fields to digestive tracts with nary a snag, the California farmer was a man without a face. Far better to turn a raisin into a minstrel, or a Holstein into a hot French-speaking babe, or actress Jane Seymour into a heart-healthy huckster of the pistachio nut than to stick a real farmer on the tube to be his own pitchman. This phantom state of the California farmer was, of course, by his own choosing. There was a labor contractor to deal with his workers, a coop to negotiate his prices, and a commission to tout the antioxidant wonders of his bounty.

Mark McAfee had no intention of hiding behind middlemen. Any complaint about his milk, cheese, or butter went straight to him, and when it came to marketing, he didn't send out one of his cows as shill. Click on the Organics Pastures Dairy website and there was a portrait of the farmer himself, blue jeans and ball cap, kneeling in a field of green vetch next to his wife and two grown children. So when the news media showed up on his farm that September day to document one more outbreak of deadly microbes in a long summer of deadly outbreaks, McAfee gave no thought to hiring a spokesperson. This didn't mean he didn't wince once or twice upon seeing his own wild-eyed image on the nightly news. He imagined that a few people trying to decipher his rant might have even made the connection to "that other McAfee." *Could that be Rodger McAfee's son? Sounds just like the old man. Commie father. Commie son. A thousand revolutions left undone. Wasn't that the same land Rodger used to bail Angela Davis out of jail?* As hard as the son had tried to suppress the traits of his father, the resemblance was plain to see. That loony component of Rodger had been re-fined in his oldest boy so that he wasn't so much crazy as crazy smart. And as much as he recognized the tragic missteps in his father's life and told himself that he wouldn't trace the same path, Mark McAfee was every bit as stubborn as Rodger, every bit as committed to becoming his own heretic on the land.

Like the physicians of the first half of the twentieth century, he believed that raw milk is powerful medicine. Through the chemistry of what is known in the naturopathic movement as probiotics, he had seen his milk cure asthma in kids and irrita-ble bowels in adults. This was no great leap, he insisted, only a return to the root. For thousands of years, man and cow had shared the same space. The farther we as a society had moved away from cows and soil, the sicker we had become. Without our barns and our pastures, we no longer had the "inoculation of the farm" to help us fight off the bad bugs. An emerging branch of immunology was now uncovering the evidence to back up McAfee's belief that raw fresh milk, in all its living, breathing culture, was the vaccine of the farm shipped straight to the lapsed modern city. All those little purple pills to treat old-fashioned heartburn, the belches that the pharmaceutical industry had turned into billion dollar diseases with the acronyms of war (IBS, GERD), were just a glass of raw milk removed from the rubbish heap.

"The industrialized form of agriculture is killing us," he said. "We're chronically ill, we're obese, we're sick and immune depressed. The giants of the marketplace have processed our food to death to extend shelf life and expand distribution. The raw milk revolution grows right out of this disorder. People are saying, 'We don't want factory farm foods. We don't want foods that are sterilized or pasteurized or irradiated. We want real, whole, bio-diverse, enzyme-rich foods from natural sources.'

"We're talking about a massive paradigm shift. It's the difference between killing everything to make it well versus growing good things to counter the bad. It's antibiotic versus probiotic. It's nuking Mother Nature versus trusting Mother Nature."

Microbes aren't some foreign invaders. They exist by the billions in each speck of fertile soil on McAfee's pasture. There are good bacteria and bad bacteria, and it is pure hubris to think we can get rid of any of them, at least for very long. Like us, they have been infused with the spirit of Manifest Destiny, only they are infinitely more equipped to go places we could never think of going. To the ocean vents that shoot 480-degree water from the earth's core, for one. By giving us both disease and our immunity to disease, they give us life. Of the few hundred basic strains of *E. coli*, only a handful actually make us sick. The rest colonize our gut and allow us to digest all that food from the factory farm. Incredibly, the sheer mass of bacteria in all its forms rivals the sheer mass of all other living forms put together. They run the earth. We are their guests. The trick, McAfee believed, isn't to kill the bad ones by sterilizing the farm in the manner sought by the spinach police. The trick is to build up a system, a foundation, where the good bacteria hold the malevolent bacteria in check.

The entire operation at his Organic Pastures Dairy, which sits a dozen miles west of Fresno, is devoted to this notion. To get there from Los Angeles, you have to first trek through the mega-milking land of Tulare County. Metal roofs the size of football fields cover giant slabs of concrete, where tens of thousands of cows, stall by stall, lie confined in their own waste. Troughs of corn run from one end to the other, and immense lagoons brim with shit water. At sundown, when the cows get a little riled up, clouds of fecal dust hang for hours in the air. Car windows shut tight, vents closed, the awful smell still finds a way inside. Only after navigating out of that thickness and finding the clear of McAfee's dairy does it sink in how strange is the scene in front of you:

Cows, not cattle, were roaming a green expanse of California pasture. Hundreds of Holsteins and Jerseys were feeding straight from the land, dropping their excrement into a mix of sweet clover, Bermuda and Johnson grass. The cow pies weren't washed into a concrete sluice and shunted to some open pit to stew in the sun. McAfee left the piles in the field, where they were ground into fertilizer by a millstone of microbes. Because the cows never left the pasture, he had built a one-of-a-kind mobile milking barn that actually traveled to them. "No one has ever heard of 'free range cows,'" he said with a grin. "But there they are. Those happy cows on TV— that's a million dollar picture that the California dairy industry dreamed up with computer animation. It's a brilliant ad, but the whole thing is bullshit. Even cows at big organic dairies live in confined pens and maybe are let out to roam now and then. But these cows—they've all got a name—are truly happy cows."

In the same way that the factory farm bred the pig to fit the precise contours of a slaughterhouse saw, so too was the cow pushed to evolve in a way that defies nine thousand years of history with man. Cows ate grass, not grain, and yet because we turned the Midwest into a subsidized wasteland of corn, corn became the mainstay of the cow's diet. All that starch doesn't go down easily. It so acidifies the cow's rumen that the animal burns up from the inside. In our dogged pursuit to squeeze ever more from each unit of production—the average cow pumps out three gallons a session, 728 sessions a year—we milk the animal until it drops. Doses of antibiotics notwithstanding, cows are becoming sick with pneumonia and mastitis, their milk filled with pus. Creameries don't seem to care because all those bacteria are cooked dead anyway by the machines of pasteurization.

Because of the wear and tear, cows are dying at four and five years of age, half the life they lived in the 1960s. More and more Holsteins are having a difficult time getting pregnant a second time. Frustrated dairy farmers are using the genetically engineered hormone BST as a way to take full advantage of a cow's single lactation. They are milking some cows four hundred days straight and then culling them out for meat. Downer cows, the very Holsteins that pose the most risk to humans for mad cow disease, are loaded into trucks up and down the San Joaquin Valley and transported to slaughterhouses, where they are turned into hamburger patties for schoolchildren. Bowing to the beef lobby (honorable men fully capable of policing themselves), George W. Bush pulled the last of the teeth from the Department of Agriculture's regulatory bite. The ranks of inspectors and vets have grown so thin and the procedures so lax that the trafficking of downer cows has become a new California niche industry.

Is it any surprise, then, that the industrialization of the cow has saddled us with very toxic strains of *E. coli* that have spread from dairy to vegetable field to city? By nature, *E. coli* are highly promiscuous and capable of evolving at the slightest provocation. The introduction of antibiotics made the bacteria more willing to mate outside their gene pool as a means to give their progeny the traits to survive. Scientists now surmise that the rather low doses of antibiotics in dairy herds have failed to kill the hardier strains of the bacteria. Instead, the antibiotics have accelerated the process by which the survivors exchange DNA with their more menacing cousins. This is how *E. coli* came to mate with a bacteria known as Shigella, which hailed from the family that produced cholera. Strains of O157:H7 were actually delivering the Shiga toxin.

High-energy grain feed played a significant role in turning the pathogen into a mobile force of attackers. The slight acid in a cow's lower tract used to be enough to kill the bacteria, which caused no harm to the cow. But with all that corn now in the diet, a cow's upper tract churns a continuous bath of acid. So much acid that the bacteria evolved into a strain that resisted acid. This coat of armor allows O157:H7 to survive the journey from a cow's four stomachs to its lower tract and out its rear end into the world of humans. Here, in a sneeze of self perpetuation, the pathogen finds easy vectors in our food chain.

At Organic Pastures Dairy, by contrast, the cows are given no BST and no antibiotics and live an average of eight years, producing a steady, if unspectacular, two gallons each milking. McAfee almost completely eliminated corn from the feed, choosing instead to supplement his pasture grass with home-grown organic alfalfa. By using the feed that nature intended, he was confident that he had shut off the main valve of O157:H7. In all the years of testing his manure and milk, he had never come across the pathogen. And yet he was always aware that it might be lurking in some corner somewhere. His theory of living systems is predicated on the possibility that the slightest shift in wind or sun or food or water may bring the bacteria his way. McAfee knew that he had just come out of one of the hottest summers on record in the San Joaquin Valley, the summer of 2006 in which tens of thousands of dairy cows had died due to heat stress and sickness.

What if the immune system of his own herd had been weakened just enough that O157:H7 had been afforded a point of entry? What if those sick children had consumed a batch of his milk produced in 105-degree heat of late August that was tainted? Yes, the milk sampled by the state never tested positive for O157:H7. But McAfee knew a strange thing about his milk that made him wonder. It was so mercurial, so alive, that it could change faces right inside the bottle. As a test, he had once infected his milk with a pathogen and then measured its presence over the next several days. Incredibly, the toxin became less and less prevalent each day before vanishing altogether. What if that late August milk, in an act of dissembling, had erased its own O157:H7 fingerprint? What if the pathogen was there when the children drank the milk on day 8 but was gone by day 15, when the state tested it?

McAfee, who had been a decorated paramedic before returning to his father's land and opening the dairy six years earlier, wanted to know for himself. So a few days later, on the morning of September 25, 2006, he got into his red Volvo S80, caked with mud and manure, and headed to Loma Linda, where the toxin produced by O157:H7 had marched out of the stomachs of two Southern California children and into their kidneys. Each one was being kept alive by dialysis.

Tony and Mary Martin didn't come to raw milk in the usual fashion. They didn't drink it as kids on the farm, nor did they have a child with asthma or autism. They weren't followers of naturopathic guru Dr. Mercola or Jordan Rubin's Back to the Bible diet or Weston A. Price's philosophy of unadulterated animal fats. Tony Martin taught government at Corona High and Mary was one of the school's guidance counselors. For years, they had tried to have a child of their own until one day a student, pregnant and not wanting to abort, surprised them with an offer to allow them to adopt her child. They attended the birth and promised to raise the boy with every advantage, including a strict diet with only the healthiest of foods. "We know what the food supply in America is like," Tony said. "We did our best to stay away from all the junk and eat as much organic foods as we could."

Whenever Chris Martin drank pasteurized milk, he got a cold. Even pasteurized organic milk gave him congestion. Every medical website his mother turned to declared the same thing: Milk doesn't produce mucous and doesn't cause colds. Any connection was an old wives' tale. Not until she stumbled onto the online world of naturopathic healing did she find a theory that explained Chris's reaction to milk and offered a remedy. The bacteria killed by pasteurization releases histamines that cause some drinkers to suffer an allergic response. Likewise, pasteurization destroys the all-important enzyme lactase that helps humans digest the sugars in milk. The good news was that lactose-intolerant groups, which include a majority of Asians, blacks, and Latinos, could drink raw milk without a problem.

As Mary Martin kept searching, she came on the website for Organic Pastures Dairy, with its blue skies and green pastures

and cows named Farah and Tasha. "Dairy Foods As Nature Intended. Beyond Organic. The Barn that Mooooves. Join the
Raw-volution!"

The dairy was "family owned and operated and inspired"
and there was the portrait in the pasture of McAfee, his wife,
Blaine, and their two children, Aaron and Kaleigh. She
scrolled down and read the testimonials from customers whose
lives had been changed by drinking the dairy's raw milk and
raw colostrum and eating its raw butter and raw cheese.
Eczema was gone. Asthma was gone. A pain in the knee that
had stolen sleep for years was gone. "Finally, I'm Motrin-
free!" What especially caught Martin's eye were the bacterial
counts that the dairy had put up on its website for all to see.
Every batch of milk was tested, and every batch, it seemed,
measured far below the 15,000 per/ml standard for bacteria
counts. This is the mark for raw milk set by the state of California—a far more stringent standard, by the way, than the one
set for milk destined for pasteurization.

"Top to bottom it was impressive," Mary said. "It was eight
bucks a half gallon, but we had gotten used to spending a lot
for natural foods."

There was one caveat: a government warning label on each
container stated that raw milk poses a risk of bacterial illness,
especially to children and the elderly. But Mark McAfee had a
reasonable answer for that. Some people got sick from raw milk
because they had been so starved of living food that they lacked
the proper flora in their gut to handle it. Raw milk was the perfect source for "seeding and feeding" beneficial bacteria such as
Lactobacillus. A first-time drinker might come down with a bout
of diarrhea but not to worry. "This is rare and should be considered very normal," McAfee wrote. "After all, the intestine

has never seen such an incredible introduction of new and diverse beneficial bacteria and does not have any idea what to do." If McAfee's pitch had the sound of an elixir barker, more and more scientific research, especially in Europe, was pointing to healthy gut flora as a key to a healthy immune system. As for the presence of pathogens in his milk, it was possible but "highly unlikely," McAfee wrote. If this were to happen, "they die off and do not grow" in our milk.

Seven-year-old Chris Martin had been drinking McAfee's milk for only a few weeks when his parents came home from the Sprouts health food store in Temecula with a new container, dated September 10. It was Labor Day weekend, and he drank a glass on Saturday and two more on Sunday and Monday. He was feeling fine and ate a spinach salad and then headed to tae kwon do with his father. After class, he felt exhausted and went straight to the couch with a fever. The next morning, the fever was gone but he couldn't control his bowels. He went to the toilet nineteen times that day, his stools runny and full of blood. Then he began to vomit. His parents rushed him to Kaiser Hospital in Riverside, where a sample of his stool was taken. One of the physicians left orders that until the results came back, the boy was not to be given antibiotics. In the case of O157:H7, the Martins learned later, antibiotics often cause a mass kill of the bacteria and a mass release of the Shiga toxin. Such quantities of the poison could shut down a child's renal system and march right on to the lungs, heart, and brain.

It would take five days before the sample came back showing the presence of *E. coli*. In the meantime, Chris had been transferred to another Kaiser in Fontana. There the doctors, believing he had colitis and not factoring in the possibility of O157:H7, ordered two antibiotics. "His blood was normal and then they hung those two antibiotics from the line and all of a sudden his blood work exploded," Tony Martin said. "The Shiga toxin was accumulating in the kidneys. His red blood cells were popping like balloons."

Chris was transferred to Kaiser Sunset with a condition known as hemolytic uremic syndrome, or HUS. Doctors wanted the Martins to know that their son might need a kidney transplant. Because Kaiser didn't have the capacity to do kidney dialysis, Tony Martin spent the next forty-eight hours demanding that his son be sent to a hospital that did. There was no better facility for a child suffering kidney failure than Loma Linda University Medical Center. "I am an absolute maniac at this point. There is not a doctor or nurse or patient on that floor who doesn't know me," he said. "I am watching my son dying, and this whole bureaucracy is moving in slow motion."

It took another several hours for Kaiser to approve the paperwork to airlift the boy to Loma Linda. Doctors there wasted no time hooking him up to a dialysis machine, but a pool of fluid already had built up near his lungs. "All that toxin in his system and his little chest is pounding. I can literally see it rise and fall, 180 beats a minute. The doctors said he was on the verge of congestive heart failure. 'We need to take over for him now,' they told us. So they intubated him and put him on a respirator, and we waited. For days and days, the world just stopped. There was nothing but me and my son and my wife and that room."

When news of the *E. coli* spinach outbreak filtered in, Mary Martin naturally suspected that the O157:H7 attacking her son's body had come from the spinach salad they had served to Chris a day before he got sick. She called the health food store and told the owners what had happened and asked that the spinach be removed from the bins. Then a few days later, in the waiting room of the intensive care unit, she overheard another mother talking about her own nightmare: Her ten-year-old daughter, Lauren Herzog, had been stricken with *E. coli* poisoning; antibiotics were given, and HUS ensued. The two mothers compared notes. The girl hadn't eaten spinach but had consumed a glass of raw milk from a dairy near Fresno. Organic Pastures Dairy.

The coincidence seemed too much. The Martins now concluded that it was the raw milk, not the spinach, that had sickened Chris. Yet there was a hole in the epidemiology. His stool sample, for whatever reason, didn't show O157:H7, much less the unique substrain that had stricken Lauren Herzog. While state health investigators considered it highly probable that both children suffered from the same milk-borne pathogen, they had neglected to test the raw milk Chris had consumed. And a test of the raw milk Lauren drank failed to turn up the O157:H7 that appeared in her stools. "We were pretty sure it was the milk, but we weren't positive," Mary Martin said. "That's when we found out that two more kids in San Diego had become ill after drinking the same batch of raw milk."

As the raw milk recall began to grab its own headlines, Mark McAfee showed up unannounced at Loma Linda Hospital. A broad-shouldered man over six feet tall, he was wearing jeans and brown leather Clarks when he made a beeline to Mary Martin and introduced himself. He had a nice warm smile on a round face and seemed genuinely concerned. Still, she couldn't help but think he was there on a mission to exonerate his milk. He had a dozen questions. How long had Chris been drinking the milk? Had he showed any signs of trouble before? How much of the new milk did he consume before he got sick? What was the time lag? Before she could give a full account, her husband walked up. Tony Martin hadn't had a good night's sleep in three weeks. "Do you know what it's like?" he asked, standing eye to eye with McAfee. "My son drank a glass of your milk and now he's fighting to live."

McAfee said he did. When his nineteen-year-old daughter was a child, she came down with a rare viral infection that nearly took her life.

"You don't have a damn clue what we've been through," Tony Martin replied. "My son is on a breathing machine, and I can't even communicate with him."

McAfee wanted to tell him about all the children whose lives had been changed for the better because of his milk, but he held back.

"I hope you have insurance," Martin said. "Because I can guarantee you one thing. If it turns out that your milk did this to my son, I'm coming after you. I'm going to own your dairy."

It was late August, a month before the state's recall, and Mark McAfee stood on the back of a flatbed trailer in the middle of an almond grove, listening to a bagpipe player blowing the strains of "Amazing Grace." Only a scattering of family and friends had come to pay last respects to Rodger McAfee, the farmer whose half century of protest against the U.S. government included driving his tractor across California and dumping it into the Pacific Ocean. Among the mourners gathered under a hay loft were three of his five wives—one white, one black, one Latino. There was Andrew McAfee, the youngest of his four surviving sons who now lived in North Carolina, where he sat as the principal French horn for the Raleigh symphony. There was the Mexican boy Rodger had adopted and taught how to fly and play chess and grow organic almonds on a farm he had bequeathed to his Our Land Self-Help movement. There was Richard Chavez, Cesar's younger brother, and Dolores Huerta, cofounder of the United Farm Workers Union. And there were the urban farmers who had just lost their ten acres in Los Angeles, despite the public protests of actress Daryl Hannah. They were now farming a twenty-acre plot in Fresno that Rodger had given them.

His two middle sons, Eric and Adam, once part of the McAfee traveling horn band and the McAfee Balkan dance troupe, were among the missing. They were venture capitalists in the Bay Area who had never quite forgiven their father for allowing his lefty causes to consume the family. He had never quite forgiven them for becoming multimillionaires. "I think if they were here, they'd tell you that their incredible success has something to do with the DNA they got from my father," Mark McAfee said, putting the best possible spin on a family feud that had followed his father to the grave. "But whereas me and Andrew took the good with the bad, my two other brothers just saw the demons."

The eulogies did not attempt to capture his abundant life: How Rodger, the son of two teachers from a long line of Presbyterian missionaries, dropped out of school and traveled to Israel to live on a kibbutz when he was fifteen. For the rest of his life, he would try to graft the communal spirit of Beit Hashita onto the soil of the San Joaquin Valley, a place that could not have been more averse to the Jeffersonian ideals of small plots and yeoman farmers. "He was a visionary with all these ideas and all this energy," said his first wife, Darlene, the mother of his sons. "But his energy could never stay put in one place."

It was on a return trip to the kibbutz in 1960 that Mark was conceived in a wood shack beside the kosher cows. The boy was just a few months old when his father read a book by C. Wright Mills called *Listen, Yankee*, a rally cry for the Cuban revolution. Rodger packed his wife and child into a raggedy Cessna and flew to Havana to offer his expertise to Castro himself. The Bay of Pigs invasion was only a few months past; the Cuban missile crisis just a few months away. Castro's men didn't know what to make of the earnest six-foot-two, 210-pound country boy. They grilled him for six hours about his politics and then took him on a weeklong tour of their farms. When it was over, he wrote a term paper on how they could improve their agricultural practices. They thanked him profusely and ushered him and his family back to their Cessna. Landing in Florida, he blithely told customs agents that they were returning from a wonderful week in Havana. It would take the signature of Attorney General Bobby Kennedy to finally release him from jail.

Back home, he joined an angry pack of agrarians protesting the federal government's refusal to enforce acreage limits on California's big subsidized farms. Even after his parents traded 100 acres near Fresno State University for 1,200 acres on the valley's west side, he acted like no big farmer the UFW had ever met. "When Rodger first came along, it was so early in the game that our own Latino people weren't sure about our union," Dolores Huerta recalled. "No Chicanos from L.A. dared join us. But Rodger gave us his time and his money. He stood alone."

He tried to be a simple dairy farmer, but it only reminded him of how much he missed Beit Hashita. In the summer of 1969, he decided to return there with Darlene and their five sons. They worked their way from one kibbutz to the other, but something wasn't right. Israel had changed. The soul of the kibbutz had changed. The perpetual war with the Arabs, he confided, had turned his old lefty friends into oppressors of the Palestinians. Without telling his wife, he sneaked off with son Mark and traveled to Cyprus to meet with Syrian intelligence officers. When he returned to northern Israel a week later, his kibbutz hat was merely a cover. "He drove to every military outpost that Israel had in the desert. He memorized how many tanks, how many personnel, how many checkpoints and then reported everything back to the Syrians," Darlene recalled. "It broke my heart. The kibbutz. He had lost his boyhood dream."

They were visiting a Greek island when he bought a twenty-foot boat, painted it red, white, and blue and set sail for the promise of communist Albania. That night, somewhere in the Adriatic Sea, they nearly drowned. As Darlene handed over each of her sons to the Albanian rescue crew, she told Rodger that she would no longer play companion to his craziness. With or without him, she was taking the kids back to the farm in Raisin City. He agreed to return with them, and it seemed to work for a while, but only until he found a new brightly lit cause in the Vietnam War. On the front lines of the protest marches, he was the hick who carried a peace sign taped to a Louisville slugger. He was the munitions expert who set off a bomb that blew up a trailer that the military was using to recruit college students.

On one trip to San Francisco, Rodger was so taken with Angela Davis, the Black Panther sympathizer and communist, that he offered to put up his four hundred acres as collateral to bail her out of jail. The next day, the national media came calling, and McAfee showed up on TV sets with cow shit on his boots and a military assault rifle in his right hand. "When *Good Morning America* and the others started knocking on the door, I pleaded with him. 'Rodger, just don't tell them you're a communist. Just tell them Angela deserved the right to bail,'" Darlene said. "But he went right on TV and told everyone, 'I did it for my sister. For my fellow communist.'"

Overnight, the McAfees became pariahs in the farm belt. Mark, a sixth grader, was milking cows early one morning when he heard gunshots strike the barn. Outside the stalls, he discovered that nine of their Holsteins had been poisoned with strychnine. That week, he and his brothers were escorted off school grounds to the shouts of "Good-bye commies." As the death threats grew, real commies from all over the country, armed to the teeth, showed up to help. Rodger put them to work on his dairy and sent his wife and children into hiding. One evening, Darlene and the boys were driving to town when a bale of hay dropped off a farm vehicle and landed in front of them. The brakes locked up, and the car flipped over. David, the youngest McAfee horn player, the star of the Balkan dance troupe, not a scratch on his face, was dead. The mechanic told Rodger that the brakes had been tampered with. He went on believing for the rest of his life that some redneck dairyman had found the lowest way to get even with him.

He spent his last twenty years entrenched in a fight with the federal government over water wells it had dug on his ranch in Merced County—wells that turned up dry. Then one afternoon in late August, just down the road from where David had died, he was cruising in his old Mercedes when a car ran a red light and struck him head-on. A drunken Mexican farmworker, of all people, had killed Rodger McAfee.

His memorial service ended with his adopted son, Miguel, flying a Cessna 152 over the almond orchard and scattering his ashes. He was now part of the soil, Mark McAfee said, part of the microbes. "I spent a lot of years running from him, but look at where I ended up, a maverick just like him, trying to subvert the way we produce our food and milk. In my own way, I'm probably more radical than he was. I may even be more dangerous than he was. Because I know what I'm trying to change."

McAfee didn't know it then, but the forces of nature were about to subvert him. Snaking through his mobile milking barn and into his 1,200-gallon stainless steel tank was a batch of raw milk that shared at least one trait with the tainted spinach: Both had come to life in one of the hottest California summers on record.

"ALERT: RAW MILK NEEDS YOU NOW. Our access to raw milk is at stake!"

It had been eight days since officials with the California Department of Food and Agriculture had pulled his milk from thirty-six Whole Foods markets and scores of smaller stores around the state. What concerned Mark McAfee wasn't so much the $8,000 to $10,000 in sales he was losing each day but what the recall was doing to his dairy's reputation. If state health officials had conclusive evidence tying his milk to the five sick children, they weren't sharing it with him or the public. Frustrated, McAfee papered the Internet in late September with an urgent call beseeching raw milk lovers throughout the state to come to a rally at his dairy.

On the eve of the protest, he had never been more worked up. "This is a war between me and the state. What they're attempting to do, bottom line, is an assassination on our brand.

They're trying to attack us as bioterrorists and baby killers." He threatened a $100 million lawsuit to clear his company's name and restore the honor of raw milk itself. The fact that he even had to call it "raw milk," he said, was a concession to slander. It was milk the way we had been drinking cow's milk for thou-' sands of years. It didn't need the word "raw" placed in front of it. The other milk was the milk that needed an adjective: pasteurized milk.

Raw milk, McAfee said, was never a problem until humans chose to huddle in the big city. New York and Boston, not the dairy farm, had given his milk a bad name. In the mid-1800s, in one of the first industrial-scale mockeries of the principle *what we feed our livestock we feed ourselves*, the manufacturers of whiskey sought an easy place to dump their slop. Next to their downtown stills, they built barns with enough cows to consume vast amounts of used-up mash. Distillery slop made for awful milk, thin and blue, and they threw in all sorts of junk in the bottle to make it thicker and whiter. No amount of chalk, though, could cover up the tuberculosis, diphtheria, and typhoid lying wait inside. Through the 1890s, more than a quarter of the babies in New York City died each year before their first birthdays, many of them due to tainted milk.

Had Louis Pasteur been alive, he might have pointed out that the germ-killing heating process he invented to sanitize beer and wine could easily be used for milk. Instead, the crusade for pasteurization fell to one of the more remarkable men in turn-of-the century America. Nathan Straus was a Bavarian who had arrived in New York City after living in a log cabin in Civil War Georgia. He and his brother had bought Macy's and built it into the world's largest department store. As city parks commissioner and then president of the board of health,

Straus devoted his public life to cleaning up New York's tenements and erecting shelters for the homeless. After two of his children died of bacterial infections linked to raw milk from the family cow, Straus took it upon himself to sell the science of pasteurization to the nation. He opened dozens of distribution depots where families could purchase, for only a few cents, bottles of milk sterilized at 145 degrees for thirty minutes. In the early 1900s, thanks to Straus's hectoring, New York and Chicago became the first municipalities to pass mandatory pasteurization laws. When infant mortality rates dropped by two-thirds, scores of other cities did the same.

This is how the nation split into two milk camps, a rivalry so entrenched that it touched off newspaper wars in places such as Kansas City, where the *Star* (pro-raw) and the *Post* (pro-pasteurization) went toe to toe in banner headlines. Arguing that heat destroyed much of milk's nutritional value, raw milk forces boasted their own formidable voice in Henry Coit, a New Jersey pediatrician whose son also had died from drinking contaminated milk. Raw milk, Coit argued, didn't have to answer for the diseases of slop milk. Solving the problem was no more complicated than weeding out the filthy dairies. In every region of the country, Coit created medical milk commissions staffed by physicians and vets who made sure that dairymen kept to the strictest hygiene standards. Only raw milk with bacteria counts below 5,000 per cubic centimeter earned the "certified" label from Coit's local boards.

Then World War II broke out and all those sons of dairy farms went off to fight. The best milk was now the milk that could ship and hold the shelf the longest. As the balance tipped toward pasteurization, national magazines carried lurid accounts of deadly epidemics skulking across America in crates of raw milk. Though most of the stories turned out to be urban myths, state after state began to outlaw raw milk. By 1986, when a federal court ordered the FDA to stop the interstate shipment of raw milk, fewer than half the states still allowed farm fresh milk to be produced and sold locally.

McAfee's milk never had been illegal in California. Still, he knew he operated with little government tolerance for error. Shadowing him always was the ghost of Alta-Dena, once the largest producer of both pasteurized and raw milk in the nation. The Southern California dairy had shipped millions of gallons of raw milk to hundreds of thousands of loyal drinkers during a half century of operation. Time and again, state health officials claimed the milk made customers sick, only to learn that tests could not definitively link a single illness to the Stueve brothers' cows in Chino. "We had eight trials where plaintiffs claimed that they or someone in the family got sick or died from drinking Alta-Dena raw milk," said company attorney Raymond Novell. "And eight times we won." This didn't stop the state, however, from issuing more than two hundred recalls of the dairy's raw milk. Bankrupted by the bad headlines, the Stueves shut down for good in 1998.

If McAfee had positioned himself as heir to Alta-Dena's high mission, he operated a very different dairy. The Stueves, who didn't allow their herds to graze on pasture, believed that wholesome milk comes from keeping a cow clean on the outside. So they ran the dairy version of a car wash, using thousands of gallons of water and 20,000 towels a day to remove all traces of manure. McAfee tried a similar approach, only to watch his bacteria counts skyrocket. A spotless udder wasn't the point, he discovered, if all that water and wiping simply transferred microscopic fecal matter to the teats. "Now we use very little water and no wiping," he said. Before and after milking, each teat was dipped in an iodine solution. Otherwise, McAfee relied on grass feeding to keep pathogens from harboring in his cows.

In the land of monster dairies, McAfee was a bit player, accounting for less than 700,000 pounds of the 38 billion pounds of milk produced each year in California. The dairy industry could have chosen to dismiss McAfee as a crackpot, but it decided instead to keep a wary eye on him. It was one thing to brag about your happy cows grazing on pasture and quite another to declare that grass feeding actually produced a more nutritious milk. In the mind of the giants, who poured their milk into one shared pipeline, all distinctions in fat or vitamin content were obliterated by homogenization, the pulling apart and remodeling of milk. Any talk of superior quality was viewed as an unseemly brand of nonconformity.

"Milk Is Milk" shouted the billboards made to look like milk cartons along a stretch of Highway 99 through Tulare County, where the dairy cows outnumbered people. "Claims on the outside don't change what's on the inside!"

It wasn't quite the same as leveraging your land to get a commie Black Panther out of jail, but Mark McAfee, in the measure of the milk lobby, was a serious misfit who needed to be stopped.

Three thousand miles away, in the basement of a Virginia farmhouse, Alex Avery, a libertarian with a science degree, was still perfecting his "milk is milk" message. He and his father, Dennis, the author of *Saving the Planet with Pesticides and Plastics*, ran the Center for Global Food Issues. The elder Avery had worked thirty years as a USDA economist before establishing the center as an arm of the Hudson Institute, the neoconservative think tank. Now father and son were teaming up to protect the factory farm from encroachment by McAfee and the other "cranks and thieves" of the nation's growing organic movement. Their billboards, like everything else at the center, had been underwritten by the agricultural behemoths Monsanto, DuPont, and John Deere. If the money seemed unwisely spent—the signs had been planted, after all, in a San Joaquin Valley that hardly needed arm twisting on the wisdom of the mega dairies—the younger Avery was embarking on a much grander plan with his "Milk Is Milk" blog.

"The organic crowd hates me because I'm a scientific debunker of their myths," Avery explained. "The food purists are a lot like a cult. Every time I attack their faith, they want to string me up. And no subject brings more irate mail than when I go after the raw and organic milk folks."

To make his larger point, Avery liked to boast that the heirloom tomatoes he grew in his backyard—using not synthetic fertilizers but manure scraped up from his horse stables—tasted far superior to anything he could buy at the supermarket. But what happened in his garden had nothing to do with real agriculture. Applying organic methods to food production was simply a recipe for global hunger. "Let the organic folks have their niche. But if we're going to double the food supply over the next fifty years, it's not going to be done through compost piles. It going to be done by factory farms using synthetic fertilizers and pesticides."

For Avery, yield trumped everything. This is how he could argue that cows stuck in pens on mega dairies were far healthier than the cows found grazing on McAfee's farm. They were healthier by the only measure that counted in Avery's mind: they generated more milk per unit. And unlike the tomatoes in his backyard and the ones sold at the supermarket, all milk was equal in taste and nutritional content, no matter the inputs. "Organic milk. Conventional milk," he said. "The only difference is the price they put on the carton."

As a scientific debunker, Avery lagged a little behind the science. The dairy labs at Utah State, for one, already had established that the feed given to a Holstein can significantly change the nutritional profile of its milk. Cows that graze exclusively on grass produce a milk that contains nearly double the beta carotene, omega fatty acids, and vitamin content as conventional milk. What goes into a cow, it seems, has everything to do with what comes out. This is why milk sold under the Horizon brand, whose mega dairy cows ate organic corn, was a poor cousin, at least nutritionally speaking, to the milk at Organic Valley, whose cows came from smaller dairies and ate real grass.

"The difference is the feed," Tilak Dhiman, the dairy science professor who conducted the Utah State study, said. "You can raise a cow organically and give it organic feed, and the milk you get is no different than the milk from a conventional cow. But as soon as you give a cow access to fresh grass, the nutritional quality of the milk and the meat greatly improves. Milk isn't milk. Milk and beef is what a cow eats."

None of this came as a surprise to the customers who drove to McAfee's dairy to buy their organic raw milk directly or purchased it from health food stores in Berkeley and Santa Monica or had it delivered across state lines as "pet food" to get around the FDA's ban on the interstate traffic of raw milk for human consumption. Think of that nutrient-rich grass-fed milk, only without the heat that kills all its bacteria, and you have McAfee's raw milk—the milk that cured their children of asthma and their husbands and wives of irritable bowel and Crohn's disease.

Several dozen of these raw milk enthusiasts, some from as far away as Seattle, gathered on a hot summer day in 2006 in front of McAfee's dairy to protest the state's quarantine. All food carries risk, they chanted. To remove the risk, you have to remove the earth. Even then, a vegetable grown, say, in a hydroponics setting, if touched by the wrong hands, can harbor a microbe menacing to humans. For every outbreak of Listeria or campylobacter linked to raw milk over the past twenty years, the protesters cited a similar outbreak traced to pasteurized milk. If the wider public could accept the notion of yogurt or kefir with three or four types of live bacteria, they wondered, why not raw milk with ten times as much good stuff?

"We're getting more orders than ever before from all over the state," McAfee told the crowd. "The government only succeeded in pissing the people off."

Just hours before, McAfee had learned that the state of California had officially lifted its quarantine and he was back in business. Whatever circumstantial evidence tied Organic Pastures to the *E. coli* illnesses—and it was not insubstantial—the fact remained that not a single lab test had traced the pathogenic fingerprint back to the dairy. McAfee chose to see this as vindication, but even as his plastic jugs of raw milk were being returned to the market shelves, the state was quietly building an even bigger case to shut him down.

"I've been working twelve hours a day on nothing but McAfee," said John Dyer, a lawyer for the California Department of Food and Agriculture who was leading the charge.

"Some of our guys don't like raw milk, but I'm not one of them. I grew up on the stuff. So as far as I'm concerned, there's no witch hunt." State investigators in the field were still endeavoring to find the smoking gun, but Dyer was inclined to file the case even if they fell short. "We don't need to trace the O157:H7 fingerprints back to Organic Pastures because we've got other evidence that points to the milk as being the only common factor that made those kids sick. It's a unique strain of *E. coli*, a serotype different than what we found in the spinach. So for McAfee to say these children became ill after eating spinach or some other food is playing fast and loose with the facts."

Early Halloween morning, as the herdsman called out in the dark (part whistle, part Spanish singsong) for the cows to come to the mobile barn for their 5:00 A.M. milking, a team of state investigators and veterinarians took aim at McAfee's dairy. As they parked their Toyotas along a dirt road that sliced through the pasture, here came the headlights of McAfee's Volvo from the opposite direction, heading down the same road that connected his house deep in the pasture to the trailers that served as his office and creamery. "Welcome, everyone," he said, sounding downright chipper for a man whose farm was being raided.

The ladies and gentlemen of the state government team, dressed in moon-walking biohazard suits, quickly set up a lab with four large Igloos, boxes of latex surgical gloves, and Ziploc bags and then waited for the cows to be milked. Holsteins and Jerseys hadn't been bred for their brilliance, only for their prowess as lactating beasts, but the herd knew precisely where and how to move without any fuss. The first dozen cows, heat misting off their bodies, filed in one behind the other and then stepped backward into their respective stalls. The discharge of snot and shit, loose and runny, didn't stop once they were inside. Three milkers, men from Mexico, doused each nipple with a splash of iodine and then slapped on the suction cups. Fifteen minutes later, the milk was sloshing inside a chilled stainless steel tank that would be transported back to the trailers and filtered one time before bottling.

As each milked cow moseyed down a chute and back into the pasture, she was stopped by a state investigator whose right arm was gloved from finger to elbow. He then reached a full two feet inside the animal's rectum and pulled out a fist full of the freshest dung. "You sure this is enough?" he asked the vet standing nearby. "Because if it isn't, I have some more here for you." McAfee stood on the side wearing an ironic smile. "They're frustrated like crazy, hunting for that strain," he said. "What they don't realize is that if it was here, it showed up for just a moment in late summer and was gone. Poof."

It took four hours to extract the evidence from 225 milking cows. The investigators and vets left that day believing that McAfee, in an eleventh-hour cover-up, had administered a massive dose of antibiotics to kill off any evidence of the *E. coli* strain. Their suspicions had been aroused by the runny consistency of the samples, a cow's version of diarrhea that they weren't accustomed to seeing unless a Holstein was coming off a fresh round of antibiotics. What didn't occur to the state team—what seemed plain to McAfee and others who had been around bovines fed a diet of natural grasses—was that this was cow shit the way God intended it to be.

The results of the state's samplings wouldn't be known for another two weeks. In the meanwhile, state officials had informed the FDA that McAfee was breaking federal law by transporting his products across state lines in the guise of pet food. "He's saying it's cat food, but since when do cats eat raw butter," Dyer, the state lawyer, said. State investigators surfing the Internet were convinced that McAfee was using his website to hoodwink the public about the cleanliness of his operation. In some weeks, state labs tests showed, the raw milk at Organic Pastures had exceeded the standard bacteria counts by more than tenfold. "The highest bacteria count we allow is 15,000. His counts have been as high as 200,000," Dyer said. "While it's true that those counts are measuring good bacteria, they can also be measuring bad bacteria, the stuff that made these kids sick."

The high counts, McAfee countered, were rare—only thirty-six times in a four-year period. At worst, the extra bacteria might be causing the milk to sour a little early. "I'm still waiting for the state of California to produce a single test showing that the bacteria in my milk is anything but beneficial. Until they do that, they're just telling me what I already know: that my milk is loaded with probiotics."

McAfee did not waver even as the news broke that two eight-year-olds in San Diego County and a five-year-old named Adam Chafee in Nevada City had been stricken with the same sub strain of O157:H7 that had made Lauren Herzog sick. The San Diego kids and Chafee had been drinking raw milk from Organic Pastures and became ill around the same time as Herzog and Chris Martin. They suffered a few days of diarrhea and vomiting—no antibiotics were given—and recovered quickly. Their parents, some of whom remained believers in the healing powers of raw milk, decided the risk was no longer worth it. "I have family in Vermont who are dairy farmers, and every summer I grew up drinking raw milk," Wendell

Chafee, Adam's father, said. "We visited Vermont this summer, and we were all drinking raw milk without any problems. So when we got back to California, we decided to make it part of our diet. Adam had four or five half gallons before the bottle that made him sick. Nine times out of ten, probably more, that milk is fine. But a small risk is still too big for a child. When we get back to Vermont, we'll still drink it from the family bulk tank. But that's all."

The one link that seemed beyond dispute was that each of the five children had been a newcomer to raw milk, and this common background raised an intriguing question: What if the sick kids had too little time to truly change the flora in their guts, at least to the extent that the good microbes can wage a successful war against the bad ones. If so, then the lesson for people thinking of trying raw milk might be one of diminishing risk. If you can survive that first month or two without ingesting *E. coli* or some other nasty microbe, you are well on your way to building an iron gut that becomes a pathway to a healthier immune system. Even McAfee conceded as much. "There's a chance, especially in children new to raw milk, that they can drink a batch and get sick. And the next door neighbor, a raw milk drinker from way back, can drink the same milk with no problem. In fact, this is what happened in San Diego. But when you talk about risk, how many recalls of beef have we had because of salmonella? This summer alone we've had tainted spinach, tainted iceberg lettuce, tainted carrots, tainted tomatoes. You put a glass of raw milk in front of me, and I'll bet on it every time. That tiny infinitesimal risk is outweighed by a ton of benefits."

Tony Martin watched Lauren Herzog leave Loma Linda Hospital in early October after four weeks in intensive care. It would take another month, eight weeks in all, for his son, arms and legs the size of sprinkler pipes, to follow her out the door. Chris faced an uncertain future. One-third of the children with HUS continue to be afflicted with kidney problems through adulthood. "Five kids. The same batch of milk. The same symptoms. Four of them with an identical pattern of O157:H7," he said. "Am I convinced it was the raw milk? Let me put it to you this way. You could put a gun to my head and say, 'If you don't give your son a glass of raw milk every day, you're a dead man.' I would choose to be a dead man."

In the end, investigators were frustrated in their efforts to find a definitive link between McAfee's dairy and the five sick children, and a sort of truce was declared: The state of California would pay Organic Pastures $15,000 for the milk it had pulled off the shelves, and McAfee would agree not to sue. A few days before Thanksgiving, standing over his bottling line, marveling at the industrial flow of more raw milk sales than ever before, McAfee was certain of one thing: State agents would be back, and so would the feds. "I don't want to spend my life the way my father spent it, fighting America, fighting the government, fighting local conventions. I want to believe it's going to turn out differently for me. But these guys have a political agenda, nothing short of outlawing raw milk, and they're not going to rest until they've got my head mounted on their wall."

chapter nine | Home Front

Ever since the Twin Towers came crashing down and the cloud of jihad fogged the land, the crop dusters swooping low over the San Joaquin Valley have taken on a new menace. Even here, tucked away in the farm fields of middle California, fear has settled into the ground. Harvest to harvest, one year to the next, we watch tens of thousands of illegal migrants stream into our vineyards and orchards to pick the crops. Not a single suicide bomber is ever among them. Still, we can never be certain if it is our vigilance or just dumb luck that keeps us safe.

I am a native of this valley, fine-tuned to its quirks, but it wasn't until the fall of 2004 that I saw the fear take a different turn. On a Friday evening, as the nation debated whether George Bush or John Kerry would better keep the terrorists at bay, I came across a curious piece of theater playing out along the busiest intersection in Fresno. A group of antiwar protestors, no more than fifty by a generous count, huddled on one corner of Blackstone and Shaw, waving "Honk for Peace" signs. On the opposite corner, an equal number of evangelical Christians and right-wing Jews held up U.S. and Israeli flags and shouted "Jew haters" at the peaceniks. It didn't occur to me, at least not that first day, to stop my car and ask how a quiet vigil against the war in Iraq could be seen as an act of anti-Semitism.

At the synagogue where my two sons had gone to pre-school, members had begun to look at each other with suspicion in the weeks after the 9/11 attacks. The more ardent conservatives at Temple Beth Israel were showing up in full military dress to guard the front gates. Their distrust had grown to such a pitch that even the top choice to be the new rabbi had the look of a traitor. In a meeting with temple elders, the unsuspecting rabbi was asked about peace in the Middle East, and he ventured the opinion that perhaps the leaders of Israel deserved the leaders of Palestine, seeing as they both had their birth in terror. The rabbi was promptly shipped back to South Carolina, never to be heard from again.

In an irrigated desert where they had come not to farm the loam but to sell dry goods, clothes, and jewels, Jewish families had blended so thoroughly into the landscape that the old-timers could recall only a single deli that served matzo ball soup a half century ago. Here, halfway between Los Angeles and San Francisco, it was even more true that the temple meant everything. As the town's only Reform congregation, Temple Beth Israel had stood out for decades as one of the few local institutions willing to raise a voice for liberal causes. Back in the 1960s, temple lefties marched with Martin Luther King Jr. and protested the Vietnam War. Though the majority of the synagogue's thousand members still counted themselves as

Democrats, not even the most liberal among them cared to march with Peace Fresno. The war in Iraq was a different war.

The temple's loudest voices now belonged to a committed band of Republicans led by Stuart Weil, a frog farmer who ran the local branch of the American Israel Public Affairs Committee, the powerful Washington lobbying group known as AIPAC. I had first spotted Weil on Blackstone and Shaw at a 2004 rally to reelect Bush, sporting a sign that read "Liberate the Iraqi People." He was a fifty-two-year-old man with braces on his teeth and a ponytail that hung down from a bald crown. The ponytail wasn't born of some midlife crisis. Like a religious man's yarmulke, it was there to remind him of a constant presence. In his case, that presence wasn't God but the Palestinian intifada, the never-ending assault of suicide bombings in Israel that had transformed his whole way of thinking, right down to his views on abortion.

A few days after the street corner rally, I found myself standing inside a corrugated tin shed in the middle of almond orchards and citrus groves, where Weil tended to a million African frogs of the dwarf variety. He was a quirky mix of energies. He refused to talk about the methods he used to propagate more of the Congo species than any other breeder in the world—frogs destined for fish tanks across North America. Yet he had no problem discussing the various means by which he was mating evangelical Christians and Jews in the same united fight against Democrats and Muslims. Tapping into the valley's deep reservoir of Pentecostal churches, a legacy of the Dust Bowl migration, Weil made friends with preachers and ex-military men who were so passionate about Israel that they considered themselves part of an army of Christian Zionists.

I hadn't known such a legion existed, at least not in California's farm belt, until I turned the radio dial one evening to KMJ-AM and made the acquaintance of John Somerville. He was a retired marine colonel who lived in the hills above Fresno and clung to a worldview that had been decreed by God himself: nations that supported Israel received God's blessing. Nations that crossed Israel received God's curse. It was no more complicated than that. He believed the least hint of wavering on the part of the United States—any pressure to remove Jews from their biblical West Bank lands or carve out a Palestinian state—would be met with a hurricane-like calamity. He possessed the charts, natural disasters precisely linked to acts of betrayal against Israel, to prove it.

As I poked around the edges, I began to see that Ground Zero isn't simply a massive crater hole in the earth of New York City. There are smaller pockmarks all across the nation. Strange as it sounds, the war on terror and the war in Iraq were playing out with a particular intensity in the raisin capital of the world. The locals saw no special irony in the fact that we were fighting for our piece of the Homeland Security pie with every bit the vigor of New York or Washington, D.C. If a case had to be made about our region ranking as a place of special needs, we could certainly make it. There was the Fresno factor, for one, our collective ability to master the exaggerated form. Where else in America could you take a twenty-minute drive and go from white suburbia with its brand-new schools, football stadiums, 8,000-square-foot houses, and giant evangelical compounds to the inner city with its gangs and drug-infested neighborhoods to the dead silence of the vineyards in winter's hibernation? No other region produces more milk and more meth than our valley. If you want to examine the burgeoning political power of the exurbs, come here. If you want to study the hand-to-mouth sub-sistence of rural America, come here. If you want to see concentrated poverty unlike any other city—Fresno number one, New Orleans number two—or witness the nation's highest per capita IV drug use, come to our inner city.

We are a strange place that God has walled off from the rest of California. Our separation has the effect of creating the illusion that fear couldn't possibly reach here when in fact the opposite is true. Decades ago, Japanese Americans regarded the Central Valley as a place that might protect them from the fate of the internment camps. They left the cities and joined family members on farms only to discover that fear was even more irrational here. Their white neighbors swore that Japanese growers were placing white caps over their vegetables not to protect the crops from frost but to guide kamikaze pilots toward our military bases. As the trains arrived to take the Japanese to their Arizona camps, their fields were picked clean by the fear mongers. People still referred to the valley as "the other California," and as far as politics went, it is true that we have more in common with Oklahoma City than with Los Angeles. Up and down Highway 99, the church was a kind of state. The mayor, police chief, and city manager of Fresno were all Promise Keeper Christians, men who didn't hesitate to publicly invoke Jesus' name to explain their success or scrub their past clean. Still, there was a farmer's honesty, a rural genuineness, if not naïveté, that came with the land. Unlike people in the big city, folks in the valley didn't bother to disguise their words. In coffee shops and greasy spoons, you could hear them talking about issues such as race, class, and immigration in the most raw and rancorous form, as if they were sitting in their own living rooms with only family around. In this way, the valley became my ideal place to watch the war on terror as it twisted and defined America.

Night after night during the buildup, Colonel Somerville did his best to sound reasonable. To break up any tedium, KMJ added the voices of Victor Davis Hanson and Bruce Thornton, two classics professors at Fresno State who had spent their careers punching holes in the cult of multiculturalism. Since 9/11, their shared premise—that Western culture need not apologize for its superiority—had morphed into a call for war against Islam. Hanson, a raisin farmer whose family had worked the same piece of dirt since 1872, had become the hawk of the month for the Bush administration. Culling the lessons of the ancient Greek battles (the Peloponnesian War took twenty-seven years and that didn't count all the plagues), Hanson's writings had the effect of providing a historical cover for invading Iraq. Vice President Dick Cheney was so pleased that he invited Hanson to his house for dinner. Great nations, Hanson averred, need to wage great wars to remain great. As the statue of Saddam came tumbling down a few weeks later, it was hard to dispute Hanson's boast that no campaign in the history of combat had gone so smoothly and with such dispatch.

The afterglow of "shock and awe" worked on us like a soporific. People, at least most of those who lived in our valley, had lost patience for any details beyond the declaration of "Mission Accomplished." That a real war had replaced the doctored-up first one didn't seem to register. What was happening now in Iraq, the image of one clear madman replaced by a hazy blob of insurgents and tribal lords, was little more than an abstraction. Yes, we had our own Navy air base rising out of the cotton fields, and poor kids from valley towns were signing up in strong numbers. If the SUVs were any clue—

their rear ends magnetically dressed in "Support Our Troops" ribbons made in China—the war was everywhere. And yet it was nowhere. No homegrown kid, no Okie or Hmong or Mexican or Armenian, had come back in a flag-draped casket. You don't belong to a place, William Saroyan once said, until one of your family has been placed into its ground. I wondered if maybe the same could be said of this war. It wasn't going to be our war until we had given up one of our own. As spirited as those rallies tried to be on the corner of Blackstone and Shaw, they had the sound of something hollow. Then on a cold November morning in 2004, as President Bush was counting the "political capital" he had earned in his reelection and was making plans to spend it, I picked up the *Fresno Bee* and saw the news: two local boys from Buchanan High, best friends, had died in Iraq. On the eve of a massive battle to overtake Fallujah, the two Marines went out on a late-night mission that ended with a bomb blast.

Growing up in a valley where so many dreams were hemmed in by the fields, Jared Hubbard and Jeremiah Baro had the fortune of being suburban boys. Their fathers weren't migrant farmworkers following the crops but a policeman and a loan officer who chose to live in Clovis, an old rodeo town where masses of white people from Fresno had fled. Here the schools were big and gleaming and the athletic teams among the finest in the state. But after graduating from high school, the football star and standout wrestler seemed unsure what to do next. One thing was certain. Wherever one would go, the other would follow. It was Jared and Jeremiah, spotter and sharpshooter, right up to that November 3 night in Ramadi, when an insurgent detonated a hidden bomb from afar. It must have hit just so because of the eight Marines walking along both sides of the road, only two—Hubbard and Baro—were killed.

The funeral was held on Veteran's Day at a Catholic church in Fresno. The mourners included a congressman, state senators, the mayor of Clovis, the mayor of Fresno, scores of law enforcement officers from both cities, hundreds of family, friends, and teachers, and a dozen boys, now men, wearing their old Buchanan lettermen's jackets. Past the strawberry fields and new housing tracts, in a cemetery that faced the Sierra, seven Marine riflemen fired three times each and a bugler played Taps. As their parents held tight the U.S. flags handed them, Lance Corporal Hubbard, twenty-two, and Corporal Baro, twenty-one, were buried side by side.

Not much separated the two fathers in those first weeks. Jeff Hubbard put up a new flagpole along the front walkway of his two-story stucco house, flying the U.S. flag on top and the Marine flag on the bottom. He was a big, stout man with a balding head and owlish glasses whose impulse was to hunker down and say, "Heck with the world. Let me grieve." His wife, Peggy, believed it was important to share Jared's story, so as a favor to her, he put aside his distrust of journalists and welcomed me into their home. He had only one condition: "Ask anything you want about Jared, but please don't turn him into a political pawn. I know this war is controversial and we just came through a nasty election. But I'd appreciate it if you wouldn't. We supported his decision to join the fight."

As they recalled that decision, they couldn't help but wonder how things might have turned out had they raised their children with the goal of college. Whenever the subject of higher education came up, their three sons and one daughter pointed to members of the extended family who had found success without a college degree. Jared, the second son, showed the most interest and aptitude in school. In fact, his parents were under the impression that he was about to enroll at Fresno City College when he walked into the kitchen that day and blurted out that he was thinking of joining the Marines.

Jeff Hubbard had policed the neighborhoods of Clovis for almost thirty years, but he rarely played hard-nosed cop with his kids. Even when Jared came home with his eyebrows and tongue pierced, the disappointment he registered was a quiet one. This time, as Jared talked about feeling adrift, his father cautioned him. Take the military test and see how you score. If you score high, you can become an officer and skip the front line. Jared ended up acing the exam, but he still insisted on being a grunt. "How could I put my foot down?" said Jeff Hubbard. "He wanted to serve his country and go in with his best friend." As we sat in the kitchen, I didn't realize that their youngest son, Nathan, nineteen, had been listening to our conversation. He was lying on the couch just a few feet away, a guitar at his side. Suddenly he popped up, a smallish figure in a wool beanie and poncho, and gave a tug to his Abe Lincoln beard. He was out of school and between jobs, and he sensed an opening with his parents. "I've always thought about joining myself," he said nonchalantly. "I'm just not going to talk about it right now."

Peggy, a petite woman with a bob of blond hair, had been sitting quietly beside her husband. The few words she had spoken had come in a raspy whisper. Suddenly her voice grew loud and clear. "No. No way, Nathan. You're not going."

He took off the poncho and lifted his T-shirt sleeve. Above the bicep, he wore a tattoo of three interlocking ravens. The three brothers—he and Jared and the oldest, Jason, an undercover cop—had gotten the same symbol of Celtic fidelity etched into their arms. "There's lots of things popping in my head. Go there and honor him and maybe a little vengeance pumping through my blood too," he confided. "But I can't do that to my family. I can't put them through that."

I thanked them for their time and drove a mile or two down the road to an apartment where the second father, Bert Baro, sat in front of a plasma TV he had hung high in the living room, a day and night flicker of Fox News. He was a small pit bull of a man who grew up fighting on the streets of Manila. As he watched the tube, he popped another beer and shook his head at the spectacle of the antiwar protestors. The fight against terror was a matter of will, he said, and communist doubters were breaking our will. "People say communism is dead in America. Bullshit. They've just changed their coats. How do you defeat the most powerful nation in the world? You do it from the inside."

His wife, Terry, knew where he was going and tried with a half smile to stop him. "Bert . . ."

"I don't care how advanced we are. I don't care how Christian we are. We have to get medieval with these people."

I wondered if what he had in mind was the treatment of inmates at Abu Ghraib prison.

"Abu Ghraib?" he sneered. "That's not medieval. Yeah, we shamed them. So what? Yeah, we ran them around naked. So what? We didn't go chopping their hands off. We didn't go around castrating them."

"That's medieval?"

"Yeah, that's medieval. That's the difference."

"Do you think we have the appetite for that?"

"When they start exploding bombs here, we're going to be just like every other human being in the world. We're going to act with the exact same methods. And I'm kind of hoping that bomb comes. Because I want to wake people up."

How much of Baro was a show intended to flush out the "liberal" reporter in me, I couldn't say. I saw no need, though, to tell him that my father's father, Aram Arax, had been one of those communists in the 1940s. In a valley hostile to organized labor, it took little more than a subscription to the *Daily Worker* to turn a citizen into a subversive. Hoover's men followed him to bookstores and a Labor Day picnic along the Kings River. "Subject Aram Arax was observed eating a shish kebab sandwich," one entry read. Every year, FBI agents in Fresno wrote headquarters in Washington asking if they should continue to follow him. Every year, the bosses wrote back, "Yes." They followed him for forty-five years, until he was blind and wearing diapers.

I didn't bother telling Baro that my own lesson in jihad had come at an early age, at the knee of that same grandfather. Jihad is what brought my family to America. Grandpa was fifteen years old when the government of Ottoman Turkey began a genocide against its Armenian population. As he hid in an attic in Istanbul, more than a million Christian Armenians were being slaughtered by Muslim Turks and Kurds. "Where is your Jesus now?" they taunted, ravaging Armenian villages that had preceded their arrival by eight hundred years. As a kid, I wondered why my grandfather wrote his poems in Armenian and shouted his obscenities in Turkish. No word, he taught me, was more vulgar than *giaour*. It was the reason Armenians paid a special tax to the Turks and couldn't bear arms or testify against a Muslim in court. It meant infidel.

Years later, I was rummaging through his desk when I discovered a half-written poem, "I Am Looking for a Turk." It described his longing to find a Turk with the courage of poet Nazim Hikmet, a Turk who might be willing to stand beside him at the Martyrs Eternal Flame in Soviet Armenia. Never finding that Turk became one of the great disappointments in my grandfather's life. A month before he died, I sat in the kitchen while Grandma made plans for Thanksgiving dinner. As she ran down the menu list, I innocently asked who was going to carve "the turkey." Grandpa rose up out of his mist and began to shout. "Turkey? Turkey? You give me five thousand good men and I will kill those bastards." He had forgotten that a secret army of young Armenians had tried to do just that in the decade prior, assassinating Turkish diplomats and bombing airports around the world. His fighters for justice had been hunted down by the FBI as terrorists.

What the genocide and Red Scare had in common, I reasoned, was fear. The pashas had manipulated the Turkish masses, selling over and over the notion that Armenians were conniving with Russia to destroy the Ottoman Empire. The communist peril, the enemy within, the dominos toppling in Southeast Asia, they too were rooted in the peddling of fear. Years later, when the CIA finally conceded that all those terrifying assessments of the Soviet military buildup had been embellished by the Armageddon brigade—men such as Richard Perle, Paul Wolfowitz, and Richard Pipes—it was too late. We had spent billions of dollars trying to keep up with a phantom.

None of this history offered much help, of course, on that morning of 9/11. My wife, an early riser, had come into our bedroom and awakened me. "You're never going to believe what's happening." We sat, like everyone else, transfixed by the images on TV. We even let our three-year-old son Jake watch. On the third day, he grabbed his Legos and built two towers that he took to bed with him at night. A week later, sensing a new fear at Temple Beth Israel, I insisted that my wife pull Jake out of the preschool. I reminded her that we weren't Jewish and had chosen the school mostly because it was safe and nurturing.

"You're nuts," she said. "We're in Fresno. They're not coming here."

"How do you know where they're coming?" I shot back. "This is America's greatest farm belt."

When the flag went up—on car antennas and back bumpers, on T-shirts and lapels, on houses in our neighborhood that never flew the flag before, so many flags that my eleven-year-old son Joseph wanted us to fly one too—I figured it was patriotism finding its most facile form. "The flag has become a cliché," I explained to the kids. "And the easiest thing to hide behind is a cliché." I knew it was more troubling than that when I began to see the mega churches selling flag and cross as one image, the blanket that swathed the crucified body. Driving along Highway 99, I came upon a car with two flags flapping in the wind, one from each window. As I pulled closer, I could see that it was a family of Sikhs inside, the father and sons wearing their customary turbans. The flag wasn't just a declaration of loyalty for them. It had become a convenience, the cheapest and most direct way of proclaiming to the anti-Muslim bashers in our midst, "Don't mistake us for them."

I had watched in a kind of numbed state as we made our way, fugue-like, through the spring of 2002. The war on terror was doing strange things to the place where I grew up, but it took me a long time to discern any pattern. Had anyone asked me back then whether some larger movement was afoot, whether the religious and secular were merging and odd new alliances were forming out of fear, I wouldn't have seen it. Over the next two years, right up to the Bush-Kerry election, I hardly had a clue that some kind of communal madness was playing out in my backyard.

Our biggest manufacturer, Pelco, didn't punch out tractors but video surveillance systems that guarded some of the most important buildings in the world, the Twin Towers among them. President David McDonald, the born-again son of a Virginia preacher, was now richer than our richest farmer. If his two-hundred-acre estate in the foothills above Fresno seemed like déjà vu, there was good reason. McDonald had stolen the design of the spiral staircase from *Gone with the Wind* and the pool from Hearst's castle. As for the elaborate security system that watched over Eaglecrest, documenting all but the domestic violence, he alone took credit.

In the weeks after 9/11, McDonald sprang to action like no other CEO in America. He published a special glossy edition of the company magazine filled with the heroism of the fallen and built a grand memorial garden outside his office window. For the dedication, he chartered five jetliners dubbed Hero 1, 2, 3, 4, 5 respectively and flew out more than a thousand firefighters and cops from New York City—nonstop booze the whole way. They stumbled past 403 empty chairs, each adorned with a yellow rose and the name of a fallen comrade, and huddled at the base of the memorial. Then the same firefighter who had raised the American flag over Ground Zero three months earlier raised a super-size version over Pelco. That night, McDonald treated 4,200 guests to a steak and scampi dinner under heated tents at Eaglecrest. What began as shared prayer ended with firefighters and their new friends from Fresno fornicating on a hillside studded with security cameras. The bill for the weekend was $1 million. As PR goes, it was a steal. McDonald was working to sell a new camera, one that could recognize the face of a terrorist, a lens that would be tucked into untold corners across America. "We learned September 11 that we cannot take freedom for granted," he said. "We are more vulnerable than we ever thought."

Under the cloak of the Homeland Security Act, Sheriff Richard Pierce created an antiterrorism unit that knew exactly where to set its sights: the ragtag members of Peace Fresno. The group's leaders were so hungry for new recruits that they didn't think to question the earnest young man named Aaron Stokes who showed up one day eager to assist. For two months, Stokes sat through planning meetings and passed out fliers at antiwar rallies, and then he vanished. The peace activists didn't see his face again until several months later when the *Fresno Bee* ran a story about a fatal motorcycle accident. The photo of the victim was a dead ringer for Aaron Stokes. Only his name was Aaron Kilner, and he was a sheriff's deputy assigned to the antiterrorism unit. What was an undercover cop doing at the cookie and green tea socials of Peace Fresno? The sheriff played coy. "For the purpose of detecting or preventing terrorist activities, the department may visit any place and attend any event that is open to the public."

If Peace Fresno was feeling beleaguered, it had less to do with the cops than with the Jewish community, a onetime ally. Democrats at Temple Beth Israel had not only abandoned the antiwar cause, but a few were joining a pro-war movement under the banner "United We Stand with Israel." At a kickoff rally at Woodward Park, Jews and Christians stood hand in hand on a grassy knoll, looking a little like bride and groom at a shotgun wedding. For the Christians, the union made all the sense in the world. Returning biblical Israel to the firm grasp of Jews, after all, was a vanguard of the Second Coming. The Jews, on the other hand, were willing to take their chances on Armageddon as long as the Christians supported Israel in the here and now. Leading the rally's battle cry that day was an old Nazi hunter and retired Israeli general named Shimon Erem, who had driven up from Los Angeles to address the crowd. "Jesus tore down the walls of hatred which separated gentiles and Jews and made us one," he shouted. "And anyone who fights against this defies Jesus Christ. We are one, and we are going to remain one."

As if on cue, a few dozen peace activists came marching up the hill, only to run into a wall of Israel supporters. Scott Hawkins, who would later describe himself as a "Mormon Zionist," noticed a sign in the crowd that called for a Palestinian homeland and went belly to belly with the biggest peacenik he could find. "You want to get past me?" he said. "I guarantee you there will be blood." As the protestors retreated, his wife, Sandra Duffy Hawkins, a district director for the California Republican Assembly, began to shout. "Jew haters. Jew haters. You're just like Hitler."

Among the speakers that evening were Somerville, the retired Marine colonel from the radio, and Hanson, the classics professor at Fresno State. More than the others, Hanson had glimpsed in 9/11 a shot at taking his modest scholarly career into the stratosphere. He had grown up in a family of left-leaning Democrats; his mother, Pauline, a respected judge, was the first woman to sit on the state appellate court in Fresno. It didn't seem to matter that the closest Hanson had come to war himself was a dormitory skirmish over the Vietcong flag while he attended UC Santa Cruz in the early 1970s. Or that he had made his name in the valley not as a war hawk but as a cranky farmer who wrote poignantly about the struggles of the yeoman agrarian. The weather, the insects, the price of a ton of raisins—he now had traded in all those vicissitudes for a new certainty.

"In the post-9/11 world, there is no margin of error when dealing with a madman," Hanson had said. "Saddam Hussein is more dangerous to the civilian population of the United States than was either the more formidable Hitler or Tojo. Saddam simply requires a dozen sleeper agents with suitcases of anthrax to pollute with microscopic spores multimillion-dollar high-rises, killing and infecting thousands."

In the new world envisioned by Hanson, a reality he rendered in hyphens (Islamic-Fascist-Wahabist-Jihadist terror), the aims of the United States and Israel were no longer merely compatible. What had been a strategic alliance in the 1990s was now something much more sacred. Since 9/11, the two countries, much like Christians and Jews, were brothers in the same war against Islamic fundamentalism. What was good for the United States was good for Israel; what was good for Israel was good for the U.S. All lines were symmetrical lines. All roads ran parallel.

Hanson had signed up, media agent and all, with an ascending movement of neoconservative writers and policy wonks in Washington and New York who were pushing the notion that the United States and Israel could be made safer by waging preemptive war in the Middle East. The movement's core consisted mostly of Jewish Americans and a few white Christians who called themselves, with no small hubris, the Project for the New American Century. Having been relegated to the sidelines during the Clinton years, they regarded the three thousand victims of 9/11 as their "I told you so."

Professor Hanson's new pals had written to President Bush in April 2002 to press this new reality. "Israel's fight against terrorism is our fight. Israel's victory is an important part of our victory. As you have said, every day that Saddam Hussein remains in power brings closer the day when terrorists will have not just airplanes with which to attack us, but chemical, biological or nuclear weapons." The designers of the New American Century—William Kristol, Richard Perle, Norman Podhoretz, Eliot Cohen, William J. Bennett, Martin Peretz, Richard Pipes, Frank Gaffney, Reuel Marc Gerecht, Kenneth Adelman, Rich Lowry, Gary Bauer, Stephen P. Rosen, Donald Kagan, and R. James Woolsey—would soon have their war.

In January 2003, as the Marines prepared to storm Baghdad, the beaten down ranks of the valley's antiwar movement gathered in a small hall at Cal State Fresno. They had come to hear a USC linguistics professor talk about her previous life as an Israeli peace activist. The theme of Hagit Borer's lecture, though hardly novel, still had the capacity to wound. Zionism and democracy are incompatible, she declared, and Israel's occupation of the West Bank and Gaza Strip is akin to apartheid. "If you say a Zionist state cannot be democratic, you're immediately branded an anti-Semite," Borer told the crowd. "And if you're like me, you are branded a self-hating Jew."

A small, frail man, who had been fidgeting in the front row, began to boil. Then he blurted out in Hebrew, "Yes, that's what you are."

"Excuse me?" Borer said.

"Self-hating Jew. Yes. That's what you are."

Borer decided to ignore the man and shifted her eyes to the middle of the room. She tried to take a question, but he persisted. He stood up and began shaking his finger, not at Borer this time, but at Vida Samiian, the dean of arts and humanities. It was Samiian who had organized the event with her husband, Sasan Fayazmanesh, a Fresno State economics professor. The couple had grown up in Iran and protested side by side against the Shah while students at UCLA in the late 1970s.

"It's all your fault," the man shouted at Samiian. "It's all your fault."

Samiian could hear the indignation in his heavily accented words, but she had no idea who the man was. John Krebs was a former county supervisor and Democratic congressman who had taken on corrupt developers and subsidy-grabbing farmers before his zeal sank his political fortunes in the late 1970s. His father had been an early Zionist who left Germany before the Holocaust and settled amid the Arab villages of British-controlled Palestine. When it came time to kick out the British and build a Jewish nation, Krebs joined an underground movement that rejected the terrorist tactics of more radical Jewish groups. After living a half century in the United States, he didn't support the policies of Israel's Likud government and no longer gave money to AIPAC. But the suicide bombings in Israel had bled away any sympathy he had for the Palestinians.

"Palestinian terror, Osama bin Laden terror, I don't see any difference," Krebs would later explain. "I see it as an anti-Western mentality."

In this respect, Krebs's logic was no different than the logic of the neoconservatives with whom he otherwise vehemently disagreed. The reality was that neither the PLO nor Hamas had ever staged an attack against the United States, either here or abroad. The lecture series at Fresno State tried to advance the idea that Arafat and bin Laden were different, that the Palestinian grievance against Israel was about dispossession and statehood, not Al Qaeda–like jihad. But for a speaker such as Borer even to imply that a Palestinian suicide bomber carried in his heart a different—daresay more authentic—cause was too much for even a Jewish liberal such as John Krebs to hear.

Krebs left the lecture intent on taking action against Fresno State. This is how he came to join forces with Stuart Weil, the frog farmer who headed the local AIPAC. With a stack of angry e-mails backing them, Krebs and Weil appealed to top university officials. President John Welty couldn't very well cancel the remaining antiwar speakers or bar a planned Palestine Day. So in an effort to mollify the Jewish community, Welty freed up $7,000 to bring in a speaker with a very different view: Daniel Pipes, the Middle East scholar who had written, among other provocations, that "all Muslims, unfortunately, are suspect." True to his word, Pipes had started his own Campus Watch website that drew up a list of university professors he believed were terrorist fellow travelers.

Samiian and Fayazmanesh feared that inviting Pipes wouldn't be enough to quiet their critics. Sure enough, the neocon muckrakers began digging. High-speed grapevines buzzed with postings about "Cal State Palestine" and the two Iranian professors who, depending on the blog, were either Marxists or fascists or worn-out paranoids. No neocon was more vigilant about such dangers than David Horowitz, a 1960s liberal with Berkeley bloodlines who now ran FrontPageMagazine.com. Horowitz had a flair for outing un-American professors whose commie bios were just a mouse click away from the pictures of big-breasted coeds selling "Hippies Smell" T-shirts. Horowitz wasted no time sending a reporter to Fresno, or at least a reporter whose computer could google the word "Fresno." The reporter found out that a little old lady, two decades dead, had bequeathed the money used by the university to pay for the pro-Palestinian lecture series. Dots connected to dots. Enough dots to declare that Mrs. Hamish (it apparently didn't matter that her actual name was Harnish) was tied to the National Lawyer's Guild. In the 1930s, according to FrontPageMagazine.com, the guild was funded by Joseph Stalin. Seventy years later, it had links to Saddam Hussein himself.

"One wonders if the farming community of Fresno, California, is well enough represented by this local community of Marxists and anticapitalists who run with and support the terrorists of the PLO," the FrontPage story read. Before it was over, Professor Fayazmanesh would find himself on Sean Hannity's website, beneath the headline "Terrorist Prof at California State University, Fresno."

In the summer of 2005, as the news from Iraq shifted and folded, growing more optimistic and then more dim, I drove out to Clovis to visit Jeff Hubbard, the father of the slain soldier. He greeted me at the door in a "U.S.A. United We Stand" T-shirt and sat me down, as before, at the kitchen table. We talked about how football had shaped three generations of both our families. My younger brother was the head coach at our alma mater, and Hubbard was looking to get back to the Pop Warner ranks. His only hesitation was knowing that he'd be overwhelmed with old images of coaching Jared and the rest of the Garfield Cubs. "I don't want to forget my son, but I don't want to keep him so alive that I'm sitting here all day long in the past," he said.

He hadn't been to the cemetery in months even as his wife, Peggy, went every chance she could. She worked long hours at Vons arranging floral bouquets for customers and extra ones for the grave. When he did make it out there, the flowers always told him how long it had been since Peggy's last visit. The flowers almost always were fresh. He would stare into the headstone at a son who had grabbed the best features from both of them and try to think of something to say. "When I'm saying stuff, it comes out like I'm talking to him. But I'm not really believing he's hearing it. I know I'm just talking to myself. I don't want to say that death is the final thing. I want to say I don't know if it is or it isn't. 'Gone.' I don't know what that means."

His wife had rejoined one of the mega churches on a long avenue of mega churches near their house. He was an agnostic and found no comfort behind the compound walls. "I mow the lawn. I weed the flower beds. I feed the fish, take care of the dog. Then the day is done."

He understood how Bert Baro, the father of his son's best friend and companion in death, had found solace in taking the hardest, pro-war line. It didn't work for him. Night after night, as he replayed the explosion that took Jared's life, sifting the details still coming in from his platoon, adding to them details of a war growing more costly and bloody by the day, he began to ask questions that he couldn't share with Peggy. Did we sacrifice our son for a worthy cause? Was the desire to see that Jared died for something simply a formula for other sons dying for nothing? Honoring the dead by insisting on more dead was the worst kind of selfishness. And yet for all his doubt, he had a difficult time believing that the fictions that had gotten us into war made the war itself a lie. "I keep thinking that maybe there's a reason for going to Iraq that our leaders just couldn't share with us," he said, shaking his head.

Over the next two hours, Hubbard and I wrestled with every aspect of the war. At first, it felt wrong to push the father of a dead soldier, and I apologized for treading on his grief with questions of politics, questions he had forbidden in our first meeting. But he said grief had done a funny thing. He had lost his patience with the Bill O'Reillys of the world, the way they spun their questions into loyalty oaths. More and more, he was turning to lengthy articles and books to find answers. He was searching for some ground, he said, that neither the left nor the right had found. He was searching even as he told himself that such a truth could never be grasped by the father of a dead soldier.

On the fireplace next to the kitchen table sat his son's Marine Corps portrait, photos from the 2000 championship football team and the watch that, despite the bomb blast, was still telling perfect Iraqi time, eleven hours into the future. As I watched him steer from the clearness of that death to a place where everything became muddled, it occurred to me that I was not just seeing the real face of war but hearing the honest debate we never had as a nation. Watching his struggle, I felt as if I owed him a good look into my own struggle, first as a citizen and then as a journalist whose feelings about the war also had grown more confused over the past year.

I told him I was not unlike so many other Americans who had been reluctantly moved to the side of war when Colin Powell went before the United Nations and detailed the evidence of Saddam Hussein's arsenal and ties to terror. That the evidence turned out to be false changed everything for me. The fiction wasn't Bush or Cheney lying about the contents of a particular intelligence report. Rather, the way they picked and hyped only the intelligence that fit their desired end was a malicious disregard for the truth. The whole process became the lie. "The administration didn't want a real debate," I said. "Given the climate of 9/11, they knew that fear trumped everything. So they exploited our fears with mushroom clouds and biological clouds and clouds from our own crop dusters."

He agreed that it wasn't simply a matter, as the hawks would have it, that because those reasons turned out to be false, we could replace them with more valid reasons and, ex post facto, feel good again about the war. By not vetting those other reasons when they should have been vetted, before the war, we had lost the ability to vet them altogether. He wondered if his son would have volunteered to fight, if Americans would have even backed the invasion, if the air had been sucked clean of fear and the idea of exporting democracy had been the only imperative. Tragically, there was no way of knowing because he could never return to those prewar days and have that conversation with Jared. "I never believed that Saddam was connected to Al Qaeda. And I think the war is probably creating more terrorists than we're killing right now," he said. "But when you're facing that kind of evil—people who want to destroy your way of life—you have to put down the gauntlet somewhere."

Each night, after he stripped away the rhetoric on both sides, he was left with one question above the rest: "Can we win this war? I don't mean the hype about exporting freedom. I don't mean the simplifications like 'we're fighting over there, so the terrorists aren't here.' But is it doable to stabilize that country and help the Iraqis choose a better system? Not our system but their system."

The more I listened, the clearer it became that for Hubbard, at least, the war had moved beyond the falsehoods of Bush and Cheney. It was now bigger than their ability to screw it up. He understood how the lies had brought their own just desserts, turning so many Americans against the war. Yet all the talk of bringing home the troops reminded him, oddly, of the Golden Gate Bridge over San Francisco. "Once you start, you don't stop halfway over the bay just because it's costing more than you projected and men have died along the way," he said. "If the bridge can be built, you need to reach the other side."

Before I left, I asked him about his youngest son, Nathan, who had seemed so lost during our last visit. Was he still talking about honoring Jared by going to Iraq? "I haven't heard anything about it lately, and I kind of want to leave it alone. It's hard to hold Jared in the light we hold him and then turn to his little brother and say, 'If you choose the same path, it's wrong.' But he also needs to know that life has changed since Jared was killed. This family is not the same. This war is not the same."

I stepped inside Stuart Weil's giant tin shed expecting to hear the chirp of 1.2 million tiny frogs singing Congo love songs. As it turned out, a radio blared ranchero music, and the frogs did their chirping low and mostly at night. "Welcome to frog nirvana," Weil said, shaking my hand. A female in the wild produced 50,000 eggs during her lifetime. Maybe two or three turned into frogs. Here, amid a labyrinth of open-air tanks, pumps, heaters, and filters, with no predator to elude except an occasional pathogen from the sky, that same female gave birth to 50,000 tadpoles. A crew of Mexican workers made sure the big boys, the breeders, got what they wanted.

This left plenty of time for Weil to pursue his real passion: building a Christian-Jewish bulwark.

Since the launch of the war on terror, the balance of power inside Temple Beth Israel had shifted. Weil and his group of right-wingers had taken over important posts and were using the synagogue's email list to promote lectures by gay-bashing Christians and pro-war Jews. Barry Price, a former temple president, was among a group of liberals not sure how to respond. A few years earlier, during a High Holiday address, Price had stood up to Weil's group, voicing his concerns about their strong anti-Muslim sentiments and lust for war. "Some of the right-wingers got up and walked out," Price recalled. "I was labeled a traitor. I was called ignorant and naive."

The Iraq war had put temple lefties in a bind, raising questions they weren't keen to address. Was the decision to topple Saddam Hussein motivated in part by America's devotion to Israel? Was it relevant that several of the neoconservatives who pushed hardest for war inside the Bush-Cheney administration—top defense aides Paul Wolfowitz and Douglas J. Feith and consultant Richard Perle—were Jews who had worked for years to marry the security concerns of the United States and Israel? "It was the one topic that people were most afraid to touch," Price said. "The progressives in the temple had ceded the field to the vocal Jews on the right. We were cowed into silence."

Sitting in his office in his khakis and tennis shoes, brow furrowed and head cocked, Weil now wondered if I might be betraying some prejudice for even raising the question that a love for Israel had motivated Jewish war hawks in the Pentagon. He rejected the notion as a new version of the old canard that Jews operate with dual loyalties. "Is that how your liberal friends talk when you're together?" he asked, eyes narrowing. He stopped short of calling me an anti-Semite, if for no other reason than our seventeen-year-old daughters attended the same high school and were close friends. He believed the term "neoconservative" had become a liberal code word for "Zionist." If the neoconservatives got us into war, the translation read: "The Jews did it."

I was hoping Weil could tell me why merely raising such a question smacked of anti-Semitism. Why couldn't Americans question our relationship with Israel when it was that relationship that caused so much of the Arab world to hate us? Was it anti-Semitic to suggest that our union with Israel made us less safe at home? Even the 9/11 Commission, for all its timidity, had found that our siding with Israel in the Palestinian conflict had made us a target. Yet delving into the matter somehow landed you on the Anti-Defamation League's list of Jew haters.

Weil sat still and nodded here and there as I dug in deeper. To argue that Wolfowitz, Feith, and Perle weren't Zionists or that their desire to protect Israel didn't color their advocacy of the war was to ignore their own resumes. Feith, for one, had been honored by the Zionist Organization of America for being a "pro-Israel activist." This was just a few years before he set up the rogue operation in the Pentagon to gather the intelligence to sell the war.

I told Weil he needed to look no further than his own AIPAC to see how high the stakes had become. Federal agents suspected that top AIPAC officials, in the months leading up to the war, had been spying on behalf of Israel. The FBI probe was connecting back to the very unit headed by Feith and his gang.

"You really think that AIPAC is a den of spies?" he asked.

A part of me whispered to myself that it was best to leave it there. This wasn't the time or the place. Our encounter, after all, was occurring several months before two professors would author a controversial study on the Israel lobby and its role in pushing for the invasion of Iraq and a similar attack on Iran. That study would grow into a national book and help bring the subject out in the open. Weil and I had no such cover. We were dealing with a topic that, at least for a Gentile pressing a Jew, seemed verboten. Even so, the air in frog barn remained friendly, and Weil followed every wince with a smile that told me we were still okay.

I explained that the federal probe into AIPAC was hardly the first time that neoconservative zeal for Israel had become a matter of national security. Among the more fervent hawks urging President Bush to remake the map of the Middle East were Stephen Bryen and Michael Ledeen. Both men were founding directors of the Jewish Institute for National Security Affairs (JINSA) and had joined the powerful American Enterprise Institute, the pro-Israel think tank. Back in the late 1970s, Bryen had to resign from the Senate Foreign Relations Committee staff after the FBI learned he was showing classified documents to his friends in Israeli intelligence. In the early 1980s, Ledeen used his own close ties to Israel to act as a middleman in the arms-for-hostages deal with Iran, raising questions at the National Security Council about which country's interests (Israel or the United States) he was serving. Two decades later, Ledeen had emerged as a shadowy figure in an elaborate scheme to link Saddam Hussein with yellowcake uranium from Niger—one of the principal falsehoods that led to the war.

"Where are you getting this stuff?" Weil asked, his face now twisted into a perturbed knot. "It's all so conspiratorial."

It had been Bush and Cheney who made the call for war, he said, not any Jewish advisers whispering "Zionist commands" in their ears.

He was right, of course, that the vice president and president didn't need much cajoling when it came to Israel's security as a consideration for war. Before he took office, Cheney sat on the advisory board of JINSA, fully committed to its mission of cementing strategic U.S.-Israeli ties. As for Bush, his attachment went even deeper. His reverence for the Jewish state was the reverence of a born again.

Weil swiveled his chair around and turned his attention once again to his computer screen, sending one missive and then another into the Christian-Jewish ether. He said he was a man now free from the straitjacket of Temple Beth Israel. As chairman of the new local chapter of the Republican Jewish Coalition, he no longer needed the rabbi's blessing to promote his own causes. "I do everything now under the RJC. You'd be surprised how many prominent Jews support me with money but anonymously, because they don't want to risk the wrath of the liberals."

He had hope for me, as well. Just as the second Palestinian uprising had opened his eyes, he predicted a similar awakening would one day strike me. "You're not beyond saving," he said with a cackle. With a rescue in mind, he invited me to the 2005 Friend of Israel award dinner in Fresno the following night. At the previous year's dinner, my first as his guest, Weil had promised to double the modest crowd of one hundred by "tapping into the evangelical community." As I walked into this year's affair, I could see that Weil had more than made good on his vow. Preachers and flocks from several big churches were spreading chopped liver on crackers with their new Jewish friends. Weil got up and enumerated the Republican Jewish Coalition's recent events: a pastors' forum and a speech by the evangelical former mayor of Fresno and a retreat with Bridges for Peace, a Christian Zionist group whose members believed that Hurricane Katrina was divine judgment on the U.S. for pushing Israel to resume talks with Palestinians.

Weil then introduced Bill Manders, the old KMJ radio host who had experienced his own awakening a few years back when Weil and friends sent him on a paid trip to Israel. Manders recalled how he had returned from his stay with a newfound appreciation for the challenges the Jewish nation faced. Iraq, as far as Manders was concerned, was only the first front in a much longer war. "When is someone going to step forward and say, besides me on the radio, why don't we drop a nuclear bomb on Iran and blow them off the face of the earth?" The crowd applauded and shouted, "Yeah."

The time had come to honor this year's winner of the Friend of Israel award. It was none other than John Somerville, the short, well-built, old Marine colonel I first encountered on the radio three years earlier. He thanked Weil for the honor and made it plain that his passion for Israel came from the Bible but extended to the realms of politics and war. "A true friend is not knocked off his perch when Israel is denounced for rough treatment of the Palestinians or when an Israeli politician is found to have his hand in the till or when Mossad carries off a dirty trick," he said. "A true friend of Israel does not have to rework the ethical arithmetic in order to reckon whose side he is supposed to be on. A true Christian Zionist has the requirement of faith to prefer the blessings of Israel to all others. To be a Christian Zionist is to be an unconditional lover of Israel and of the Jewish people."

Was it our vigilance or dumb luck or some beautiful combination of the two that kept us safe? For the longest time, that's how I had framed the question. As the anniversaries of 9/11 came and went, each one marking another year without incident, I began to consider another possibility. Maybe the threat wasn't such a threat, after all. Maybe it had been hyped and sold like everything else. The calculation that we faced a greater risk simply because 9/11 had happened always struck me as wrongheaded. If thousands of migrants from Mexico were finding a way across the border, why hadn't a single suicide bomber made the same trek? If our vigilance was as shoddy as Hurricane Katrina suggested, why not a single hijacker? Could it be that those nineteen men wielding box cutters were the best and brightest that Al Qaeda had to offer? Could it be that they got lucky that day, and we were now assuming a risk based on a once in a blue moon reality? Maybe the question of terror is like sizing up the threat we face from the San Andreas fault. Pressure builds and builds over decades until an earthquake finally erupts. Energy spent, the fault goes silent again, but for how long? In those periods of slumber, we do not alter our lives measurably because of fear of the Big One. We have found a way—call it healthy denial—that allows us to live with the awareness that the earth beneath will surely rupture again. Is it so hard to find that same perspective when it comes to terror? Then I turned on the TV and saw the foaming anger that the war in Iraq has unleashed in the Muslim world, and I went to bed understanding that we have made more real the very threat we feared. None of our vigilant deeds, none of the civil liberties we have so willingly tossed to the cause, matter in the wake of what we ourselves made true. The Muslims on the tube are insane, the war is a war of cultures, the war is a war without end.

In the fall of 2005, a news release from the Los Angeles Army Recruiting Battalion office came over my fax machine. It was headlined "To Serve Our Country," and it announced the recruitment of two more valley boys into the military: Nathan C. Hubbard, nineteen, and Jason R. Hubbard, thirty-one. Their situation, the release noted, "is a special one." Jason and Nathan's brother, Jared, had joined the Marines in December 2001. During his second tour of duty, Jared "gave the ultimate sacrifice." The statement included remarks from the man who had recruited the brothers. "Words can't describe what they are doing," said Darren Mayes. "This is the true meaning of service to our country."

I hadn't talked to Jeff Hubbard in several weeks, and the news knocked me back. Not only had his youngest son acted on his bravado and signed up, but so had his oldest boy, a sheriff's detective with a wife and newborn son. The next day, I drove out to Hubbard's house and found him alone watching a Monday night football game. There was nothing diminished about him, not his firm handshake or clear eyes or his sheer energy for talking. Because he had a philosophical side, I didn't expect to find him in any sort of despair. Nevertheless, I wondered how a man who had lost so much and whose feelings about the war had grown more conflicted could possibly have given his blessing to two more sons signing up for Iraq.

Since the day the three Marines came knocking at the door ten months ago, he told me, he knew that one son, if not both, would follow in Jared's footsteps. "They didn't tell us, 'Okay, we're now driving over to the recruiter's office.' But we knew it was coming. Remember those conversations in the kitchen with Jared. Well, we had those same conversations with Nathan and Jason."

A part of him wanted to tell them no, that they had already paid their price as a family, that if they were trying to honor their brother or pursue some silly notion of revenge, it wasn't enough of a reason to go. It wasn't enough to put him and their mother through a new round of torment. Instead, he sat immovable in his chair, dulling his words, finding a certain wisdom in his belief that it wasn't right to hold one decision captive to another. What happened to Jared was its own world. Call it bad timing or bad luck or perhaps it had been God's will. Each son, though, deserved his own hearing, apart from anything that had come before or might come after. So he listened as Jason and Nathan talked not about revenge but about duty in a time of war.

He told me this stoically, his face filled with resignation, as if the course of action of those around him, those he wanted to protect, was out of his control. "How do you try to change someone's mind when you know that changing their mind is all about you, not them?" he asked.

This didn't sound right to me. It sounded like either the most selfless gesture or the most selfish one. We had built enough rapport over the previous year that I decided to challenge him. "Jeff, this isn't some tattoo or tongue piercing. You tell them, 'You're not going to do this. You're not fricking doing this to me or your mom. Jason, you've got a new wife and baby. You've got a great job catching drug dealers. That's your service to the country. And Nathan, you go to school and honor your brother because you know college was his dream. That's your service.' You just don't go leaving it up to them."

He flashed a knowing grin. "When you decide to draw a line in the sand with your kids, what do you do if they decide to disobey you? Where do you go from there? Did we tell them how we felt? Of course we did. 'We would rather you wouldn't do this. We have given a lot. You don't need to do this.' We said it all."

"But you didn't put your foot down. The prerogative of the father."

"No. They told us they wanted to join to serve their country. For no other reason than it was the right thing to do. And I'm not going to let them do the right thing? The thing they believe in? I couldn't do that. I couldn't let my questions become their questions."

I pointed to the Army recruiter's press release. "Now they're using your sons for propaganda."

"I realize that. 'One brother dies and the other two follow him into war.' It bothers me. But at the end of the day, I still believe in this war. I'm not happy with the manipulations. I'm not happy that some of those manipulations still continue. But I have to believe we're trying to make that part of the world a better place. I still hold out hope that in ten or fifteen years I can walk the streets of Baghdad as an old man and say my son died for something. He really died for something."

It was late, and he followed me out to the car. We shook hands, and I thanked him for not losing his patience, for keeping his door open to me and my questions. He leaned over and stuck his head into my half-open window. "There isn't one clean answer," he said. "You don't think I know that?"

Maybe I had come for one clean answer, I wasn't sure, but who was I to push him anymore? It was enough that his struggle, set against the carnival of patriots and prophets and fear mongers, was private and real.

I took the long way home that night, past the cemetery where the two boys were buried, past the strawberry fields being turned into suburbia, past the university where all eyes were now fixed on the Bulldogs' Top 20 football ranking. I reached the corner of Blackstone and Shaw, where the pro-war demonstrators hadn't staged a rally in months, and headed west toward Highway 99. In the vineyard rows, the grape growers had set down their bunches to make raisins, praying that rain would hold off for another three weeks. In the distant sky, the crop dusters were making another late-night run over the cotton fields. As I made a last turn toward the old fig orchard where we lived, the valley rested silent, almost at peace.

POSTSCRIPT

On August 22, 2007, a Blackhawk helicopter carrying Nathan Hubbard and thirteen other infantry scouts crashed just before dawn in an oil-rich province 180 miles outside Baghdad. His brother, Jason, had been in the air only thirty seconds when he was told that the Blackhawk, part of his Army platoon, had gone down. As his helicopter hurried to the scene, he could see the scorched earth and broken pieces, as well as the frantic rescue workers. He tried to tell himself that his youngest brother, the free spirit that the Army could not break, wasn't dead. But all fourteen of them were dead. They held his funeral at the same church in Fresno where they had held Jared's. Every seat, as before, was filled. Two years and nine months had passed since that day, and 2,589 more American soldiers had been added to the list of dead, but the pastor's words had not changed. "He gave his life serving the cause of freedom in the global war on terrorism." The sun through the stained glass spilled into the sanctuary, and the recorded voice of John Wayne recited a verse about the day an American boy became a man. "I promise I'll go back to school when I've met my obligation, to you, my friends, my girl, my school, and most of all this nation," the Duke chanted. "We've got to keep the Old Glory flying." I was facing the front row, standing alongside the other Peeping Toms, but I couldn't bring myself to look Jeff Hubbard in the eye. Our last encounter, the way I had pushed him, now came back with the echo of judgment. A major general who had come to pay his respects on behalf of the secretary of the Army rose to present the soldier's Bronze Star to his parents. "Your son was willing to go the distance with any task," he said. Peggy's face was impassive, a mask of tranquility, and she could barely utter "thank-you." Jeff stood straight and tall, wearing that same quiet look of resignation. I walked out of the church unsure how such a man, who lived without the benefit of sedatives, no pills or religion, drew his solace.

The route to the cemetery had been lined with red, white, and blue ribbons tied to lampposts and trees. A little after noon, in the 107-degree heat, the crowd gathered at the gravesite. Of all the brothers who had died in Iraq, only these two brothers, side by side again, had been brothers in blood. The bagpipes played, and the last Hubbard brother held his salute until the final note. The honor guard of seven fired three rounds each. Were these the same riflemen? The funeral attendant released twenty-one white doves. Were these the same doves? An Army officer stood over the coffin, folded the U.S. flag, and handed it to Peggy Hubbard. Was this the same flag?

chapter ten | Confessions of
an Armenian Moonshiner

For all our big city lust, we still tell time by the farmer's clock. There is a season of bloom, the race between the wind and hail and the blossom trying to set into bud. There is a season of harvest, though we plant so many different crops that it never seems to end, from the earliest stone fruit in April to the latest table grape in October to the citrus of February and March. Every season comes with its own uncertainty, but no season causes more civic fret than late summer, when the raisin farmer sets down his bunches of Thompson seedless grapes in the sun and prays that no rain will fall upon them. We all pray with him, even though by that time the sky is as foul as the sky in China and every third kid is on an inhaler, and a little rain would be God's blessing. We are standing near the halfway point in our proud progression from raisin town to another Los Angeles, yet to be caught muttering any supplication but the supplication of a farmer is still a thing of sacrilege. If we are no longer farmers, we once were farmers and might be again, if we listened to our hearts.

Between the family vineyard and me stood a grocery store and a bar, a generation of waywardness. While I didn't exactly plot my return to the land, I did the best a farmer's grandson could do with a third of an acre in suburbia. Each April, I reclaimed another chunk of hardpan beside the swimming pool, planted my vegetable garden, and thinned the buds on my fruit trees. And each January, the season of fog, when the pair of grapevines outside our bedroom window went from rank to bare, I waited for the call from my brother-in-law, the one real farmer still left in our family. "The mash," he'd say in a clandestine voice, as if a crime had already begun. "It's ready."

We had been making moonshine in the San Joaquin Valley for as long as we had been growing fruit. Each immigrant group swore by a different mash. The Armenian and his raisin. The Slav and his plum. The Italian and his blood-red Alicante bouschet. My great-grandmother Azniv, who died when I was seven, was a moonshiner. She kept her bottle of *ooug-he, raki,* white lightning flavored with anise, in a burlap sack two feet under the earth of the vineyard where my father was born. Abscessed tooth, infected ear, sore throat, sinus headache, 105-degree fever, dandruff, you-name-it was alleviated by a slap or swish or rub of her sauce. My father's brother, Navo, never forgot a flu that knocked him flat on the ranch in Depression time. "I was aching head to toe, and she took that raki and rubbed it over my body, wrapped me in a towel, and put me to bed. The next morning I woke up and it was gone. I had sweated the whole thing out. Some years, when our crop came in short, we were too poor to afford a doctor. That damn raki became our medicine."

Back in Prohibition, the uninterrupted farmland between Bakersfield and Stockton ranked as one of the "wettest" regions in the country. Local boosters tried to put it off on all those old country grandmas and grandpas cooking their home brew, but Prohibition agent Tom Niceley, a valley boy, knew better. He devised a sting where he hid in the rear compartment of a black roadster that belonged to a moonshiner turned informant. As the moonshiner pulled up to the houses of top police officials and handed over his bribes, a crumpled up Niceley took notes from under the hood. It was 1924, and he couldn't believe his ears. Three immigrants from Italy were running a bootlegging syndicate that extended from the vineyards and fig orchards of the west side to downtown's Whiskey Row. They were clearing an incredible $120,000 a year; half the profit, five grand a month, was going to the Fresno Police Department. The scandal grabbed headlines coast to coast, but only one of the thirteen police officers was convicted—for a minor offense. Prohibition lifted, and the Italian kingpin went into the ice cream business.

As the old immigrants died off, moonshining went the way of blacksmithing. My grandfather Aram was too preoccupied with Soviet Armenian politics, and my father and uncle too busy with sports, to bother with the custom. Somewhere in the move from the Rolinda ranch to the Peacock Markets to Ara's Apartments nightclub, the family still got lost. I was in my early forties when I decided, maybe as a way of reaching back, to try my hand at moonshining. In the winter of 2001, I followed my brother-in-law to a vineyard outside the town of

Fowler, into a wood shack behind the main house where the farmer, one year dead, had kept an old copper still. There we pledged an oath of secrecy with four other cooks, all of them Armenian farmers, and produced our first batch of raki. I didn't play golf or fish, and it was about a sublime a day as I've ever spent with a group of guys. We stuffed our faces with Armenian cheeses and sandwiches made of *peda* bread and the thin slices of cured sirloin we called *basturma*. We passed around a box of wooden matches and took turns igniting the clear liquid that came drip-dripping out of the coiled line. If the flame burned blue, we had proof of its potency, proof of its high proof. The wet, cold air went straight through us, and standing for hours over a contraption that utilized only a single burner for heat was no way to keep warm. The real fire was in the bottle, the first batch at 160 proof and the second batch at 140 proof and then a new run where we poured the weaker stuff back into the mash and cooked it again and out came something very close to the supernatural. No heat moved faster from tongue to chest, and each shot—two, three, four— went down smoother than the last. Farmers were a suspicious, guarded lot, but this was a buzz that gave great lubrication to tender, metaphysical musings about life and death and the moral quandaries each of us felt in an age when man had never been more attached to machine, never been more alien to himself. For a whole afternoon in the world, as Saroyan might say it, farmers became philosophers and journalists poets. We waxed even as we peed, unzipping our pants right there in the vineyard beneath a big orange tree. That night, I slept like I had never slept in my life. I dreamed like I hadn't dreamed since I was kid. Was this how opium felt? I had no intention of

waking up but when I did, I could sense no headache, no slug-
gishness, just a sensation of peace that soaked through my entire body. In the pantry, I stashed an old vinegar bottle filled
with second run and over the next several months practiced
great resolve in bringing it out only on the most special occa-
sion. I figured it would last me a year, until next January's
cook. Mysteriously, I ran dry in midsummer. Only later would
I discover that my wife, dreams coming up short, had been
sneaking a little shot at bedtime.

For the sake of production, my brother-in-law ditched that
leaky copper still and replaced it with a gleaming stainless steel
pot and top designed in the shape of the Tin Man. Not only
did it distill twice as much mash each run, but it was far less
likely to blow up in our faces. We transported the behemoth
from place to place, even cooked a couple of winters in a backyard in the middle of suburbia. The plan for 2008 was to return to tradition and find a setting deep in the country. I
waited for the call from my brother-in-law, Avedis as he will be
known in this story, a tale in which the names of the cooks
have been changed to the names of their paternal grandfathers. January passed. February passed. March passed. We
were two-thirds finished with April, on a Friday the week before our annual and very solemn commemoration of the Armenian genocide, when he finally gave the word.

"The mash is done. We're taking the still to Suren's new
ranch. It's right along the river. Sunday about eleven."

"Should I bring some food? Mezza?"

"I had a lamb slaughtered and cut into chops," he said.
"Khachig has been marinating them for three days. He'll do
the barbecue and cook the pilaf."

"Sounds great, but we've never done it this late. The fog's gone. How are we going to throw off the scent of the revenue agents?"

He knew I was only half joking. "Hell, we've been cooking for the past two years in my backyard. You're the one who complained that there was no poetry back there. Suren's vineyard is along the river. It's perfect. No one's going to find us."

It was true that it was spring, that the canes on the vines had gone from vacant wood to new green, and we could drink and eat lamb in the sun and pee big streams (little streams) in the rows. But as a matter of ritual, the fog was not an easy thing to give up. Maybe there weren't any more Tom Niceleys prowling the plain, but as a student of moonshining lore, I liked to believe there was still some risk involved. Unlike our cousins in the Ozarks, we had no hills to hide in. The valley, its hog wallows, had been leveled flat by the Fresno scraper more than a century ago. Even in the country, forty acres apart, neighbors had a pretty good notion what busied neighbors. The prudent moonshiner, looking for cover, waited for the fog. Ours happened to be no ordinary vapor. "Tule fog," we called it, the curse of the Yokuts, their get-even for the white man draining Tulare Lake. *You've taken our inland sea, its fish and turtle, and turned it into cotton fields. The lake may be gone, but its mists will haunt you forever.* Each winter, as the great cloud descended, people had to be reminded all over again of its peril. In the zero visibility, they drove like monkeys down Highway 99, the deadly pileups sometimes numbering fifty and sixty vehicles.

If Avedis was all right with letting the season of fog pass and cooking the mash a good ten weeks late, then the rest of us would surely follow. He was the most precise and careful man we knew. Among farmers, he was considered one of the finest table grape growers around—his Flames and Crimsons bigger, crisper, and more colorful, if not always tastier, than the rest. The agriculture he practiced was a different one than our grandfather's. His reputation lived and died by the timing of the decisions he made in April and May—when to apply the sulfur, when to spray for mites, when to administer a first, second, and third shot of gib (gibberellin), agriculture's version of the human growth hormone. By removing the seed from the fruit, we remove its testicles, so to speak. The vine no longer produces the gibberellic acid that naturally thins every bunch and sizes and colors each berry. To replace the seed, the grape grower applies a synthetic version of the acid in a series of methodical sprayings from spring to summer. Gibbing, they called it. Avedis believed that a single small error in his coverage— one drop too heavy or too light, one day too soon or too late— was enough to change everything. Problem was, he wouldn't know how badly he had screwed up for another ninety days, when his mistakes stared up at him from the bottom of a box. "I deal in the parts per million" is how he described his life. We relied on Avedis to plan and conduct our cooks with the same sort of precision. At harvest's end, he saved five or six trays of raisins that he had no intention of eating. He dumped stems and all into a barrel, filled it with a few buckets of water, threw in five pounds of sugar and eight packets of Champagne yeast and closed the lid. Each week, with his considerable nose, he measured the ferment. Only when the raisins bloated into something that looked very much like pinto beans did he pronounce the mash ready.

As I drove out to the river that day, so clear that the Sierra popped up out of the asphalt just beyond, I couldn't help but

304 WEST OF THE WEST

puzzle over the strange turns in my life. A year ago, at our last cook, I was a married man, the father of three children living in or near the nest, a senior writer for the *Los Angeles Times* magazine, a Little League coach, and a backyard farmer. Now my marriage and career, which began in the same month in 1981, had ended in the same month in 2007. It made for the nice round number of twenty-five years, half my life. As such tales often go, mine was tedious and more than a little self-serving, and there was a temptation to trace both losses to the same cause. I had written a story in the spring of 2007 about the continued denial of the Armenian genocide, a story that editors on the national desk were considering for page one. The day before it was scheduled to run, the managing editor decided to kill it, for no other reason than I am an Armenian. I would have not believed that a man so savvy could have put forward such a sorry rationale, but he told me himself in a note. I had never had a story spiked or even gutted, and I saw no choice but to fight it. My wife, who came from a family of hardy Dutchmen, saw my public challenge to the newspaper—and its certain fate—as part of a "martyr syndrome" that afflicted not only me but my entire tribe. As it turned out, I left the paper with an apology from the publisher and a monetary settlement, but the breach at home could not be repaired. And so I moved into a condo a few blocks away, without enough open dirt to grow a tomato, and was soon joined by our seventeen-year-old son. Meanwhile, our daughter took her third year of college from Berkeley to Buenos Aires, and our youngest child, a ten-year-old boy, split his time between households. The lines my wife drew were not to be trifled with. While the house was still half mine, I was told not to trespass. When I heard that the fruit trees had set heavy, I sneaked into the backyard and tried to thin as much as I could. One of the peach limbs had broken off from all the weight, and my Meyer lemon tree was nearly dead from lack of water. In the garden, I could see that little Jake had taken my grandfather's hoe and was preparing the ground for a planting, not understanding that the window for summer vegetables had already passed.

I turned north on the other side of Dickenson and headed straight to the bluff, slowing down to let a 1931 Ford Model A pickup, candy apple red, perfectly restored, take the road in front of me. Closer up, I could see that it was Suren showing one of the boys the lay of his new land. "Almost there," he shouted out the window. "Follow us." His smile was easy, and he spoke in a Dust Bowl twang that sometimes set down on the tongue of an Armenian or Swede or Japanese living in the valley. In the cut of the vineyard, he had remodeled a sweet little ranch house, and behind the house stood a large metal shed he had filled with all his collectibles: a dozen motorcycles of various makes and vintages, autographs of legendary race car drivers and famous actors with a passion for speed, a guitar signed by B. B. King, pinball machines, antique signs, and a 1935 Ford two-door sedan resting high above on a rack. The shed was Suren's playroom. Indeed, the whole vineyard was his hobby. He did not have a farming bone in his body. His father had run a string of liquor stores. Suren built from scratch a top-selling commercial sign company. And yet he had found himself a restless man trapped in a fancy subdivision behind gates. His wife, who had saved his life once before, understood his discontent. As harebrained as his plan had sounded, she and the two children agreed to follow him into the country. "I've never felt the kind of peace I felt since moving here," he said. "I've got a farm manager who takes care of everything. I just walk the rows and take a deep breath."

Next to the pump, alongside the first row of vines, Avedis had set up the still. He was halfway into cooking the first batch. Some of the boys were already well lit.

"Nishan," they called out, using the Armenian name for Mark. "Eench ga? What's up?"

"What, you jackasses don't wait for me anymore?"

"Hey, you got those Saroyan hours. We're farmers. Gets to noon and our day is done."

The group had grown since the last cook, and not all of them raised fruit for a living. There was my younger brother, Aram, the high school football coach, and Levon, the accountant, and Kourag, the government inspector, and Arakel, his supervisor at the USDA.

"And I was worried about the feds busting in," I said, laughing.

I looked around for Khachig. Sure enough, he was standing over the barbecue, swaying his hips to a John Lee Hooker tune that blared from the sound system inside the shed. He managed to be barrel-chested and slumped-shouldered at the same time, and his manner of grilling was to stick his Fu Manchu right into the flame. When it came to lamb, he was every bit as deft as his father, who had given up after years of hard luck in the restaurant business. Khachig, lesson learned, did his grilling strictly for the church. Picnics and men's club nights.

"Kid, I'll be throwing on the chops in ten minutes," he shouted. "It's good young lamb marinated well. So they'll be done in no time."

I had made a batch of hummus and set out a plate of baby organic carrots as dipping sticks. "Organic, smorganic," Avedis said. "An excuse to pay a dollar more per bag." After sampling a handful, even he, Mr. Pesticide, had to admit that they were sweeter and crisper than the conventionally grown. And they went nicely with a hummus heavy on the garlic, lemon, and paprika.

"Goddamn, this hummus is good," Khachig said. Of course, there is no higher compliment. I thanked him, and that's when he started working on me, the lapsed one. "Why don't you join the men's society? We could sure use a hummus maker. We don't require any blood. Just show up once a month for dinner. Maybe give a little talk." Suren, the men's society president, had leaned on me the summer before at the blessing of the grape picnic. As before, I nodded and smiled, but otherwise steered clear of any commitment. My mother's father had been the priest of our church. I was an altar boy from the age of fifteen to nineteen. But once I left Fresno for my first job at the *Baltimore Evening Sun*, a strange sort of exile happened, one that had nothing to do with geographical distance. I was a journalist now. No longer could I afford all the entanglements—and there were plenty—that came with being an Armenian in America. I loved my people, but I dared not allow myself to be swallowed up, pen and all, by their ardent designs for me. Even as I returned to California and took up residence in Pasadena, amid a new world of Armenian immigrants, I plodded along a wary fringe. I became the Chinese reporter, the Hmong reporter, the Mexican farmworker reporter, the black Okie reporter, the prison reporter. Only at the end did I become "the Armenian reporter."

I walked over to the still, the Tin Man's head held down tight with vises. The first run had finished in a flame of blue. Avedis, hydrometer in hand, was taking a more precise measurement.

"It's not quite 160 proof. About 155." Not much, I could see, was staying in the bottle. Surab, the raisin farmer from Sanger, poured me a first shot. Right off, I could taste the licorice of the anise, a lacing more heavy than in past runs. "Damn, that's mighty fine."

There is a notion, backed by science, that the mash doesn't count, that no matter what goes into a moonshiner's pot— raisins, plums, Alicante bouschet—what comes out is the same white lightning. Because raisins pack a lot more sugar than plums or grapes, the alcohol comes out stronger. But as far as taste goes, the only thing that makes raki different from slivovitz and slivovitz different from grappa is the flavoring added to the mash. Maybe I was trying too hard, but once I got past the anise, I swore I could smell the raisin and taste the vineyard in our drink. One thing for sure, it doesn't mellow. Fresh from the still, two years in the bottle—it gets no better, and no worse.

In the smoke of the barbecue, my brother the coach had cornered Kourag, a former tackle. Kourag had been playing coy all afternoon, letting us know he had gotten some rare action the night before but not telling us her name or ethnic background. He was in his late twenties but might as well have been sixty the way he was glued to old country habits. "No American girl, not even an Armenian one, is going to take you," my brother poked at him. "You need to go back to Hyestan like Yeraz did."

At six feet eight, Yeraz was a giant with a squeaky voice who traveled from Fresno to Armenia with a tape measure in hand. He announced to the country's elders that the girl he was seeking to take home had to be five feet nine, no less, no more. In the land of squatty Armenians, this was, shall we say, a tall order.

Yeraz managed to find one young woman who truly hit the mark but before a spring wedding could be held, she got a glimpse of Los Angeles and ditched him. On his return journey to Armenia, his specifications grew more accommodating. His future wife could be as short as five feet seven. This time, the young woman agreed to marry Yeraz without delay, and he flew her straight back to Fresno. Two children later, he was king of his castle.

Khachig called us to the food line, and we filled our plates high and sat down in the vineyard. He had cooked the lamb chops to perfection, pink in the middle with the sear and smoke of seasoned grape wood and sweetened by wine and purple onions. As for his pilaf, it was lousy.

For a long minute, as the sun beat down gently on our faces, no one said a word. When Hagop the cabinet maker finally broke the silence, he spoke for us all, by which I mean every sentimental Armenian.

"How did we ever get away from this shit?"

He didn't mean it as a question, we all knew, but that didn't stop us from throwing out answers. Our wives, Armenian and otherwise. Our jobs, big and small. The computer. The cell phone. The hoops and loops of government and the busybody unions too.

Hagop told the story of his uncle, Harry Bedoian, who operated the family cabinet shop in town. "One day the union man came calling. He asked my uncle, 'How many minorities do you have working here?' My uncle answered, 'Three.' He said, 'What are their names?' My uncle said, 'Bedoian, Bedoian, Bedoian.' 'Those aren't minorities,' he said. 'The hell they're not,' my uncle said. 'Go out and count 'em.'"

We Armenians hail from the Caucasus and could be considered the original White Men. Yet we hesitate whenever we are asked to fill out one of those government forms identifying our race. I myself have never checked off the box for "white." I go down the list to "other" and write in "Armenian."

Levon reasoned that we suffered a peculiar fate. Even in our own homeland, where our presence preceded the original Turk by a thousand years, we were the minority. A tribe of Christians with Persia on one side and the Ottoman Empire on the other. What better explained our tragedy than the scapegoating of the minority?

"The Turks," Khachig shouted, a fourth shot of raki now coating his throat. "The Turks. Kid, I hate them for my grandfather."

"I guess we're now officially into the massacres," Suren said, raising a chuckle.

"No," Khachig snapped. "I haven't even gotten to the subject of the massacres."

Even if he hadn't been drinking, he had ample reason to feel melancholy. Just three weeks earlier, he had buried his grandmother, Zari Bekian. Born in the village of Kharpet, a refugee who migrated from Havana to Detroit to Fresno, she had been one of the oldest living survivors of the genocide, dying of natural causes at the age of ninety-nine.

"In the village, the Turks were running across the rooftops with big swords, killing every Armenian they could find," Khachig said. "And these four Armenian sisters, these short little bastards, found a way to stop them. These sisters, I've forgotten their last name, about four feet tall each, they tricked them into sex and then slit their throats. They hid knives in their belts and double-crossed them. Kid, these were great women. They killed more than a hundred Turks this way. That a boy!"

Evidently there was more to the story, details his father had passed on to him, but Khachig was having a hard time getting beyond the sex and sliced throats and near-midget dimensions of the avengers. The whole time he was talking, he was churning like one of those machines that mix dough to a Stevie Ray Vaughn tune. I couldn't help it. I was laughing and crying at the same time.

"Let me tell you," Suren said. "We had a big-ass house with big columns back in the old country. When the Turkish soldiers came, they threw the babies into the air and caught them on their swords. Then they took the men, women, and children out into the desert and let them die one by one."

"The Der er Zor," Avedis said. "The desert in Syria. That's where they were made to march."

"One and a half million dead," Hagop said. "A nation vanished from its three-thousand-year homeland. And somehow that doesn't add up to genocide."

"Why must we always compare ourselves to the Jews?" Kourag asked. "As if their Holocaust is our validation. Didn't we suffer first? Wasn't our blood spilled onto our own land, and not some borrowed land? Was it not Hitler who took his lesson from the Turk?"

Khachig was standing nearly still now, holding a shot glass in one hand and sweeping his other hand across the big blue sky. It was a posture of great speechifying that we knew well from our grandfathers, and we braced ourselves. "It's no accident that this valley looks like valley of Kharpet," Khachig said. "No accident that these mountains look like Ararat. Our coming here as refugees, what we ended up building, is a spit in the eye of the Turk. This whole day, the vineyard, the lamb, the moonshine, is a spit in his fucking eye."

My first impulse was to applaud, in part because I was the one who had egged his performance on, but I thought better. Here we were, in the comfort of America, two generations removed from our grandfathers, trying to recreate a small piece of their world. And in our attempt to keep alive what they had been through, and perhaps even understand the madness of our tribe, we could not get beyond the banal and the grotesque. We ourselves had assumed the form of caricature, repeating platitudes we had learned at the age of ten, as if gathered around us in the dust of the vineyard was an audience of strangers who had no inkling of our story. *The first Christian nation. The first genocide of the twentieth century. The forgotten holocaust.* Our clumsy performance could not be explained by drink. Throughout my adult life, I had witnessed much the same at church, at picnics, wherever Armenians of my generation came together. This is how seventy-five years of Turkish denial had stuck. We did not know how to talk to each other about the past. Our incomprehension at what the Turks had done to us nearly a century ago, an evisceration kept forever fresh by the affront of denial, a denial that portrayed us not as the killed but the killers, had left us a muttering mess. We could not distill our history, we could not extract and pass on the lessons to our daughters and sons, because our history had been left undone.

We did not spend the rest of the afternoon, thank God, spouting murder and revenge. With Martyrs Day less than a week away, we gave our nod and moved on. As the sun worked its way behind the shed, we talked about our love and hopes for our children, our abiding perplexity over what makes a woman truly happy, our irritable bowels, PSA readings, the dream houses we still planned to build, the books we still plotted to write, the farmland we still intended to buy (those who weren't farmers) or sell to a developer (those who were). We wondered if our sons and maybe even our daughters would one day dust the cobwebs off our still and strike the match. I told them about my youngest boy tending to a couple of tomato plants that had managed to come up from seeds in what used to be my garden. He would make an excellent moonshiner someday. We talked until close to six in the evening, until the third batch was finished and the mash had petered out. Not counting what had been siphoned from the spigot, and it was considerable, we had manufactured seven liters of the finest stuff. It had been a good day. We hugged each other good-bye and pledged to do it again in another few weeks, at another vineyard on the east side. As I drove along the river heading home, I knew I wouldn't be making the second cook. Summer was already in the air, and the 107-degree days of the harvest would take us right into fall, and the raisins and almonds would come in together, and right behind them would be the pomegranates and tangerines and before you knew it, after the first rain, the lid would close down on the valley and the fog would settle in, and the old Yokut would get his last laugh. I would wait until then.

chapter eleven | An Epilogue

One day not long ago, I drove into a valley deep in the mountains of Oregon, a swath of green pastures edged by wild blackberries and split by a creek that filled up a nearby lake. It seemed
a pleasant enough place in the world, a place I might even visit
again to fish the rivers of the Cascade range or soak in the 1940s
scenery of Oregon's hidden valleys. That was a trip I owed my
family, though my wife, who had known me since I was a kid,
no longer believed I was capable of such leisure. "You, a tourist
wandering the byways?" she said, scoffing at the image of me
and her and the children free at last. "You don't go anywhere
without a purpose." This wasn't altogether true—our volumes
of family photos showed otherwise—but I knew full well what
she was getting at. The road that had taken me from the middle of California to this spot on the other side of Grants Pass
was nothing if not purposeful. For more than half my life, I
had been looking to find the answers to my father's murder,

only to discover that the secret rested not in the hometown I had spent so many years prying into but here, five hundred miles away, in a tiny trailer set back in the woods alongside a creek they called Cow.

My father, Ara Arax, was gunned down by two strangers who walked into his nightclub in Fresno on a foggy night in January 1972. He was forty years old and I, his oldest child, was fifteen. Why we assumed that the police wouldn't solve the murder, I'm not sure. But that night in the emergency room, I told my family that I would. All through my twenties, as my mother lost a fight with cancer and my wife gave birth to our first child, I tracked down the names in my notebook. There were barmaids turned junkies, a bouncer who rode with the Hells Angels, and one bartender who had become a hit man. I approached each one as Ara's boy "Markie," and they confessed all manner of sin. I even wrote a book about my journey, a combined memoir and investigation that took me back to the land of my grandfather's birth, a murdered nation. No matter how deep I dug, though, I never found my father's killers, never completely put to rest the rumors of drugs and police corruption and a dad who coached Little League by day and entertained Fresno's crooks by night.

Then thirty years after the murder, I was handed a new name: Sue Gage. She was the keeper of the secrets, I was told, the woman who had set my father's death in motion. Not long after the murder, she had left California and moved to a tucked away valley in southern Oregon. She had been living outside a town called Azalea ever since, each year breathing a little easier as the trail that led back to Fresno and my father grew more and more faint.

For weeks, I debated different ways of approaching her—by deception or third party—before deciding to pick up the phone and arrange a meeting face-to-face. What tone of voice do you take, I wondered, when the person on the other end, frightened and cagey, holds answers to questions that have defined, twisted even, your adult life? What words do you let tumble out? Part of me, the son, couldn't stomach the idea of any small talk. Part of me, the journalist, knew how to soften up the wary by playing the earnest good guy. And so I dialed her number and put on my best performance. How I sounded so grateful when she told me what a pleasure it was to hear from Ara's son. How I listened so patiently as she gabbed on about the coyote unnerving her pit bull and the long-awaited vacation she was about to take with her grandkids.

Now I was headed down a last stretch of road toward her trailer, past Christmas tree farms and cows grazing the hillside and tin-roofed cabins spewing thick gray plumes of smoke. As the hilltop dipped down into the valley, the smoke became mist and the mist turned to rain. Through the windshield splatters, I could see a tiny woman in a red turtleneck and jeans standing at the side of the road. The closer I got, the bigger her smile became. I didn't know what Sue Gage looked like. She had my father's face to know me.

There was a time when I dreamed of nothing but such a moment. I'd sit in bed at night and stare at the police composite of one of the gunmen drawn from the memory of a single eyewitness. He had slicked back hair, high cheekbones, boot-shaped sideburns, and a neat mustache. I spent years lifting weights, transforming my body in anticipation of something primal that would surely come over me when I found him. I imagined how the perfect hardness of his face would melt when he realized that the man standing before him was the fifteen-year-old son.

What awaited me now wasn't that killer but a woman who had provided a gun and a half-thought-out plan to the shooters. Two of her former boyfriends, all these years later, had come clean to the Fresno police. They told the story of a minor league beauty with a cunning that made dangerous men carry out her schemes. That she had grown old like the rest of them, with a bad liver and a mouth full of bad teeth, might have led one to miscalculate the challenge she presented. But seeing her standing there in the weeds—in the rain without an umbrella, smiling, smiling—it was hard not to appreciate the cunning that remained. As I got down from my truck, she moved closer for what I expected was a handshake. Then the smile vanished. She was staring at my hand, the one holding a notebook and pen.

"Are you here as a son or as a writer?" she asked.

It was a plain question posed in a flat twang. Maybe she thought it deserved a plain answer. The answer was my life. I wanted to tell her that the son had become a writer on account of murder. He had practiced and honed all the skills of journalistic investigation across a long career for just this one moment. Son, murder, writer—we were one.

Before I could answer, she looked me cold in the eye.

"If you're looking to pin the blame," she said, "you've come to the right place."

My father taught me that the seams on a baseball serve a far greater purpose than stitching leather over cork. If you grip them right, you can make a fast ball jump halfway to home plate. Years before suburban parents began hiring personal trainers to transform their kids' core muscles, my dad preached the wonders of a fit belly button. He'd grab a bat and demonstrate how the midsection was the secret to crushing a ball like Willie Mays, who hit more than 650 home runs while weighing only 185 pounds. "When you swing, you're throwing your back hip at the ball, right? But what you're really throwing is your belly button, Markie. Explode with your belly button."

We lived in a neighborhood of fancy houses plunked down in a field of fig orchards—dad and mom, my little sister, baby brother, and me. Football season on the front grass was no different. We didn't play catch with one of those pint-size rubber balls. Dad insisted on an "Official NFL" pigskin, so fat it kept slipping out of my hands. I played quarterback on a Pee Wee football team that won the city championship. It didn't matter that I was too light to make the eighty-pound minimum. Dad had a friend mold a three-pound hunk of lead that fit into my jock strap for weigh-ins. What I lacked in pounds, I tried to make up with belly button explosions.

My father wasn't the most patient teacher. His irritations, I figured, were the irritations of a natural. If I managed to exhibit some rudimentary form of explosion, he had been born with it in full flower. How else could a five-foot-nine, 205-pound fullback from Fresno High earn a scholarship to play the line at USC? Whether he was performing his Air Force fitness program in our living room or smacking golf balls 310 yards off the tee, he approached every challenge the same: he'd gather all his power in one spot and a split second later erupt in a great unloading. Only if you looked at his mouth, upper lip curled tight under lower lip, could you see the quiet that held the fury.

One of the riddles of my childhood was finding ways to engage this energy before it turned on me or my mother. Years later, my grandfather would talk about my father's powerful life force—*hahvas* he called it in Turkish Armenian—as if it were some mythic gift and curse. His energy was something my grandfather clearly didn't share, much less understand, and he apparently never found a way to fully harness it. "You know Grandpa had a lot of faults," my grandmother told me. "He didn't have a damn head. He should have guided that boy. He was too busy dreaming."

My grandfather had survived the Armenian genocide in 1915 not by out-braving the Turks or outlasting their death marches. Instead, he dreamed away long months hiding in an attic in Istanbul, reading Baudelaire and Maupassant. He was among 20,000 young Armenian men, the Army of the Attics, who dodged the Turks by sitting still. If *hahvas* was ever a fire inside him, he found a way to smother it. "I stayed up there one year," he told me. "My life was with the poems and short stories. All these lives, these flirtations, in this two-by-four room. My life was more romantic than any other time."

This is how my grandfather spoke, his long silences giving way to sometimes grand pronouncements. None of it struck me as high flown. His language fell out in a sweetly broken English that turned words such as *very* into *vehdee*. When he let go a cuss word, he never defiled Armenian. He used his best English and Turkish instead. His favorite word was *bullshit*, which came out *bullsheet*.

He was twenty years old, a young poet with the pen name of Aram Arax, when he arrived in the San Joaquin Valley in 1920. Arax was the mother river that roared down from Mount Ararat, an odd choice for a writer whose pen would turn silent for the next fifty years. He followed the crops from field to cannery before saving enough cash to buy a twenty-acre vineyard on the west side of Fresno. My father was born on that farm in the summer of 1931 as the grapes were being laid down to make raisins.

When pressed, my grandfather would tell two stories about his second son that had the sound of allegory. Both took place on the farm after Dad had dropped out of USC his first year. Why he left college is one of those questions that become freighted with all sorts of monumental hindsight when a life turns tragic. He was either homesick (Grandma's version) or worn down by family guilt for abandoning the farm (Mother's version). This much was certain: he had come home with something to prove.

One day, his tractor got stuck on a knoll and my grandfather warned him not to touch it until he could summon help. When he returned a few minutes later, he was amazed to see that my father had moved the tractor several feet by himself. It now rested in an even more precarious position—and he was caught underneath. Dad was claustrophobic, a fear that may explain what happened next. On his knees, with a crazed look, he lifted enough of the tractor to slide free.

Then there was the day he pruned a row of fig trees and insisted on burning the cuttings. Grandpa told him the branches were too green and the wind too unpredictable. As soon as the old man left, my father poured gasoline all over the pile and lit a match. The fire landed on his clothing and he panicked and ran. By the time it occurred to him to tuck and roll, he had third-degree burns on his hands and forearms. "When he got it in his mind, he had to do it," Grandpa explained. "He had to conquer. He had to be a hero."

My mother, Flora, worried that his epic gestures might one day consume us. In the mid-1960s, we lost our small chain of grocery stores after Safeway discovered Fresno. Dad took our savings and plunked it down on a restaurant and cocktail lounge just off Highway 99. It had a strange name, The Apartments, which my father personalized to Ara's Apartments. Whenever Mom tore into him, her sarcasm dripped. "Big Ara. Ara's Apartments. Name in lights. Mentor to all the creeps and whores."

Maybe to spite her, he ripped out the kitchen and turned the restaurant into the hottest rock and roll club between Los Angeles and San Francisco. In the summer of 1971, when I was fourteen, he brought in Chuck Berry to play back-to-back shows. It's enough to say that my mother's fears came true. The bar got rough and the old clientele of lawyers, politicians, and jocks disappeared. Fresno had become a western hub for narcotics smuggling. Crop dusters would finish spraying the cotton fields and make furtive runs to Mexico. The Hells Angels moved the marijuana and pills from farm to big city. Our police chief, who was married to the town's biggest madam, didn't seem to notice. The smugglers were good about spreading their wealth. Nowhere did they spend more freely—$100 bills stapled together—than at my dad's bar.

When the phone rang that Sunday evening, I want to say I sensed some terrible news came with it. Maybe it was me, the nail biting son forever worrying about a car accident in the fog. But I had seen signs of trouble in recent months. I had watched my father lose his temper one too many times trying to keep his employees and patrons in line. Stubbornly, he kept putting out the welcome mat to all races, even as the mix of white, black, and brown proved more and more volatile.

He wasn't supposed to work that night—the day after New Year's 1972—but a phone call had summoned him. I was going to come along, but he found me in the shower and worried that my damp hair might cause a cold. "It's chilly out there. Stay inside," he said. "I'll be back in an hour." The hour passed. A female bartender was on the line. My mother screamed from the kitchen. "Your father's been shot. Your father's been shot." I bolted out the side door and ran through the fog to a friend's house down the block. I must have been howling because his brother thought a dog had been hit by a car. Five bullets had struck my father.

Murder, I would learn, has many accomplices. The doctor in charge of the emergency room at St. Agnes Hospital that night was drunk. The machine that typed patients' blood had broken. They tried administering a water solution to keep dad's heart pumping, but his blood pressure had dropped to zero. Still, he was fighting to live. He couldn't understand why they weren't taking him into surgery. "Sew me up, and I'll buy you all a drink," he said. My father kept bleeding for ninety minutes, and then he died.

I was sitting in my office—the *Los Angeles Times* bureau in Fresno—on a sunny November day in 2000 when the phone rang. Sergeant Daryl Green from the Fresno police department introduced himself, then asked if I might be willing to meet with him and a detective named Bob Schiotis. "He's been working on your father's murder. I know it's been a long time, but I think we've solved it."

"It's been twenty-eight years. My God, are you sure?"

"It's quite a story. Better that we tell you in person. How about meeting us in an hour at the old Peppermill."

Before he hung up, he couldn't resist. "You should know that these guys were thieves. It looks like nothing more than a robbery gone bad."

Ever since that first night when my sister, brother, and I crawled into bed with our mother, I had held on to the belief that he had been killed for a larger reason. Maybe it was nothing more than a kid's desire to turn his father into something grand, but it wasn't just me. The detectives had assumed the same thing back then. They traced the murder to one of two motives: To make my father pay for an indiscretion or to silence him before he could expose something illegal. The old detectives seemed certain that the gunmen had been hired to do the job.

The bar had never been robbed before. That night, no money was taken from the till, and no demand to open the safe was ever heard by the young female bartender, Linda Lewis. When I tracked her down seventeen years later in Orange County, Lewis told me the same thing she had told police right after the shooting.

It was 6:30 P.M., and the bar was empty when two men walked in. They looked to be from out of town, something in their fringe leather jackets and gloves. And they were very handsome. They ordered two draft beers and headed to the back room to play pool. Just across the way the door to my father's office was open. He was sitting at his desk working on the quarterly taxes. They played a game of eight ball and walked out.

Ten minutes passed and the two men walked back in. The place was still empty. Lewis asked if they wanted another beer. One of the men gave her an odd look, and the other headed straight back to the office and began shooting. My father fought back with everything he had. It took both gunmen to bring him down. "Every single penny was in that register," Lewis told me. "I never heard a word from those two about money. They were there to kill him."

As I drove to the restaurant to meet Green and his partner that afternoon, I thought about all the relationships I had risked trying to solve my father's life. How I had pushed my grandparents and my father's brother, not caring about their own grief, in my greed to understand all I could about him. He was my coach, that I knew, and cared deeply about his community. He outfitted an entire Little League on the poor side of town and did the same with Pop Warner football. He angered my mother by loaning hundreds of dollars to down-and-out patrons and bringing them home to share our Christmas meal. Yet murder has a way of changing what a town remembers about a man. Good as Ara was, people reasoned, he must have been involved in something no good that got him killed. I heard the whispers at school and church. *Ara Arax was involved in the drug trade. Greed got him killed.*

I spent seven years, from 1989 to 1996, writing a book that tried to uncover the truth. Over and over, what I found kept leading me toward something bigger, a conspiracy to have my father killed. Perhaps sensing the police were not to be trusted, my father in the winter of 1971 contacted a deputy district attorney and a state narcotics agent bird-dogging several drug rings based in Fresno. He confided that his bar manager and other patrons were smuggling drugs from Mexico and he was "dead set against it and wanted to cooperate." A few days later, he agreed to hold a fund-raiser for a group of reformers trying to clean up city hall.

"He was very angry and went on and on about the drug trade and how devastating it was to the kids," Linda Mack, one

of the reformers, told me. "He said there were some very influential people in town making money on narcotics. He said
the police department was corrupt and protecting the traffic.
He said there were payoffs going on, and he was going to do
something about it."

I had concluded that my father became a target for murder
while trying to expose drug smuggling operations financed by
prominent businessmen and protected by police chief Hank
Morton and his top men. My dad wasn't involved in the trade
but had heard and seen plenty from behind the bar. His phone
records showed that he placed a last long-distance call a few
days before Christmas to the state attorney general's office in
Sacramento. Whom he talked to, I could never determine. A
week later the tule fog set in and two men with the look of another place came and went like locusts, leaving behind two
empty beer glasses and a cue ball smudged with fingerprints. I
had done my best to put a face on the men who likely hired
them and why, but my conjectures weren't enough to send
anyone to court. So I left it there, believing I had at least
cleared my father's name.

Now came this phone call from the Fresno police, four
years after I had written my book *In My Father's Name*, and I
didn't know what to believe. "We got a call six weeks ago out
of the blue," Sergeant Green explained. "Some guy got
popped by drug agents in Orange County. He says he wants to
talk about an old murder at a bar in Fresno. The killers were a
couple guys out of Detroit. Not hired guns but thieves."
Green's voice wasn't smug, but what he was telling me, at least
with regard to the murder, is that I had gotten it wrong.

As a journalist, I understood that all the context in the
world didn't mean the murder was a hit. My father was talking

big stuff, telling a handful of people that his revelations would be felt "all the way to Sacramento." Yet his actions at the end may have made the murder look more fishy than it really was. The fact that my father confided to more than one person that he was afraid for his life was chilling to know, but what relevance did it have? It certainly didn't preclude the possibility that two cowboys with no particular bone to pick chose his bar from all the other possibilities and stepped inside intending nothing more than an easy robbery. It was my father who did something unexpected that sent the whole thing hurtling in another direction.

Of course, robbery was a theory I had considered—and rejected—long ago. For me to accept it now, I had to be convinced that the police department's heart was in the right spot. For one, this was the same department whose century-long corruption I had detailed in my book. Police chief Ed Winchester, who joined the force in 1967, wasn't pleased with my account of a department that had helped cover up the murder.

As I pulled into the restaurant parking lot, I could see one of the detectives reaching into his car for a folder. He had brought the names, dates, and motives from a man in the clutches of the DEA in Santa Ana. The fingerprints from criminal files in Michigan matched the fingerprints lifted from the murder scene. The case was all but closed. "I hope you understand, but we can't give you the names just yet," Detective Schiotis said.

He was fifty years old with a paunch and bushy mustache, but you could still see the eager kid in him. A cop at my gym had remarked that Schiotis was a quiet bulldog with the reputation of never once lying to a suspect or a victim's family. The toughest cases went to him, and he almost always found a way to solve them. Confronted with another long shot, his colleagues started to joke that the chances of solving it were "slim-and-none, and Schiotis."

I liked him from the first handshake, though he came off as something of a religious nut. He saw God's hand guiding his movements and detailed one uncanny break after the other that he believed helped him solve my father's case. He reached into the folder and took out two mug shots with the names covered up. That's when Sergeant Green, wiry and hard edged, the boss of the unit, addressed me. "These are the guys who took your father's life."

I didn't have to look at the photos long. One mug shot matched almost perfectly the composite of the second gunman drawn from the barmaid's memory. I waited for something to bubble up, an emotion from deep back, as I stared into the faces my father had stared into. Nothing came.

"They're heroin yahoos," Green said. "Both were in prison in Detroit and escaped. They came out to California in late 1971." One gunman had killed himself in 1982 by jumping off an eleven-story building. The other was locked up in a federal prison in the East for robbery.

"What makes you so sure of the motive?" I asked. "Detroit is a long way to come out to do a holdup in Fresno."

Green said the man in custody in Orange County grew up in Detroit. He not only knew both robbers but had lured them to California. In early 1972, the two robbers were sharing stories of their West Coast trip when they told the informant about a heist that had turned deadly at a bar in Fresno. "They said they pulled a gun on the owner and what they thought was going to happen didn't happen," Green said. "He fought them."

"So they just happen to be in Fresno for a robbery and find my father's bar on their own?" I asked.

Green believed a third accomplice, possibly the ringleader, had sent the two robbers to Fresno. This person may have known that cash from the New Year's weekend was still in the safe and provided directions to the bar and possibly even the timing of my father's movements. Green gave the impression that he didn't know the identity of this third person. Only later did I learn that it was a woman who had fancied herself a young Ma Barker and disappeared from Fresno not long after the murder. Her name was Sue Gage.

"Is this informant in Orange County reliable enough to take to court?" I asked. "Would he make a good witness?"

"Everything he's told us checks out," Green said. "He knew all the drug smugglers in town. In fact, he was one of them. You should know that he went out of his way to tell us that your dad never had a thing to do with their business. He was a good guy."

I didn't think I needed a drug smuggler coming clean under duress to tell me what I already knew. And yet I felt my eyes tear up when he said it. As we shook hands, Green told me that the years of looking over my shoulder were over. "It wasn't a contract hit, Mark. It was just a fight."

A few weeks later, on the twenty-ninth anniversary of the murder, the police chief stood before a bank of TV cameras and announced that the Ara Arax case, one of the city's longest-running mysteries, had been solved. I sat a good distance behind the reporters with my sister and brother and watched with a strange detachment. Our father, to hear it now, didn't die a hero and didn't die a villain. He was killed for no other reason than his trajectory happened to cross the path of two robbers out from the Midwest, roaming California for a taste of the sun. Had he waited that foggy night for me to finish my shower and dry my hair, their arc likely would have missed his. He would be alive today, playing golf and watching my son play left field.

As the cameras cleared out, my sister, Michelle, wondered how the police chief could call a press conference and put forward a motive on the word of one informant. Yes, the fingerprints matched and they surely had the right shooters. But the police hadn't even talked to Sue Gage or the man who drove the robbers to Fresno that day and acted as tour guide. And for all the hype, nothing the police chief said went to the heart of the mystery. Why hadn't my father or the barmaid heard one word about robbery? Why hadn't a single penny been taken?

My cousin Michael Mamigonian, who cleaned the bar when he was in high school, laughed at the notion of my father resisting a robbery with his fists. "Money didn't mean a damn thing to Uncle Ara. If these guys came in with guns and they're holding him up, he would have given them all the money and a couple bottles of whiskey as they were running out the door."

The "Arax story" led the local TV news that night and ran across the front page of the *Fresno Bee* the next morning. My father's face, his ample ears and double chin, smiled beneath a bold-lettered question: "1972 Murder Solved?" I had sat down to breakfast when our fifth grader, Joseph, called from school.

"What's up, buddy?" I asked.

He couldn't spit it out. "Grandpa," he muttered.

"What?"

"Grandpa."

By the time I got to the principal's office, his eyes were swollen red. The secretary said his outburst caught the teacher by surprise. "He's mourning a man he never knew," she said. On the way home, he ripped the tissues she had given him into shreds.

"Why did he have to die?"

I wasn't sure if this was a question about my father or a question about God. And so I decided to take the easy way out and turn it into an earthly lesson. I told him my father's calling in life was to be coach and teacher, but he never finished college. He chose the wrong business. "It's too bad he made the wrong choice or he'd be alive today," he said. "His bar was in a bad neighborhood."

His reasoning was as good as any. The town, the bar, the time, and place—it was all about bad location. We pulled into the driveway and I put my arm across his shoulder. I told him the murder and possible trial of the surviving gunman—all the stuff in the news—was my life, not his.

"How did you get through it, Dad?"

What do you tell a son who fears the fog the same way you feared it? That a few weeks after the murder, my uncle came to our house and jammed pieces of wood into every sliding window and drilled a peep hole into the front door? That the face in the composite followed me everywhere, and I'd call detectives with the license plates of look-alikes I encountered at the pizza parlor? That my mother caught me secretly recording one detective and made me promise I would stop asking questions and put away my silly notebook? That years after she died of cancer, I learned that my father had another reason for going to authorities. He was concerned about me, his ninth-grade son who had begun a pathetic little experiment with drugs?

If I answered my son's question that day, it wasn't the whole story. I didn't tell Joseph how the search for my father's killers led me back to my grandfather, Aram, and the genocide at the ' hands of the Turks that obliterated the Armenian nation from Anatolia. I didn't tell him there were four murders in our family, one in each generation, two in the old country and two in the new country. My grandfather's brother, a kind old man I knew as Uncle Harry, had killed a forty-year-old police officer in Long Beach in 1934. He pleaded the genocide, his fear of the Turkish gendarmes, as his defense. I didn't tell Joseph that I had come to see my father's murder, with the cops as accomplices, as karma's get even.

One day, I figured, maybe in the pages of my memoir, Joseph would learn that I got through it by turning my life into a supercharged mission. If my father was a do-gooder, I became his do-gooder son. In high school, I was the quarterback on the football team who rebelled and started an underground weekly that skewered the jocks and debutantes. Spray can in hand, filled with my father's outrage, I sneaked up on the house of the town's biggest developer, a man who had bought off various elected officials, and painted the words "Payola Pig."

As a journalist, I was determined not to let the murder color my views and wrote story after story about guards abusing inmates inside California prisons and how the brutality had been whitewashed by officials all the way up to Governor Pete Wilson. The series prompted legislative hearings in Sacramento and led to the indictments of a dozen correctional officers. The state prison system was forced to halt the practice of guards gunning down inmates to stop fistfights. The powerful leader of the guards' union, Don Novey, had trouble understanding how the son of a murder victim could turn into a "champion for killers." At a legislative hearing on the prison abuses, Novey angrily waved a copy of my book. I was a conspiracy nut who had sullied the reputation of one too many public servants. "When is it going to end?" the union boss pleaded to the panel of state senators.

In the spring of 2003, with the trial pending, my wife, Coby, demanded to know the same: "Seven years writing that book, seven years putting our lives on hold, and it still hasn't gone away?" she screamed.

I had moved dozens of files out of storage and back into my office at home. Returning to my late-night habits, I added new names and dates to a seven-foot-long timeline. My wife, it seemed, no longer trusted my judgment. She was sure my obsession had gotten the best of me. If I was truly considering her and the children, I would choose to let it go and trust the cops and prosecutors. I didn't see it that way, of course. My fixation on finding one clean answer may have seemed selfish and self-righteous, but I really had no choice in the matter. My father had been murdered, and I had spent the better part of my life turning this way and that way the question why. Details I had gotten wrong, details missed, details yet to come—I couldn't very well stop now.

I had the names of four people I never had before: the two shooters, the getaway driver, and Sue Gage. I went to the courthouse and pulled criminal files and began interviewing old barflies. To his credit, Detective Schiotis never once told me to keep my nose out of his case. The district attorney's office, in a move that miffed the detective, decided to strike an immunity deal with the getaway driver and Gage to shore up its case against the surviving gunman.

In the weeks leading up to the trial, Schiotis shared his own findings and tried to answer all my questions. He was the honest, never-say-die cop I had been searching for all these years. He too, it turned out, wasn't convinced of the motive or if the conspiracy included someone even closer to my father. "I'm 70 to 30 that it's a robbery," he said, "but I won't know for sure until it's over and I can sit down with the defendant."

Then on the eve of the trial, he gave me this: The getaway driver's testimony was the most important, and the reason he decided to cooperate was because he had read my book. He had been filled with guilt for two years, looking for a way to unload it. "He came *this* close to calling you a few years ago and telling you the truth," Schiotis said. "When we knocked on his door, it all came pouring out. He said he remembered you as a kid in your baseball uniform at the bar. Your book helped solve the case."

The detective saw a larger power at work, a force that connected past to present. He told a story from the late 1960s when he was a teenager practicing baseball at Hamilton Junior High. He encountered a father hitting ground balls to his young son. "It was you and your dad. I'll never forget it because he kept hitting them over and over."

I vaguely recalled that day, or a day just like it. *Charge the ball, Markie. Charge the ball.*

"I hope you don't take this wrong," Schiotis said, "but I feel it's almost destiny that this case came to me and I was able to solve it."

The trial that took place over six days in the summer of 2003 told its own story. It began, oddly enough, with a German Shepherd named Otto. Without him, I never would have had the chance to look Thomas Joseph Ezerkis—one of my father's killers—in the eye. Otto was roaming the corridors of John Wayne Airport on June 8, 2000, when his expert nose detected an unmistakable odor coming from a black tote bag carried by Ronald Young, a.k.a. Detroit Ron. That Otto even picked out Detroit Ron—one of 25,000 passengers coming and going that day—was the first of many coincidences that broke open the case. Each coincidence, it seemed, joined up with another until happenstance became a kind of fate. Everything fit so neatly that it made you wonder if Schiotis had it right: the case was God's little puzzle.

At first, Detroit Ron refused to talk about the $300,000 in drug-stained cash he was carrying. He may have looked like a leftover from *Miami Vice*—gray goatee, shaved head, Hawaiian print shirt, and Docksiders—but he hadn't survived five decades of drug smuggling by snitching. For months, he kept mum behind bars. Then his daughter died suddenly and her children needed him. His encyclopedic memory would become a way out of his jam. As he sat down with the DEA to offer up details of this new drug ring, he decided he might as well talk about that old murder in Fresno too.

The killing of Ara Arax—it too was a function of happenstance.

The testimony from Detroit Ron and a host of other rogues would unfold during the trial just as the prosecutor promised. No fishing expeditions. No surprises. His only goal was to put Ezerkis, the surviving gunman, away for life. If that meant leaving out tantalizing possibilities of other conspirators and motives detailed in my book, so be it. I was so grateful to be in a courtroom after all these years—close enough I could hear the defendant grunt—that it hardly mattered. And so I took a seat with the rest of my family and quietly watched and listened. Here is what emerged:

Detroit Ron was serving a term for burglary at Jackson State Prison in Michigan in 1971. In the cell above him was his childhood pal Thomas Ezerkis. They had grown up together on the northwest side of Detroit. Ezerkis's old man was a legendary Detroit cop. He had five children and was extra tough on Tommy, the oldest son, who began injecting heroin at age twenty. In the prison yard, Ezerkis was all ears as Detroit Ron bragged about his exploits in California. He had gone to Los Angeles in the mid-1960s and joined forces with the early drug smugglers, some of whom had grown up in Fresno. The wide-open farm town remained the base of their operations.

Ezerkis took a mental note of everything Detroit Ron told him. Then in late 1971, Ezerkis broke out of prison and headed to California to join one of the smuggling crews. Before escaping, he got the phone number of Detroit Ron's old girlfriend, a bombshell named Sue Gage who organized all the Fresno-to-Mexico runs for one group.

Ezerkis arrived in mid-December with his crime partner, Charles Silvani. They crashed for two weeks at Gage's house in North Hollywood. To raise seed money for a load, they decided to pull a few robberies. Gage loved planning the logistics of a crime, but she left the dirty work to her lovers. Her lover at the time happened to be a sweet-talking, no-honor thief from Fresno named Larry Frazier.

Gage and Frazier, like so many other gangsters, were regulars at Ara's Apartments. In fact, it was Ara who taught Gage how to shoot pool with her left hand. When she drank too much tequila one night and fired a .357 magnum at Ara's phone ("because I couldn't get a dial tone"), Ara got upset but then forgave her. Ara was sweet but business was business. Gage had spent New Year's weekend at the Apartments before returning to Los Angeles. Ara must have done five grand, she told Frazier. The cash sat in a safe behind the bar. How Gage knew this, she didn't say, but she was certain that Ara would be there at 6:30 P.M. that Sunday to open it up—with the right persuasion.

Gage handed a stolen .32-caliber gun to Silvani. Frazier gave his stolen .38 to Ezerkis. Frazier then hopped into a stolen 1968 Mercury and drove the two Detroit robbers to Fresno. They arrived late that afternoon, January 2. Frazier showed Ezerkis and Silvani the bar and told them he'd be waiting across the street in a second car at the appointed hour.

At nightfall, they struck. It was misty outside, but Frazier saw the pair running out of the bar and climbing into the Mercury. He gave them the signal to follow his car, and they drove for more than an hour through the tule fog, past the cotton fields of the west side where Frazier grew up, miles and miles until the road reached the rise of the California Aqueduct. There, beside the water that flowed to Los Angeles, Frazier huddled with the two robbers and found out what happened.

Silvani had confronted Ara in his office but never got a chance to say, "This is a stickup." Instead, Ara exploded out of his chair and charged at him like a bull. Silvani was forced to shoot. He shot several times, but Ara wouldn't go down. So Ezerkis had to step up and fire the .38. Ara wrested away the .32 and shot back, wounding Silvani in the triceps. They had no choice but to flee without the money.

"We were standing on the aqueduct," Frazier recalled. "I was mad. 'Goddamn it, why did you have to shoot Ara?' They said Ara jumped up and pulled a 'Tom Mix' on them."

Frazier took this to mean that Ara, like the famous movie cowboy of the 1930s, didn't wait for any explanation. Once he saw the gun, he made his move. On the canal bank, Frazier testified in court, he grabbed the .38 out of Ezerkis's hand and threw it into the water. Then they pushed the Mercury over the edge and watched it gurgle and sink.

With his deep-set eyes, Frazier looked like one of Dorothea Lange's haunted Okies. Defense attorney Pete Jones tried to attack his credibility, underscoring his thirty-one aliases, seven convictions in three states, an assault on a police officer, and a marital record that included bigamy and wife beating. Frazier refused to wilt.

Of all the testimony, his account of the killing struck me with the most force. My father bursting out of his chair, the panic that triggered a fury—it sounded like those old stories on the farm that my grandfather passed on to me. I had seen it myself so many times—at the golf course swinging his driver, in the living room pounding out his Air Force exercises, on the front grass teaching me baseball. My father, hard as it was to accept, had been an accomplice in his own murder. He had misread the gun in his face. All the noise he was making about exposing drug rings and police corruption had put him in a state of mind where robbery became the very murder he feared. It was the worst case of bad timing. In seven years at the bar, he had never faced the barrel of a gun. And now, on the heels of contacting state narcotic agents and the attorney general's office, comes the first gun. He is waiting for that gun. He is braced for that gun. That gun, by God, shows up in the hands of a robber.

The crime eventually came full circle. A month after Dad's murder, trailing a string of robberies, Ezerkis found himself back at Jackson State Prison, where he confessed the entire episode to Detroit Ron.

It took the jury less than three hours to find Ezerkis guilty. Jurors would later tell me that their only regret was seeing Sue Gage get immunity and go free. "We all felt that she was the one who set it up," one juror said. At the sentencing, my sister, brother, and I decided not to give any victim statements. Ezerkis, though, had something to say to us. He turned around and for the first time gave us full measure of his face. My sister said he looked like Frank Gorshin playing the Riddler. "I know that losing a parent is a traumatic experience, especially under the conditions that they lost their father. But on the same breath, I gotta tell them that I didn't do it. That's all I gotta say."

The judge sentenced him to life. As we walked out, prosecutor Dennis Peterson, a kind man who felt conflicted about the immunity deal with Gage, patted me on the back. "That's it," he said. "It's that simple."

The packet sat on my desk for months after the trial. It contained the testimony of the coroner who had taken the stand on the day I missed court. Truth be known, I didn't have the stomach to attend. I had this idea that one detail—a line from the coroner's notes or maybe the sickened face of a juror viewing the autopsy photographs—might stick and screw me up. When I finally opened the packet in the privacy of my office and began analyzing the testimony, it became clear that neither side had bothered to connect the coroner's dots. Had they done so, it surely would have complicated the robbery theory.

Of the first three shots that hit my father, at least one was fired from a longer range. This was almost certainly the first shot. Its angle is consistent with my father sitting in his chair and Silvani firing from a distance of ten to fifteen feet. He takes aim at my father's head. Dad deflects the bullet with his wrist and it grazes the top of his skull, exiting in almost a perfect line out the back office wall. This first shot, contrary to the prosecution's theory, showed that Silvani's intent was deadly from the outset. He began firing before my father ever got out of his chair and made any Tom Mix move. Dad's last words to the doctors said as much. "I was doing the books and two guys came in and just started shooting."

The fatal shot in the stomach likely came next. It was fired close up at a considerable downward angle, indicating that my father was still coming out of his chair like a lineman driving out of his stance. The third shot also struck his abdomen, its slight downward angle consistent with my father reaching a nearly upright position. Only then did he come face-to-face with Silvani, back him into the main bar area, and take away his gun. My father fired once, but before he could fire again, the gun jammed.

And then there were the other dots that the prosecution failed to connect—all the employees and patrons who lurked in the background of the story. How much coincidence was I supposed to accept? Sue Gage, who had sent the gunmen to Fresno, happened to be working with the same drug smugglers who were troubling my father. One of her cohorts, Mike Garvey, was my dad's bar manager. It was Garvey whose drug smuggling run in late 1971 had so perturbed my father that he contacted state narcotics agents. Garvey and Dad got into a dispute that December, and Dad fired him. It was Garvey who talked to Dad on the phone just hours before the murder. How did Gage know the precise time he was going to work—on a day he never went in?

Why couldn't robbery and murder be part of the same plan? If they needed to silence my father, why not lure him to work on a slow Sunday evening, rip off the money, and then shoot him? I know it isn't the simple answer. And the simple answer, they say, is almost always the right answer because it fits the small, immediate thinking of most criminals. But even Frazier, the getaway driver, had thought it was a hit after reading my book. When the detectives first interviewed him, Frazier said he had been "set up" to believe it was a robbery. The detectives told him he had to testify about what he knew back then, not what he had read in a book years later. So he gave the details of a botched robbery.

Finally, there was the reference to Tom Mix. I had never sat through one of his movies, yet the idea that the legendary cowboy made a habit of charging at villains who held guns on him somehow didn't ring right. I tracked down a man named Mix in Texas and was pleased to learn that he was not only Tom's second cousin but his biographer as well. I told Paul Mix why I was calling, and there was a long pause as he searched his memory. "Let me see," he said. "What you're describing sounds darn close to one of Tom Mix's most enduring films."

It was a 1932 talkie called *Justice Rides the Plains* and featured a crooked sheriff, a treacherous business partner, and villains who attack Mix inside a saloon and ambush him on the open trail. A bullet grazes his hand. A tomahawk is thrown at his head and he ducks. Mix never loses his cool as he fights back. Maybe I was putting too fine a point on it. Maybe the robbers only meant that my father tried to pull a hero's stunt—a "Tom Mix"—and forced their hand. But Paul Mix said his cousin's legend wasn't a metaphor for stupid heroics.

"Tom Mix was the good guy no matter what hat he was wearing," he said. "He fought only when he was backed into a corner, only when he had no other choice."

Inside a bird's nest of a trailer in the Oregon mountains, it didn't take long for Sue Gage to turn on me. She kept talking about what a good man my father was. I kept pressing her about her close connections to bar manager Mike Garvey and Fresno's drug smugglers. This whole period was an aberration, she said. Her first husband died in 1967 while serving in the Navy, and she returned to Fresno with her baby daughter. She was lonely and a friend introduced her to the crowd at Dad's bar. Before she knew it, she was running between Fresno and Hollywood, living with wanted men.

Then one day, with no warning, two guys from Detroit showed up. "Detroit Ron sent them from prison without ever telling me. I let them stay at my house in Hollywood. Very nice and polite guys. And then Larry Frazier comes over and they start plotting. I figured they were going to rip off drug dealers."

She blamed herself for naively giving her gun to Silvani and maybe innocently mentioning that she had spent New Year's weekend at a busy Ara's Apartments. She said it was a week or two later, while attending a party in Los Angeles, that she learned my father had been killed. A bunch of Fresno outlaws were discussing the murder when Frazier suddenly pulled her into a closet. "He told me the two guys from Detroit killed Ara during a robbery. I didn't want to believe it. We swore to each other to never tell another soul. And I would have never told. I would have went to my grave."

I wasn't buying it. "Frazier tells it differently. He says you put the whole thing together. You knew my father was going to be at the bar. You knew the precise time."

"That's a lie," she shouted. "Yes, I had a role, but my motivation was to get rid of those guys, to send them on their merry way with a gun. Happy trails."

"You set it up, Sue."

"Listen," she said, pounding the tiny table wedged between her bed and the refrigerator. "I'm an old lady. I've had twenty-six years of being a citizen, and I'll be damned if you're going to implicate me in a murder."

"You've already implicated yourself."

"I don't think this is a good idea. I thought I was seeing Ara's son. But you've got too much reporter in you."

"What did you expect? Your fucking greed changed my life."

Her hard face twisted into a cruel sneer. "Get over it," she said. "Get over it. Dead is dead. My daughter doesn't even remember her father's funeral."

That daughter had the benefit of an answer. Her daddy died in the hull of a Navy ship after breathing fumes from a cleaning solvent. "Where do you get off preaching to me?" I shouted.

My right hand was poised just inches from her face. For the first time in my adult life, for the slightest moment, I wished I was someone else. Not a father. Not a husband. Not a reporter. "Listen lady, you've got a lot of gall. If my parents had raised a different son, you and I wouldn't be talking right now. Where in the fuck do you get off sounding callous?"

"Callous?" she said, backing down. "That I am. That I am. I haven't slept with a man in ten years. I'm pretty shut off."

Her voice had softened, and I bored in. I described my father's talks with drug agents, how the first shot was fired at his head before he ever made a threatening move.

"What? No one ever told me that."

"Does that sound like robbery?" I asked. "Why was no money taken?"

"Wait, wait, wait," she said, looking confused. "There was no money taken?"

She seemed on the verge of going in another direction. I thought she might tell me that these guys returned from Fresno that night with some payment, after all. But before I could reach in with another question, she stopped herself short. Then it was as if she had entered some trance, a place beyond all my probing. There was no shaking her out of it.

"No, it's just an old song. Ara taught me how to play pool left-handed. He wasn't like the rest of those guys. It was a robbery. I gave the gun not knowing. Maybe I'll write a book myself and call it 'The Closet.' Because it was in a closet when I first learned about them killing your dad, and it's in a closet where I've kept it ever since."

I got up and headed to the door. The rain had stopped, and she followed me all the way to the truck.

"My biggest crime was to keep you in the dark. I could have fixed all this when you were much younger. I could have come forward and fixed it, but I wasn't a snitch. I owed that to you. I'm sure you've had a long and strange journey."

In the absence of an answer, Rilke once wrote, try to love the questions themselves. And so I ask myself if I am a son clinging to an answer that wraps my father in glory. Is it true, as a friend once told me, that as long as I keep open the question of who killed him and why, I don't have to put him away? Has the want of an answer become my way of keeping my father alive?

I am now seven years older than he was the night he left us. I have three children of my own, the oldest a daughter who has lined her bedroom floor with college applications. Whether she understands it or not, she has lived with her grandfather's murder all her life. She was two years old when we moved back to Fresno to begin my search. How foolish was my promise to keep the past separate from our lives, as if it could be stored in those boxes and file cabinets and brought out only at night, when my daughter and wife slept and I was free to work on my puzzle. Yes, I did right by my father, but for too many years, the best of me was taken from my own family.

The role of Ara's boy "Markie" no longer comes so easy to me, the forty-seven-year-old man. My mother would be happy to know that I have made a life apart from my search. I have written a new book, a grand telling of another family's history, and tend to my fruit trees and vegetable garden. My sister and brother honor our parents in their own way. Michelle teaches at a middle school in Fresno and Donnie is the head football coach at our alma mater. They both wonder, for my sake, if I have put it to rest. Maybe I have.

Ezerkis now lives in one of the California prisons I once exposed for its abuses against inmates. He has written me three times, promising to come clean with the truth, but first I must deliver $1,500 to his prisoner account. "I am the only person alive who was in the bar that night," he says. "That hatched up story of a robbery gone bad. Crap! You and I know that no such thing ever happened." His sister calls to tell me he is dying of liver disease, and when she hangs up, the image of a last confession behind bars starts to play in my mind. But I have yet to wire the cash or request the form required by the prison for a visit. Not long ago, I picked up the *Fresno Bee* and read that the bar, now known as Los Compadres, had been gutted by arson fire. It sits only ten minutes from my house, and I keep thinking I need to drive by and take a look, but the road never seems to wind there. A while back, a dentist friend called to say that one of his patients, a person not prone to fabrication, had new information about my father, a "key" that would unlock a whole other door. I keep her phone number on a corner of my desk with the other keys, accumulating a fine layer of dust and guilt.

A year or so after the trial, Detective Schiotis left the police department and joined the state Department of Justice. He tells me he hasn't forgotten my questions—they are good ones, he says—and pledges to take a hard second look at Gage and Garvey. "It's still open as far as I'm concerned." I like hearing those words, but I don't expect they'll ever amount to much.

It does feel funny letting go, as if I am letting go of the most alive part of me. As facile as it may sound, I want to say that the truth of my father's murder is less important to me now than the truth of his life. I no longer believe that the act of robbery, if true, means that he died for nothing. What was in his heart at the end counts for something. His fervent wish was for the town he loved to be a better place, and he was willing to risk a lot to see that happen. I no longer believe that all I am is a response to the murder. The older I grow, the more I think that what I am, at the core, is what I would have become had my father lived.

This past spring, my son Joseph made the move to the big diamond—ninety feet between bases and sixty feet, six inches from pitcher to home plate. Not an easy adjustment for a thirteen-year-old, much less one still shy of puberty. In the batting cage, I sometimes let my irritations show. All the years playing and coaching and learning from the best, and I return to my father. "Joe, you're swinging too polite. Your power comes from the belly button. Explode with the belly button, son. Explode."

GARY KAZANJIAN

Award-winning author and journalist Mark Arax has written two previous books, *The King of California*—a *Los Angeles Times* bestseller and Best Book of the Year—and *In My Father's Name*. He is a contributing writer at *Los Angeles* magazine and a former senior writer at the *Los Angeles Times*. He teaches nonfiction writing at Claremont McKenna College and lives in Fresno.

PublicAffairs is a publishing house founded in 1997. It is a tribute to the standards, values, and flair of three persons who have served as mentors to countless reporters, writers, editors, and book people of all kinds, including me.

I. F. STONE, proprietor of *I. F. Stone's Weekly*, combined a commitment to the First Amendment with entrepreneurial zeal and reporting skill and became one of the great independent journalists in American history. At the age of eighty, Izzy published *The Trial of Socrates*, which was a national bestseller. He wrote the book after he taught himself ancient Greek.

BENJAMIN C. BRADLEE was for nearly thirty years the charismatic editorial leader of *The Washington Post*. It was Ben who gave the *Post* the range and courage to pursue such historic issues as Watergate. He supported his reporters with a tenacity that made them fearless and it is no accident that so many became authors of influential, best-selling books.

ROBERT L. BERNSTEIN, the chief executive of Random House for more than a quarter century, guided one of the nation's premier publishing houses. Bob was personally responsible for many books of political dissent and argument that challenged tyranny around the globe. He is also the founder and longtime chair of Human Rights Watch, one of the most respected human rights organizations in the world.

• • •

For fifty years, the banner of Public Affairs Press was carried by its owner Morris B. Schnapper, who published Gandhi, Nasser, Toynbee, Truman, and about 1,500 other authors. In 1983, Schnapper was described by *The Washington Post* as "a redoubtable gadfly." His legacy will endure in the books to come.

Peter Osnos, *Founder and Editor-at-Large*